ENGLISH
FOR EVERYONE
PRACTICE BOOK
ENGLISH GRAMMAR GUIDE

Author

Tom Booth worked for 10 years as an English-language teacher in Poland and Russia. He now lives in England, where he works as an editor and English-language materials writer. He has contributed to a number of books in the *English for Everyone* series.

Consultant

Tim Bowen has taught English and trained teachers in more than 30 countries worldwide. He is the co-author of works on pronunciation teaching and language-teaching methodology, and author of numerous books for English-language teachers. He is currently a freelance materials writer, editor, and translator. He is a member of the Chartered Institute of Linguists.

ENGLISH FOR EVERYONE

PRACTICE BOOK

ENGLISH GRAMMAR GUIDE

    conditional

negative   verb

 comparative   Aa

     noun

DK

US Editors Jennette ElNaggar, Lori Hand
Project Editor Ben Ffrancon Davies
Senior Art Editor Amy Child
Illustration Square Egg
Jacket Designer Surabhi Wadhwa-Gandhi
Jacket Editor Emma Dawson
Jacket Design Development Manager Sophia MTT
Producer, Pre-production Robert Dunn
Producer Jude Crozier
Proofreader Steph Lewis
Managing Editor Christine Stroyan
Managing Art Editor Anna Hall
Publisher Andrew Macintyre
Art Director Karen Self
Publishing Director Jonathan Metcalf

DK India
Senior Art Editor Chhaya Sajwan
Senior Editor Arani Sinha
Assistant Art Editors Sonali Mahthan, Vidushi Gupta
Editor Nandini Devdutt Tripathy
Assistant Editors Udit Verma, Andrew Korah
Jacket Designer Priyanka Bansal
Jacket Editorial Co-ordinator Priyanka Sharma
Managing Jackets Editor Saloni Singh
Senior Managing Art Editor Arunesh Talapatra
Managing Editor Soma B. Chowdhury
Pre-production Manager Sunil Sharma
Senior DTP Designers Tarun Sharma, Harish Aggarwal
DTP Designer Manish Upreti

First American Edition, 2019
Published in the United States by DK Publishing
1745 Broadway, 20th Floor, New York, NY 10019

Copyright © 2019 Dorling Kindersley Limited
DK, a Division of Penguin Random House LLC
23 24 26 25 24 23
023–314180–Jun/2019

A catalog record for this book
is available from the Library of Congress.
ISBN 978-1-4654-8466-6

DK books are available at special discounts when purchased in bulk
for sales promotions, premiums, fund-raising, or educational use.
For details, contact: DK Publishing Special Markets,
1745 Broadway, 20th Floor, New York, NY 10019
SpecialSales@dk.com

Printed and bound in China

For the curious
www.dk.com

FSC
www.fsc.org
MIX
Paper | Supporting
responsible forestry
FSC™ C018179

This book was made with Forest
Stewardship Council™ certified paper –
one small step in DK's commitment
to a sustainable future.
For more information go to
www.dk.com/our-green-pledge

How to use this book

This practice book is a companion to the *English for Everyone: English Grammar Guide*. Each unit in the book tests the language taught in the *English Grammar Guide* unit with the same number.

GRAMMAR GUIDE UNIT

PRACTICE BOOK UNIT

EXERCISES

The exercises are carefully graded to drill and test the grammar presented in the corresponding *Grammar Guide* unit. Working through these exercises will help you understand and remember what you have learned.

Exercise number Every exercise has a unique number so you can easily find the relevant answers.

Exercise instruction A brief instruction tells you what you need to do.

Sample answer The first question of each exercise is answered to make the task easier to understand.

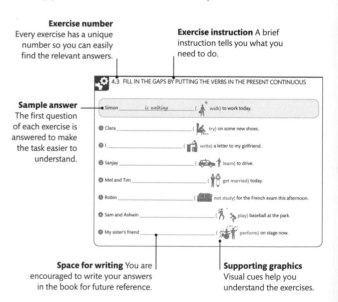

Space for writing You are encouraged to write your answers in the book for future reference.

Supporting graphics Visual cues help you understand the exercises.

ANSWERS

An Answers section at the back of the book lists the correct answers for every exercise. Turn to these pages whenever you finish a unit or exercise to see how well you have understood the teaching point.

Exercise numbers Look for the relevant exercise number in the Answers section to mark your work.

Contents

01 The present simple

The present simple is used to make simple statements of fact, to talk about things that happen repeatedly, and to describe things that are always true.

1.1 FILL IN THE GAPS BY PUTTING THE VERBS IN THE PRESENT SIMPLE

Jessica _____ *walks* _____ (walk) around the park every day at lunchtime.

1 Tony _____ (make) a huge breakfast for his family on Sundays.

2 I usually _____ (eat) my lunch at 1pm at an Italian restaurant.

3 Fiona _____ (meet) her friends at a café on Thursday evenings.

4 We sometimes _____ (play) tennis with our friends on Saturday mornings.

5 My cousin _____ (start) work at 6am every morning.

6 The shop assistant _____ (leave) work at 6pm in the evening.

7 You _____ (drink) a lot of coffee every morning.

8 Paolo usually _____ (read) a book in the evenings.

1.2 MARK THE SENTENCES THAT ARE CORRECT

Steve usually finishes work at 5pm. ☑
Steve usually finishs work at 5pm. ☐

1 Greg workes in a factory. ☐
Greg works in a factory. ☐

2 My dad watches TV every evening. ☐
My dad watchs TV every evening. ☐

3 Michel plays the piano beautifully. ☐
Michel playes the piano beautifully. ☐

4 Jane brushs her hair in the morning. ☐
Jane brushes her hair in the morning. ☐

5 Selma gos shopping after work. ☐
Selma goes shopping after work. ☐

6 Imran washes his clothes on Sunday. ☐
Imran washs his clothes on Sunday. ☐

7 Mary teaches French at a college. ☐
Mary teachs French at a college. ☐

1.3 FILL IN THE GAPS USING "AM," "IS," OR "ARE"

They ___are___ here for the party.

1. I _____ a doctor at the local hospital.

2. Vicky _____ my eldest child.

3. We _____ from a town in Scotland.

4. Both my parents _____ lawyers.

5. You _____ a very good friend.

6. I _____ an American.

7. That policeman _____ so tall.

8. She _____ twenty-three years old.

9. It _____ cold outside.

10. I _____ fifteen today.

11. Our cat _____ black and white.

12. We _____ very excited.

13. They _____ students from France.

14. Jim _____ an architect.

15. My sister-in-law _____ from Japan.

16. I _____ so hungry!

17. You _____ very lazy.

18. My children _____ so tired.

19. I _____ forty-three years old.

20. They _____ late for work.

21. Claudia and Paolo _____ Italian.

22. My grandfather _____ retired.

23. We _____ from Pakistan.

24. Paul _____ disappointed.

1.4 FILL IN THE GAPS USING "HAVE" OR "HAS"

He ___has___ a lot of homework to do.

1. Jack _____ a new car.

2. Jennifer _____ Abbie's bag.

3. We _____ a beautiful farm.

4. I _____ three sisters.

5. Bob _____ toothache.

6. My house _____ a large garage.

7. They _____ a new laptop.

8. We _____ so many books.

9. My dad _____ red hair.

10. You _____ an old phone.

11. My neighbors _____ a daughter.

12. Juan's house _____ three floors.

13. That bird _____ big eyes.

14. I _____ a new baby.

15. We both _____ headaches.

16. They _____ the same dress.

17. My grandparents _____ chickens.

18. You _____ a friendly cat.

19. My town _____ two museums.

20. Yuko _____ a painful back.

21. Our dogs _____ lots of toys.

22. We _____ an English class tonight.

23. Vineetha _____ a new haircut.

24. I _____ dinner at 6pm every day.

1.5 MATCH THE PICTURES TO THE CORRECT SENTENCES

| Hannah takes beautiful photos of the places she visits. | Reggie bakes the most incredible cakes. | Emil leaves the office at 6pm each day. | Brad goes camping in the forest every summer. |

1.6 FILL IN THE GAPS USING THE WORDS IN THE PANEL

Katya _____ *teaches* _____ young children how to read.

❶ I _____ work at 9am during the week.

❷ You _____ an engineer.

❸ Maria _____ coffee with Jules in the morning.

❹ They _____ to work by train.

❺ My dad _____ 67 years old.

❻ Robert _____ work at 7pm.

❼ We _____ an English lesson later.

❽ Paul often _____ a film in the evening.

❾ Emma _____ to bed early on Sundays.

watches	is	are	goes	have
go	start	has	finishes	~~teaches~~

02 The present simple negative

To make negative sentences using "be" in the present simple, "not" is added after the verb. For other verbs, the auxiliary verb "do not" or "does not" is used.

2.1 REWRITE THE SENTENCES, PUTTING THE WORDS IN THE CORRECT ORDER

French. | not | I | am

I am not French.

4 my | not | are | dogs. | They

_____

1 doctor. | is | She | a | not

_____

5 are | You | Egyptian. | not

_____

2 are | New Zealand. | We | from | not

_____

6 is | my | This | computer. | not

_____

3 not | My | American. | is | dad

_____

7 engineer. | an | am | I | not

_____

2.2 FILL IN THE GAPS USING "DO NOT" OR "DOES NOT"

Michael _____*does not*_____ have a dog.

1 You _____ work in the library.

2 He _____ eat meat.

3 Val _____ watch TV in the evening.

4 I _____ play football very often.

5 We _____ get up early on Saturdays.

6 My grandparents _____ have a car.

7 Nico _____ work in the factory.

8 She _____ go to work on Fridays.

9 I _____ go to restaurants very often.

10 You _____ have a cat.

11 They _____ work outside.

2.3 REWRITE EACH SENTENCE IN THE NEGATIVE USING CONTRACTIONS

| She is happy with her meal. | She's not happy with her meal. | She isn't happy with her meal. |

1. He is a teacher. _____ _____
2. Carla is very tall. _____ _____
3. You are from Australia. _____ _____
4. They are farmers. _____ _____
5. We are happy. _____ _____
6. You are lawyers. _____ _____
7. She is a doctor. _____ _____
8. It is very cold outside. _____ _____

2.4 MARK THE SENTENCES THAT ARE CORRECT

He does not likes baseball. ☐
He does not like baseball. ☑

1. I don't like Sam's cooking. ☐
   I no like Sam's cooking. ☐

2. You doesn't look very happy. ☐
   You don't look very happy. ☐

3. Antonio does not live in Madrid. ☐
   Antonio do not lives in Madrid. ☐

4. Phil don't drive a car. ☐
   Phil doesn't drive a car. ☐

5. I'm not a doctor. ☐
   I amn't a doctor. ☐

6. Diana doesn't have a computer. ☐
   Diana don't has a computer. ☐

7. I don't like cats. ☐
   I like not cats. ☐

8. Paolo does not get up at 6am. ☐
   Paolo do not get up at 6am. ☐

9. My dad don't feels well. ☐
   My dad doesn't feel well. ☐

10. They isn't from China. ☐
    They aren't from China. ☐

11. My friends don't like chess. ☐
    My friends doesn't like chess. ☐

2.5 REWRITE THE SENTENCES IN THE NEGATIVE

> This book **is** very interesting.
> _This book isn't very interesting._

1 Amy **works** as a receptionist in our office.

_____

2 I **like** going to the health center.

_____

3 Your company **is** very successful.

_____

4 You **play** the guitar very well.

_____

5 Jean **cooks** the dinner in the evening.

_____

6 This TV show **is** very interesting.

_____

7 Sonia and Rick **live** in Paris.

_____

8 My son **is** a firefighter.

_____

9 Our house **is** very big.

_____

10 Sandra **works** late on Fridays.

_____

11 My husband and I **relax** on weekends.

_____

12 Edith and Sam **like** dancing in their free time.

_____

03 Present simple questions

Questions in the present simple with "be" are formed by swapping the verb and subject. For other verbs, the auxiliary verb "do" or "does" must be added before the subject.

3.1 FILL IN THE GAPS USING "AM," "IS," OR "ARE"

_____Are_____ you a chef?

① _____ you the new teacher?

② _____ she your sister?

③ _____ we nearly home?

④ _____ I on the list?

⑤ _____ your dogs friendly?

⑥ Where _____ the front door?

⑦ _____ Carlo still a teacher?

⑧ _____ we late for the party?

⑨ Where _____ my shoes?

⑩ _____ that Shelly's new car?

⑪ Who _____ the manager here?

⑫ _____ I too late for the concert?

⑬ When _____ your birthday?

⑭ _____ he here for the presentation?

⑮ Where _____ the bathroom?

⑯ _____ I supposed to be at work?

⑰ Why _____ they angry?

⑱ _____ it time to eat yet?

⑲ _____ they coming to the seminar?

3.2 FILL IN THE GAPS USING "DO" OR "DOES"

_____Does_____ he work in a hotel?

① _____ Laura have a brother?

② _____ they know your address?

③ _____ Craig still live in Dublin?

④ Where _____ your mother work?

⑤ _____ they know your father?

⑥ _____ the restaurant serve fish?

⑦ _____ you still have my book?

⑧ _____ your house have a garage?

⑨ _____ we have enough time?

⑩ How _____ Ben travel to work?

⑪ _____ your parents have a car?

⑫ When _____ the lesson end?

⑬ _____ you work on Saturdays?

⑭ _____ she play any instruments?

⑮ What _____ you want for dinner?

⑯ _____ I need to wear a dress?

⑰ What _____ he want this time?

⑱ _____ they know what time it is?

⑲ Where _____ she buy her clothes?

3.3 MARK THE QUESTIONS THAT ARE CORRECT

Does she goes to your school? ☐
Does she go to your school? ☑

① Does Danielle plays baseball very often? ☐
Does Danielle play baseball very often? ☐

② Do you know how to play the electric guitar? ☐
Do know you how to play the electric guitar? ☐

③ Does your daughter know how to drive a car? ☐
Do your daughter knows how to drives a car? ☐

④ What time does you get up in the morning? ☐
What time do you get up in the morning? ☐

3.4 REWRITE THE SENTENCES AS QUESTIONS

You play the piano.
Do you play the piano?

① She likes going to the theater.
_____

② Carlo likes Chinese food.
_____

③ You like gardening.
_____

④ He knows how to play chess.
_____

⑤ Cleo has breakfast every morning.
_____

⑥ Jim has a lot of homework this weekend.
_____

⑦ They live in London.
_____

⑧ It rains often here.
_____

⑨ Peter enjoys taking photos.
_____

⑩ Sally knows how to swim.
_____

⑪ They play golf on Saturdays.
_____

04 | The present continuous

The present continuous is used to talk about continued
actions that are happening in the present moment.
It is formed with "be" and a present participle.

4.1 MATCH THE PICTURES TO THE CORRECT ANSWERS

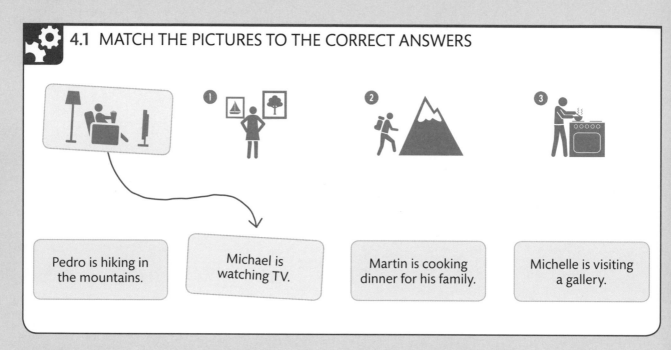

Pedro is hiking in
the mountains.

Michael is
watching TV.

Martin is cooking
dinner for his family.

Michelle is visiting
a gallery.

4.2 FILL IN THE GAPS USING THE WORDS IN THE PANEL

The children _____ *are playing* _____ football.

① You _____ a beautiful red dress.

② Matilda _____ a travel book about Brazil.

③ My cat _____ the apple tree.

④ I _____ such an interesting book.

⑤ Hetty and Paula _____ some orange juice.

⑥ Phil _____ for his piano lesson.

am reading

~~are playing~~

is climbing

is practicing

is reading

are wearing

are drinking

4.3 FILL IN THE GAPS BY PUTTING THE VERBS IN THE PRESENT CONTINUOUS

Simon _____*is walking*_____ (walk) to work today.

1. Clara _____ (try) on some new shoes.

2. I _____ (write) a letter to my girlfriend.

3. Sanjay _____ (learn) to drive.

4. Mel and Tim _____ (get married) today.

5. Robin _____ (not study) for the French exam this afternoon.

6. Sam and Ashwin _____ (play) baseball at the park.

7. My sister's friend _____ (perform) on stage now.

4.4 MARK THE SENTENCES THAT ARE CORRECT

Diane is buying a new house. ☑
Diane buys a new house. ☐

1. Sam and Pete not playing cards in the living room. ☐
   Sam and Pete aren't playing cards in the living room. ☐

2. The children eat pizza once a week. ☐
   The children are eating pizza once a week. ☐

3. Julian is wearing a suit for the meeting. ☐
   Julian is wears a suit for the meeting. ☐

4.5 MATCH THE BEGINNINGS OF THE SENTENCES TO THE CORRECT ENDINGS

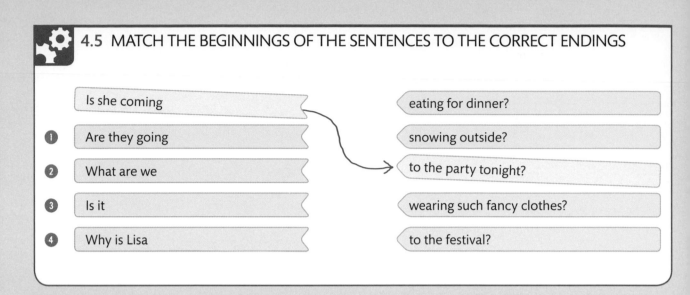

Is she coming — eating for dinner?

① Are they going — snowing outside?

② What are we — to the party tonight?

③ Is it — wearing such fancy clothes?

④ Why is Lisa — to the festival?

4.6 REWRITE THE SENTENCES, PUTTING THE WORDS IN THE CORRECT ORDER

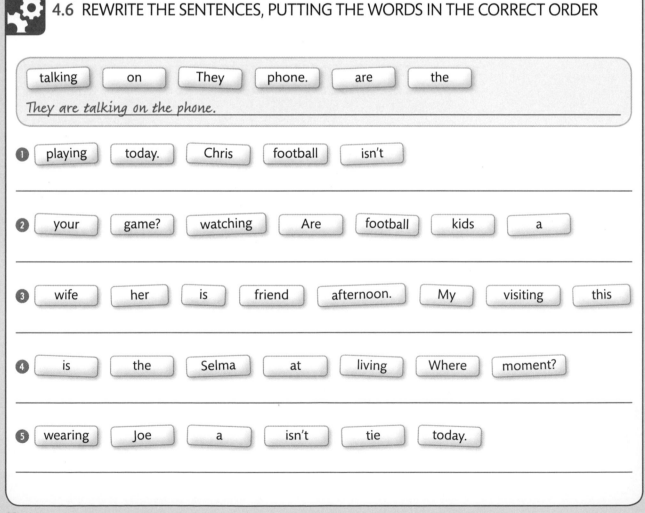

talking | on | They | phone. | are | the

They are talking on the phone.

① playing | today. | Chris | football | isn't

_____

② your | game? | watching | Are | football | kids | a

_____

③ wife | her | is | friend | afternoon. | My | visiting | this

_____

④ is | the | Selma | at | living | Where | moment?

_____

⑤ wearing | Joe | a | isn't | tie | today.

_____

4.7 REWRITE THE SENTENCES AS QUESTIONS

> She is eating an apple.
> *Is she eating an apple?*

1 They are driving to the beach.

_____

2 You are going swimming.

_____

3 She is watching a movie.

_____

4 Nelson is going shopping.

_____

5 Ben is listening to classical music.

_____

6 Chrissie is climbing the tree.

_____

7 Sven and Olly are singing.

_____

8 You are drinking apple juice.

_____

9 They are playing tennis.

_____

10 My son is reading a book.

_____

11 Pavel is speaking Russian.

_____

12 You are wearing a dress.

_____

4.8 REWRITE THE SENTENCES AS NEGATIVES

> We are enjoying the show.
> *We are not enjoying the show.*

1 I am going to the zoo.

_____

2 The dog is chasing a cat.

_____

3 They are walking their dog.

_____

4 Angela is wearing a dress.

_____

5 We are playing chess.

_____

6 I am eating Chinese food.

_____

7 James is wearing your shirt.

_____

8 You are reading a book.

_____

9 She is cleaning her room.

_____

10 Ed and Gus are watching a movie.

_____

11 I am speaking French.

_____

12 It is raining outside.

_____

05 Present tenses overview

The present simple and present continuous are used in different situations. There are different ways to form questions and negatives with these tenses.

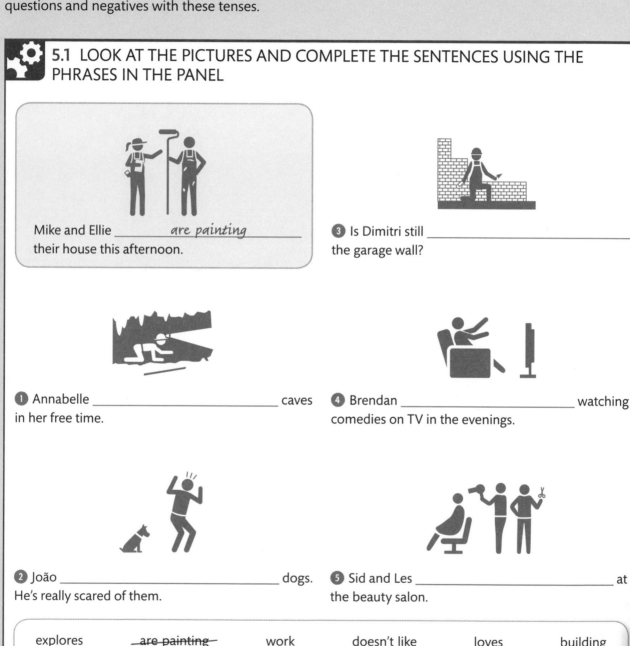

5.1 LOOK AT THE PICTURES AND COMPLETE THE SENTENCES USING THE PHRASES IN THE PANEL

Mike and Ellie _____*are painting*_____ their house this afternoon.

❸ Is Dimitri still _____ the garage wall?

❶ Annabelle _____ caves in her free time.

❹ Brendan _____ watching comedies on TV in the evenings.

❷ João _____ dogs. He's really scared of them.

❺ Sid and Les _____ at the beauty salon.

| explores | ~~are painting~~ | work | doesn't like | loves | building |

5.2 CROSS OUT THE INCORRECT WORDS IN EACH SENTENCE

  Jim ~~tries~~ / is trying to build a chair.

① Kit **goes** / is going scuba diving with her friends on Fridays.

② Ben and Kelly **dance** / **are dancing** at the club tonight.

③ Sai **puts** / **is putting** the dishes in the dishwasher each evening.

④ Bruce **waits** / **is waiting** to go for a walk.

5.3 FILL IN THE GAPS BY PUTTING THE VERBS IN THE PRESENT SIMPLE OR THE PRESENT CONTINUOUS

Alastair usually ___*plays*___ (play) tennis, but this afternoon he ___*is playing*___ (play) badminton.

① Mary _____ (not send) letters often, but she _____ (write) one to her mother now.

② I _____ (work) from home today, but usually I _____ (work) in an office.

③ We usually _____ (go) to Spain on vacation, but this year we _____ (go) to Mexico.

④ Helen _____ (work) in an elementary school. She _____ (teach) math right now.

⑤ I _____ (not eat) meat very often, but tonight I _____ (have) a steak.

⑥ It _____ (not rain) often in California, but today it _____ (pour).

⑦ My cousin _____ (perform) on stage now. I _____ (love) her voice.

⑧ Rajiv _____ (wear) a T-shirt now, but he always _____ (wear) a shirt at work.

⑨ My dad _____ (sleep) now. He _____ (be) tired after the journey.

⑩ Juan normally _____ (start) work at 8am, but today he _____ (go) to the dentist.

⑪ Bob _____ (take) a taxi to work this morning, but he usually _____ (take) the bus.

5.4 MATCH THE BEGINNINGS OF THE SENTENCES TO THE CORRECT ENDINGS

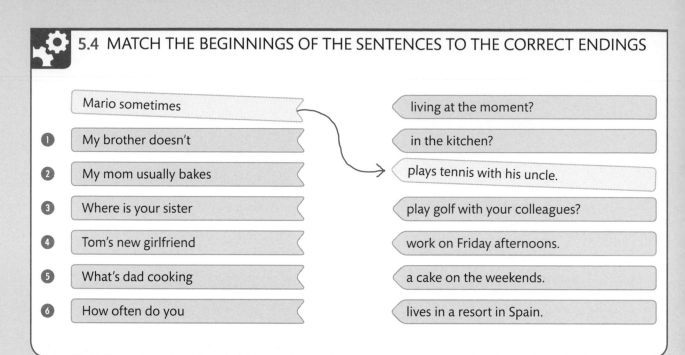

Mario sometimes	living at the moment?
① My brother doesn't	in the kitchen?
② My mom usually bakes	plays tennis with his uncle.
③ Where is your sister	play golf with your colleagues?
④ Tom's new girlfriend	work on Friday afternoons.
⑤ What's dad cooking	a cake on the weekends.
⑥ How often do you	lives in a resort in Spain.

5.5 REWRITE THE SENTENCES, PUTTING THE WORDS IN THE CORRECT ORDER

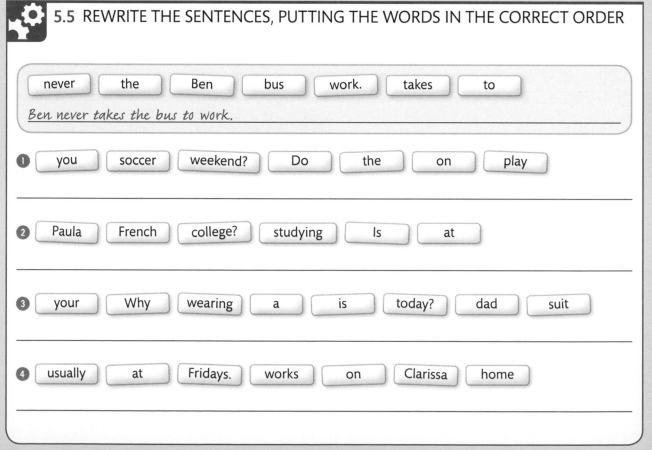

never | the | Ben | bus | work. | takes | to

Ben never takes the bus to work.

① you | soccer | weekend? | Do | the | on | play

_____

② Paula | French | college? | studying | Is | at

_____

③ your | Why | wearing | a | is | today? | dad | suit

_____

④ usually | at | Fridays. | works | on | Clarissa | home

_____

5.6 MARK THE SENTENCES THAT ARE CORRECT

Do Christina still have a cat? ☐
Does Christina still have a cat? ☑

1. Lou wakes up at 7am each morning. ☐
   Lou wake up at 7am each morning. ☐

2. Henry is performing at a country and western club tonight. ☐
   Henry are performing at a country and western club tonight. ☐

3. Tanya doesn't feels well, so she's not coming to the party. ☐
   Tanya doesn't feel well, so she's not coming to the party. ☐

5.7 REWRITE THE SENTENCES, CORRECTING THE ERRORS

Unfortunately, Mr. Clarke **doesn't understands** Russian.
Unfortunately, Mr. Clarke doesn't understand Russian.

1. Steve **read** in bed before he **go** to sleep.

2. Lisa and Tim **goes** to the gym after work.

3. My mom **plays** golf with her friend this afternoon.

4. Vernon **don't like** snakes. He really **hate** them.

5. We often **are going** to the café by the park.

6. Craig **walking** in the mountains with Rob this week.

06 Imperatives

Imperatives are used to give commands or to make requests. They can also be used to give warnings or directions.

6.1 FIND MORE IMPERATIVES IN THE GRID AND WRITE THEM UNDER THE HEADING

```
G G N I D R A W B Y R U N
N S A I H E L P T A K E V
N W E M J S M D S M A R D
G I V E E R T I S T A R T
S K A M E B O T R Q I N G
W R I T E Y A D F G I N D
W R L O L A O Z B E G I N
P W O R K N V O N S E N D
T C D H T N D E G J A Q I
E H I J L I S T E N U S S
R E C E P S T I I G G E D
G E F D B C A H T J J L M
Q K P P Y T U R N D I W G
E D I S R Y A D F A E N T
M Z L O L A O Z I O R I Z
C O M E S N V O N O E Y D
T C D H T N D E G J A G I
E H I J A R E A D E O S S
R E C E A E E I S N G K O
B S M I L E H E I D J L M
```

IMPERATIVES

_____ *write* _____

1 _____

2 _____

3 _____

4 _____

5 _____

6 _____

7 _____

8 _____

9 _____

10 _____

11 _____

12 _____

13 _____

14 _____

24

6.2 MATCH THE PICTURES TO THE CORRECT SENTENCES

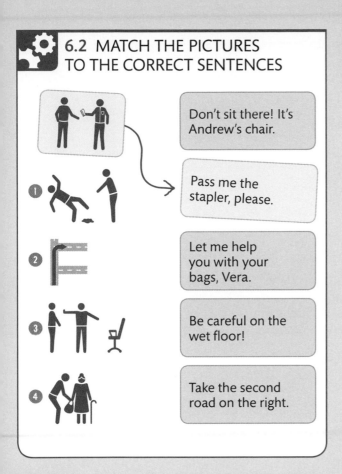

Don't sit there! It's Andrew's chair.

Pass me the stapler, please.

Let me help you with your bags, Vera.

Be careful on the wet floor!

Take the second road on the right.

6.3 MATCH THE BEGINNINGS OF THE SENTENCES TO THE CORRECT ENDINGS

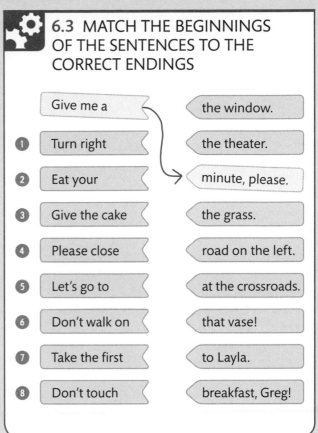

Give me a	the window.
1 Turn right	the theater.
2 Eat your	minute, please.
3 Give the cake	the grass.
4 Please close	road on the left.
5 Let's go to	at the crossroads.
6 Don't walk on	that vase!
7 Take the first	to Layla.
8 Don't touch	breakfast, Greg!

6.4 REWRITE THE SENTENCES, PUTTING THE WORDS IN THE CORRECT ORDER

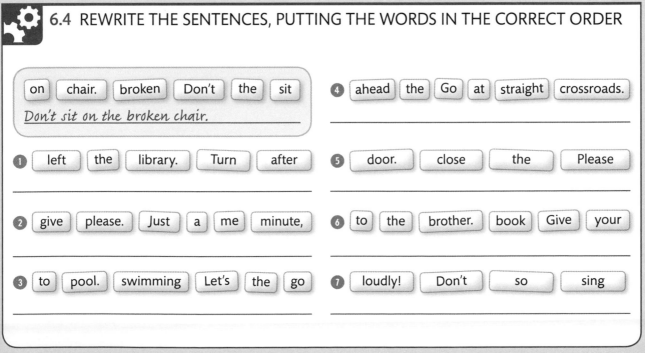

on   chair.   broken   Don't   the   sit

Don't sit on the broken chair.

1 left   the   library.   Turn   after
_____

2 give   please.   Just   a   me   minute,
_____

3 to   pool.   swimming   Let's   the   go
_____

4 ahead   the   Go   at   straight   crossroads.
_____

5 door.   close   the   Please
_____

6 to   the   brother.   book   Give   your
_____

7 loudly!   Don't   so   sing
_____

25

07 The past simple

The past simple is used to talk about completed
actions that happened at a fixed time in the past.
It is the most commonly used past tense in English.

7.1 FILL IN THE GAPS USING THE PAST SIMPLE VERBS IN THE PANEL

After work, Phil _____ *listened* _____ to music.

1. I _____ my bedroom this morning.

2. We _____ football in the afternoon.

3. After his dinner, Alex _____ a movie on TV.

4. My wife _____ her parents yesterday.

5. Lucia _____ with her friends at the party.

played

~~listened~~   watched

visited   danced

cleaned

7.2 MATCH THE BEGINNINGS OF THE SENTENCES TO THE CORRECT ENDINGS

After I finished work ————→ I decided to go for a swim.

1. Terry usually takes the metro to work,   so I checked my email.

2. I arrived at work early   the old town and visited the museum.

3. In the morning we walked to   but yesterday he walked instead.

4. Angela cried when she   after she finished her dinner.

5. We usually go to France   then started reading his new book.

6. Jemma washed the dishes   heard the sad news.

7. Roger listened to some music   but last year we traveled around Russia.

7.3 REWRITE THE SENTENCES, PUTTING THE WORDS IN THE CORRECT ORDER

| hurried | catch | The | last | to | the | children | bus. |

The children hurried to catch the last bus.

1. | so | felt | to | she | Amy | doctor. | sick, | went | the |

_____

2. | walk | I | but | to | usually | the | yesterday | I | café, | drove. |

_____

3. | laughed | Martin's | she | joke. | Mia | heard | when |

_____

7.4 CROSS OUT THE INCORRECT WORD IN EACH SENTENCE

 Jason ~~steped~~ / **stepped** off the bus and headed toward the café.

1. Simone **tryed** / **tried** to open the door, but it was completely stuck.

2. Elena **decideed** / **decided** to wear a nice dress to the dinner party that evening.

3. Chan **washed** / **washd** the dishes after she and Dan had eaten.

4. Stephan and Klara **hurried** / **hurryed** to catch the last train home.

5. The waiter **dropped** / **droped** the dishes onto the floor.

6. Megan **carryed** / **carried** the files into the office.

7.5 FILL IN THE GAPS BY PUTTING THE VERBS IN THE PAST SIMPLE

When I was a kid I _____ *had* _____ (**have**) two hamsters named Kim and Star.

1 Marilyn _____ (**go**) with Clive to the exhibition at the gallery.

2 I _____ (**see**) Phil and Dan at the party last night.

3 Sheila _____ (**swim**) across the lake to the island.

4 I _____ (**drink**) a large bottle of water after the race.

5 We _____ (**drive**) to a beautiful resort in the mountains.

6 Carol _____ (**put**) her cup down on the table.

7 Seb _____ (**do**) his homework on the bus to school.

8 Omar _____ (**buy**) a scarf for his wife at the market.

9 She _____ (**draw**) a beautiful picture of a cherry tree.

7.6 FILL IN THE GAPS USING "WAS" OR "WERE"

Irena and Jon _____ *were* _____ students together in Madrid.

1 You _____ at Paulina's party on Saturday.

2 Joanna _____ very tired after the flight to Australia.

3 My parents _____ delighted when I passed all my exams.

4 There _____ so many people waiting to buy a ticket.

5 I _____ upset when I lost my purse.

6 Liam _____ a pilot for more than 40 years.

7 There _____ a loud bang in the kitchen.

8 My cousins _____ famous dancers in the 1990s.

9 We _____ at the convention last year.

> Sam **goes** running with friends in the local park.
> *Sam went running with friends in the local park.*

1 Robin **wants** to go skiing in the winter.

_____

2 Julie and Scott **drink** a lot of coffee at the café.

_____

3 Eli **goes** camping in the woods last summer.

_____

4 Jon **plays** rugby on Saturday afternoon.

_____

5 I **watch** TV dramas until late last night.

_____

6 We **go** to a jazz club to listen to live music.

_____

7 Sadiq's dog **barks** in the yard all evening.

_____

8 The pollution in my city **is** very bad.

_____

9 Angelo **eats** an apple for his lunch.

_____

10 Kyle **makes** his bed after getting up in the morning.

_____

11 Tina **plays** the piano with her little brother.

_____

08 The past simple negative

The past simple negative is used to talk about
things that did not happen in the past. It is always
formed the same way, unless the main verb is "be."

8.1 MATCH THE BEGINNINGS OF THE SENTENCES TO THE CORRECT ENDINGS

I didn't walk to work today.

because she felt tired.

① Emily didn't go to the party

Jenny didn't call him on his birthday.

② The sports car cost a huge amount,

I took the train instead.

③ Ben was upset because

so we didn't buy it.

④ My uncle didn't enjoy the film

she didn't talk to anyone at the party.

⑤ The teacher shouted at me

because he hates science fiction.

⑥ Katie is very shy, so

because I didn't do my homework.

8.2 MARK THE SENTENCES THAT ARE CORRECT

Joanne and Greg didn't knew which road to take to get to the restaurant. ☐
Joanne and Greg didn't know which road to take to get to the restaurant. ✓

① Zehra didn't played football yesterday. She went fishing. ☐
Zehra didn't play football yesterday. She went fishing. ☐

② Michael did not like the burger he ordered, so he sent it back. ☐
Michael not liked the burger he ordered, so he sent it back. ☐

③ I didn't went out last night; I stayed in and watched TV instead. ☐
I didn't go out last night; I stayed in and watched TV instead. ☐

8.3 CROSS OUT THE INCORRECT WORDS IN EACH SENTENCE

> Lloyd **wasn't** / ~~weren't~~ happy with the new computer he'd just bought.

1. There **wasn't** / **weren't** enough sandwiches for everyone.

2. I **not did** / **did not finish** mowing the lawn because I was tired.

3. The book **wasn't** / **weren't** interesting, so I watched TV instead.

4. Joe **didn't make** / **didn't made** enough potatoes for everyone.

5. The students **not understood** / **didn't understand** the teacher.

6. There **wasn't** / **weren't** many people at the concert last night.

7. It **wasn't** / **weren't** very warm outside, so we stayed at home.

8. My brother **didn't enjoy** / **didn't enjoyed** the movie very much.

8.4 WRITE EACH SENTENCE IN ITS OTHER FORM

> Paula **was** on time for work today. | *Paula wasn't on time for work today.*

1. We **spoke** to Ellen. | _____

2. _____ | They **were not** happy.

3. They **were** late. | _____

4. _____ | I **didn't wait** for Carl.

5. Lola **understood**. | _____

6. _____ | Brendan **wasn't there**.

7. They **paid** the bill. | _____

8. _____ | Hugh **did not talk** to me.

9. Claire **ate** the cake. | _____

10. _____ | She **didn't go** swimming.

09 Past simple questions

Questions in the past simple are formed using "did."
For past simple questions with "be," the subject and
the verb "was" or "were" are swapped around.

9.1 MATCH THE STATEMENTS TO THEIR QUESTION FORMS

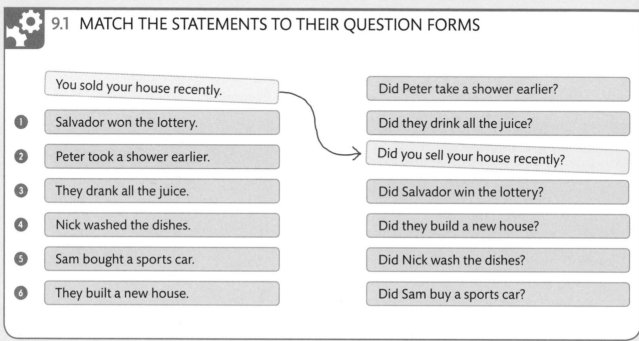

You sold your house recently.

Did Peter take a shower earlier?

1. Salvador won the lottery.

Did they drink all the juice?

2. Peter took a shower earlier.

Did you sell your house recently?

3. They drank all the juice.

Did Salvador win the lottery?

4. Nick washed the dishes.

Did they build a new house?

5. Sam bought a sports car.

Did Nick wash the dishes?

6. They built a new house.

Did Sam buy a sports car?

9.2 MATCH THE PICTURES TO THE CORRECT QUESTIONS

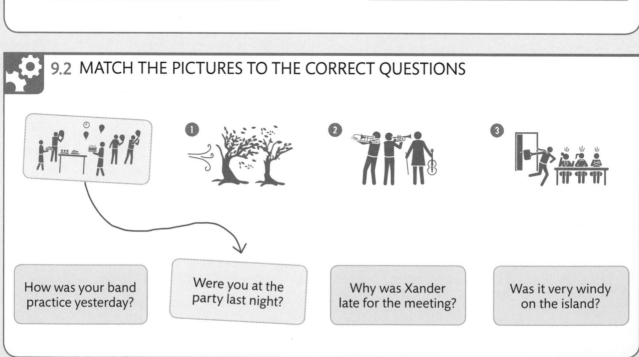

How was your band practice yesterday?

Were you at the party last night?

Why was Xander late for the meeting?

Was it very windy on the island?

9.3 REWRITE THE SENTENCES, PUTTING THE WORDS IN THE CORRECT ORDER

you	down?	Where	broke	when	were	car	your

Where were you when your car broke down?

❶ | the | Did | for | take | walk? | you | dog | a |

_____

❷ | did | home | night? | you | last | How | get |

_____

❸ | food | the | Greece? | was | in | like | What |

_____

9.4 REWRITE THE SENTENCES, CORRECTING THE ERRORS

Did Josie went to work today? She said she was feeling unwell last night.
Did Josie go to work today? She said she was feeling unwell last night.

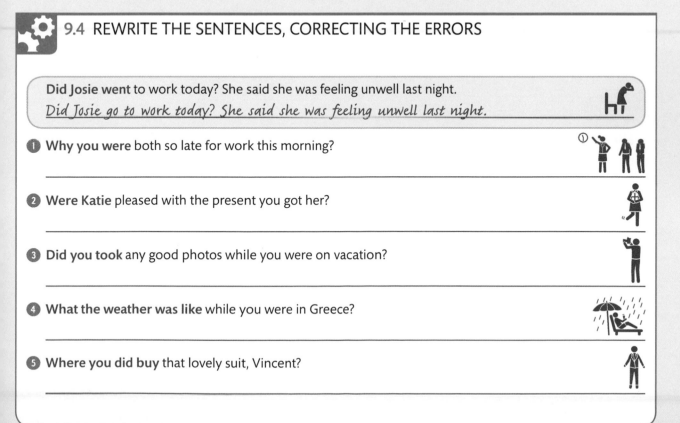

❶ **Why you were** both so late for work this morning?

_____

❷ **Were Katie** pleased with the present you got her?

_____

❸ **Did you took** any good photos while you were on vacation?

_____

❹ **What the weather was like** while you were in Greece?

_____

❺ **Where you did buy** that lovely suit, Vincent?

_____

10 The past continuous

The past continuous is used in English to talk about actions or events that were in progress at some time in the past. It is formed with "was" or "were" and a present participle.

10.1 MATCH THE PICTURES TO THE CORRECT SENTENCES

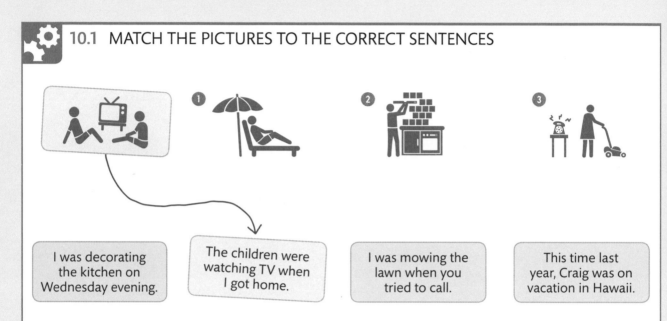

I was decorating the kitchen on Wednesday evening.

The children were watching TV when I got home.

I was mowing the lawn when you tried to call.

This time last year, Craig was on vacation in Hawaii.

10.2 CROSS OUT THE INCORRECT WORDS IN EACH SENTENCE

I **was eating** / ~~ate~~ my dinner when there ~~was being~~ / **was** a knock on the door.

1. We **were sunbathing** / **sunbathed** when it **was beginning** / **began** to rain.

2. When I **was meeting** / **met** Tracy yesterday, she **was wearing** / **wore** a lovely dress.

3. It **was being** / **was** a beautiful day and the birds **were singing** / **sang** in the trees.

4. I **was hearing** / **heard** a loud bang when I **was watching** / **watched** TV last night.

5. It **was starting** / **started** to rain while I **was talking** / **talked** on the telephone.

10.3 FILL IN THE GAPS, PUTTING THE WORDS IN THE CORRECT ORDER

| you | a | were | suit | wearing |

Why ___were___ ___you___ ___wearing___ ___a___ ___suit___ yesterday, Paul?

| in | the | hiking | were | Alps |

1 We _____ _____ _____ _____ _____ this time last year.

| he | driving | work | saw | was | when | to |

2 Colm _____ _____ _____ _____ _____ _____ _____ a deer.

| I | talking | were | when | you | to | you | saw |

3 Who _____ _____ _____ _____ _____ _____ _____ _____ yesterday?

| raining | again | wasn't | it |

4 It was cloudy yesterday, but at least _____ _____ _____ _____ .

10.4 FILL IN THE GAPS BY PUTTING THE VERBS IN THE CORRECT TENSES

We ___were walking___ (walk) in the forest when we ___saw___ (see) a bear.

1 Mia _____ (visit) Sydney while she _____ (travel) around Australia.

2 The children _____ (read) when I _____ (enter) the classroom.

3 Ravi _____ (see) an old castle when he _____ (walk) through the forest.

4 The sun _____ (shine) when we _____ (set off) on the journey home.

11 The present perfect simple

The present perfect simple is used to talk about events in the recent past that still have an effect on the present moment. It is formed with "have" and a past participle.

11.1 FILL IN THE GAPS USING "HAS" OR "HAVE" TO COMPLETE THE SENTENCES

Tess ____has____ visited France many times, but she ____has____ never been to Paris.

1 Daria _____ baked a delicious cake for everyone at the office.

2 My parents _____ decided to buy a little cottage in the country.

3 Ola _____ taken the day off and _____ gone to the new gallery in town.

4 We _____ decided when we're going to get married.

11.2 FILL IN THE GAPS USING THE WORDS IN THE PANEL

Karen ____has called____ the police about her noisy neighbors.

1 Hank _____ the letter from his college yet.

2 My children _____ the car at last.

3 Kelly still _____ her bedroom. It's so messy!

4 Danny _____ the bedroom and the living room.

5 Jess _____ Peru and Ecuador so far this year.

hasn't cleaned

has painted   ~~has called~~

hasn't opened

has visited   have washed

11.3 FILL IN THE GAPS BY PUTTING THE VERBS IN THE PRESENT PERFECT SIMPLE

Michelle _____ *has bought* _____ (buy) a puppy for her daughter.

1 Fran and Leo _____ (go) to the fair together.

2 Angelo _____ (not cook) dinner for his family yet.

3 Jenny _____ (clean) all the windows in her apartment.

4 I _____ (not meet) Nick's new girlfriend yet.

5 Morgan _____ (watch) this movie at least six times already.

6 Mr. Fernandez and his son _____ (leave) the building.

11.4 FIND EIGHT MORE PAST PARTICIPLES IN THE GRID AND WRITE THEM UNDER THE CORRECT HEADING

```
G G P I D R A O B W O T S
N S U N T I N H E L P E D
N D T M J S M D S M S R D
W A N T E D T I U T W U I
S M A Y E B O H R F U J G
E D I S R Y A S V U M N D
M Z L O W A L K E D R I Z
P A A E S N V O N S E N M
K A S K E D D E G J A G I
E H C E A R I D O N E S S
R E C M P S K I I N G E D
A N C G I V E N I J J E M
R E P E P S K D O S E N N
W A T C H E D H I J J L M
```

REGULAR

_____ *wanted* _____

1 _____

2 _____

3 _____

4 _____

IRREGULAR

_____ *given* _____

5 _____

6 _____

7 _____

8 _____

11.5 MARK THE SENTENCES THAT ARE CORRECT

Did you always live in this apartment, Vicky? ☐
Have you always lived in this apartment, Vicky? ☑

1 I have studied French in college a long time ago. ☐
I studied French in college a long time ago. ☐

2 I haven't lived in Venezuela since 2009. ☐
I didn't live in Venezuela since 2009. ☐

3 Kevin has first visited Munich in 1997. ☐
Kevin first visited Munich in 1997. ☐

4 Enzo finished the report on Friday. ☐
Enzo has finished the report on Friday. ☐

5 Sebastian is working as a chef for 10 years. ☐
Sebastian has worked as a chef for 10 years. ☐

11.6 REWRITE THE SENTENCES, CORRECTING THE ERRORS

Paula **hasn't did** her French homework yet.
Paula hasn't done her French homework yet.

1 Owen **has started** work here in 2017.

_____

2 I **have spoke** to Tina about this twice today already.

_____

3 How many countries **have you visit** so far?

_____

4 Gloria **has never trying** windsurfing before.

_____

5 Fabio **have lived** in England for more than 15 years.

_____

11.7 MARK THE BEST REPLY TO EACH QUESTION

Where is Janet today?

She's been to France, but she'll be back next week. ☐

She's gone to France, but she'll be back next week. ✓

① What's wrong, Frank?

I've just been to the dentist for a filling. ☐

I've just gone to the dentist for a filling. ☐

② Where are Rob and Susan this afternoon?

They've been to the library. ☐

They've gone to the library. ☐

③ I saw Claire come in with lots of bags.

Yes, she's been shopping with her friends. ☐

Yes, she's gone shopping with her friends. ☐

④ You look hot, Paul.

Yes, I've just been for a run. ☐

Yes, I've just gone for a run. ☐

⑤ Hi, is Sammy there?

No, she's been for a walk with the dog. ☐

No, she's gone for a walk with the dog. ☐

11.8 MARK THE BEST REPLY TO EACH QUESTION

Have you seen the new exhibition in the museum?

Yes, I saw it last weekend. ✓

Yes, I have seen it last weekend. ☐

① Have you visited the old temple here yet?

Of course, I've visited it many times. ☐

Of course, I visited it many times. ☐

② Have you tried Greek food before?

Yes, I tried it when I went to Athens last year. ☐

Yes, I've tried it when I've been to Athens last year. ☐

③ Have you lived here long?

Yes, I've moved here in 1997. ☐

Yes, I moved here in 1997. ☐

④ Have you ever seen a play by William Shakespeare?

Yes, I saw Macbeth when I went to London. ☐

Yes, I've seen Macbeth when I went to London. ☐

⑤ Have you been snorkeling before?

Yes, I've tried it twice since I've been in Malaysia. ☐

Yes, I tried it twice since I've been in Malaysia. ☐

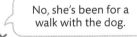

12 The present perfect continuous

The present perfect continuous is used to talk about a continuing activity in the past that still has an effect on the present moment. It usually refers to the recent past.

12.1 MATCH THE BEGINNINGS OF THE SENTENCES TO THE CORRECT ENDINGS

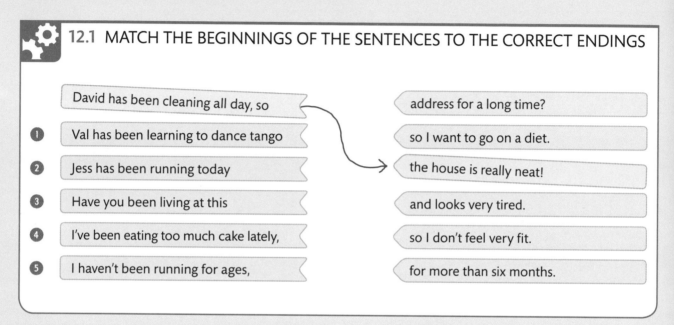

David has been cleaning all day, so — the house is really neat!

1. Val has been learning to dance tango — address for a long time?

2. Jess has been running today — so I want to go on a diet.

3. Have you been living at this — and looks very tired.

4. I've been eating too much cake lately, — so I don't feel very fit.

5. I haven't been running for ages, — for more than six months.

12.2 REWRITE THE SENTENCES, PUTTING THE WORDS IN THE CORRECT ORDER

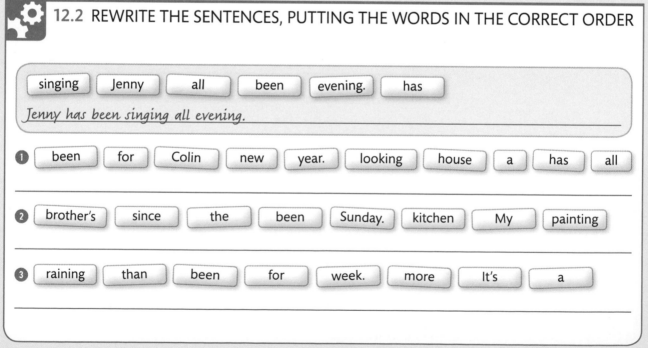

singing | Jenny | all | been | evening. | has

Jenny has been singing all evening.

1. been | for | Colin | new | year. | looking | house | a | has | all

_____

2. brother's | since | the | been | Sunday. | kitchen | My | painting

_____

3. raining | than | been | for | week. | more | It's | a

_____

12.3 FILL IN THE GAPS BY PUTTING THE VERBS IN THE PRESENT PERFECT CONTINUOUS

I _____*have been driving*_____ (drive) for hours. I'm so tired!

1. I _____ (clean) the house because my parents are coming tomorrow.

2. You _____ (build) that wall all day. Are you nearly finished?

3. Joe _____ (fish) all afternoon, but he hasn't caught anything yet.

4. We _____ (not play) tennis together for very long.

5. How long _____ you _____ (train) for the marathon, Jon?

6. Josh _____ (paint) a lovely landscape this afternoon.

7. Matt and Heather _____ (study) for their exam all evening.

8. I _____ (not read) this book for very long.

9. Jane _____ (travel) all summer.

10. _____ Robin _____ (walk) all day? He looks exhausted.

11. I _____ (try) to cook a new recipe today.

12. Ed _____ (not feel) well, so I told him to go to the doctor.

13. My friend _____ (tour) Europe with his band.

14. My manager _____ (sleep) at his desk all afternoon.

13 The past perfect simple

English uses the past perfect simple with the past simple
to talk about two or more events that happened at
different times in the past.

 13.1 FILL IN THE GAPS USING THE WORDS IN THE PANEL

George was relieved because he _____*had found*_____ his passport.

1. The play _____ by the time we arrived at the theater.

2. Ben liked Sal, even though he _____ her only a few times.

3. I _____ Indian food before, so I didn't know what to expect.

4. Justin called his sister, but she _____ to bed.

5. Edith _____ her niece for years so was delighted when she visited.

6. Amber felt so happy that she _____ her exam.

7. My uncle was upset because I _____ him recently.

8. Christine worked late because she _____ her project yet.

9. There were a lot of delays because a bus _____ .

10. When we arrived at the station, we discovered the train _____ .

11. Amy couldn't take her flight because she _____ her passport.

12. My son looked bored because he _____ inside the house all day.

13. The house looked shabby because we _____ it in years.

14. Jane was excited about going to Rome. She _____ to Italy before.

hadn't eaten	had started	hadn't finished	had left
had been	hadn't seen	hadn't called	hadn't been	~~had found~~	had gone
had broken down	had passed	had met	had forgotten	hadn't painted

13.2 MATCH THE PICTURES TO THE CORRECT SENTENCES

I had just sat down with my drink when it started to rain.

①

Yasmin was exhausted because she had just run a marathon.

②

Janine felt really cold because she'd been outside too long.

③

Tony had called for a taxi an hour earlier, but it still hadn't arrived.

④

Pete had almost finished tiling the wall by the time I got home.

13.3 FILL IN THE GAPS BY PUTTING THE VERBS IN THE PAST SIMPLE OR PAST PERFECT SIMPLE

I ____*tried*____ (try) to buy some onions, but the store ____*had run out*____ (run out).

① Craig _____ (arrive) late to work because he _____ (miss) the train.

② Marie _____ (not ride) a bike for years, so she _____ (find) it difficult.

③ Dana _____ (be) delighted that she _____ (pass) her driving test at last.

④ James _____ (prepare) breakfast when Caitlin _____ (get up).

⑤ She _____ (visit) San Francisco once before, when she _____ (be) seven.

⑥ I _____ (not meet) Karl before, but we _____ (have) lots in common.

⑦ We _____ (see) the play once before, but we _____ (enjoy) it anyway.

14 The past perfect continuous

English uses the past perfect continuous with the past simple to talk about an activity that was in progress before another action or event happened.

14.1 MARK THE SENTENCES THAT ARE CORRECT

When Fiona finally got home, she had been traveling for 12 hours. ✓
When Fiona finally got home, she has been traveling for 12 hours. ☐

❶ Maya had been working here for five years when I started. ☐
Maya was working here for five years when I had started. ☐

❷ It had been raining for a week before the sun came out. ☐
It rained for a week before the sun had been coming out. ☐

❸ I got sunburned because I been lying in the sun all day. ☐
I got sunburned because I'd been lying in the sun all day. ☐

❹ We had been to see that movie everyone talked about at work. ☐
We went to see that movie everyone had been talking about at work. ☐

❺ Vlad had been studying English for a year when he moved to Toronto. ☐
Vlad had studying English for a year when he had moved to Toronto. ☐

❻ My computer hadn't been working properly for ages, so I bought a new one. ☐
My computer didn't work properly for ages, so I had bought a new one. ☐

❼ We only found the hotel after we been driven for more than an hour. ☐
We only found the hotel after we'd been driving for more than an hour. ☐

❽ I'd trained for years before I had been winning my first marathon. ☐
I'd been training for years before I won my first marathon. ☐

❾ Carol had been cooking all morning, so she was exhausted. ☐
Carol had been cooked all morning, so she was exhausted. ☐

❿ I went to the doctor because I hadn't been feeling well all week. ☐
I went to the doctor because I didn't been feeling well all week. ☐

14.2 MATCH THE BEGINNINGS OF THE SENTENCES TO THE CORRECT ENDINGS

The floor was soaking wet because

1 Marion had been learning Spanish

2 The forest looked beautiful because

3 Kelly had been practicing all week,

4 Clive had been complaining

so her performance was perfect.

about the bad smell all week.

it had been raining all day.

for six months before she went to Spain.

it had been snowing all night.

14.3 FILL IN THE GAPS BY PUTTING THE VERBS IN THE PAST SIMPLE OR PAST PERFECT CONTINUOUS

When the package finally __arrived__ (arrive), Dave __had been waiting__ (wait) for hours.

1 Nina _____ (shop) all morning and _____ (need) a coffee.

2 Carla _____ (live) in Paris for 10 years when she _____ (meet) Liam.

3 Chris _____ (feel) exhausted because he _____ (play) football all day.

4 Phil _____ (watch) TV when the telephone _____ (ring).

5 Jill _____ (feel) ill all day, so she _____ (go) to bed early.

6 The kids _____ (watch) TV all afternoon because it _____ (be) so cold outside.

7 Jo _____ (study) for years before she _____ (pass) the exam.

8 Ahmed _____ (work) for hours before he finally _____ (leave) the office.

45

15 "Used to" and "would"

When talking about habits or states in the past, "used to" or "would" are often used. English often uses these forms to contrast the past with the present.

 15.1 LOOK AT THE PICTURES AND COMPLETE THE SENTENCES USING THE PHRASES IN THE PANEL

Ricardo _____*used to play*_____ the piano, but now he prefers the violin.

3 There _____ any factories here. There were beautiful woods.

1 I _____ in London, but I moved to Paris 10 years ago.

4 When I worked, I _____ at 5am. Now I relax in the morning.

2 When I was a teenager, I _____ fishing on Saturdays. Now I prefer photography.

5 Did you _____ a bike when you were a child?

would get up	used to live	use to ride
~~used to play~~ didn't use to be		would go

15.2 MARK THE SENTENCES THAT ARE CORRECT

Harry would be an engineer before he became a teacher. ☐
Harry used to be an engineer before he became a teacher. ☑

1. Dana was playing soccer with her friends when she was a child. ☐
   Dana used to play soccer with her friends when she was a child. ☐

2. Chris didn't use to have such long hair. ☐
   Chris didn't used to have such long hair. ☐

3. I would visit Prague three times when I was a child. ☐
   I visited Prague three times when I was a child. ☐

4. Maria used to believe in ghosts when she was little. ☐
   Maria use to believe in ghosts when she was little. ☐

5. I used to know Andre well when I was a student. ☐
   I would know Andre well when I was a student. ☐

15.3 REWRITE THE SENTENCES, CORRECTING THE ERRORS

Jenny didn't **used to** like ice cream, but now she loves it.
Jenny didn't use to like ice cream, but now she loves it.

1. I would **tried** to save money when I was at college.

   _____

2. My brother **used** read comics when he was a kid.

   _____

3. Did **use you** play computer games when you were young?

   _____

4. I **didn't used** to read novels, but I really enjoy them now.

   _____

47

16 Past tenses review

There are eight different ways to talk about the past in English. The differences between the past simple and the present perfect simple are particularly important.

16.1 CROSS OUT THE INCORRECT WORDS IN EACH SENTENCE

 Tom went to the doctor last week because he ~~has been feeling~~ / had been feeling unwell.

❶ When I saw Sam earlier this morning, he was mopping / has mopped the floor.

❷ Ron and Tim are working / have worked at the salon for more than 10 years.

❸ Danny wasn't understanding / didn't understand what the man was saying.

❹ When I was a kid, I used to be / would be scared of spiders.

❺ I love travel, but I haven't been / did not go to New York before.

❻ I discovered the loggers were cutting / had cut down almost all the trees.

❼ Pavel went outside and had built / built a snowman in the park.

❽ We were delayed, and the concert had started / started by the time we arrived.

❾ Ash had been studying / was studying Spanish for years before he moved to Madrid.

❿ We have been hiking / hiked all morning. Let's have a break, shall we?

⓫ It was a beautiful day, and the sun had shone / was shining through the window.

16.2 MATCH THE BEGINNINGS OF THE SENTENCES TO THE CORRECT ENDINGS

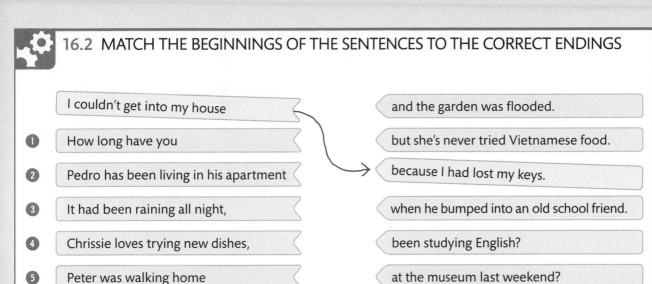

I couldn't get into my house

1. How long have you

2. Pedro has been living in his apartment

3. It had been raining all night,

4. Chrissie loves trying new dishes,

5. Peter was walking home

6. Did you go to the new exhibition

and the garden was flooded.

but she's never tried Vietnamese food.

because I had lost my keys.

when he bumped into an old school friend.

been studying English?

at the museum last weekend?

for more than six months.

16.3 REWRITE THE SENTENCES, PUTTING THE WORDS IN THE CORRECT ORDER

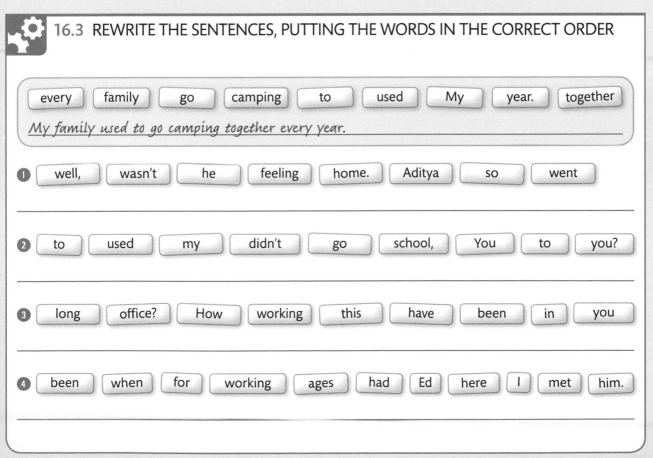

every   family   go   camping   to   used   My   year.   together

My family used to go camping together every year.

1. well,   wasn't   he   feeling   home.   Aditya   so   went

_____

2. to   used   my   didn't   go   school,   You   to   you?

_____

3. long   office?   How   working   this   have   been   in   you

_____

4. been   when   for   working   ages   had   Ed   here   I   met   him.

_____

49

16.4 FILL IN THE GAPS BY PUTTING THE VERBS IN THE CORRECT TENSES

> When Harriet _____*got*_____ (get) to the station, the train had already left.

1 When I arrived at the venue, I realized I _____ (not bring) the tickets.

2 By the time we arrived at the theater, the play _____ (begin).

3 I _____ (not see) that movie yet. Jon told me it's great.

4 Sophie _____ (cook) all morning. She's exhausted.

5 Harry looked great. He _____ (wear) his new suit.

6 Natalia _____ (sunbathe) when she noticed a monkey in a tree.

7 I _____ (not go) to the party on Friday. I was at a concert.

8 Len _____ (decorate). He has paint on his clothes.

9 Jamie _____ (practice) for months before yesterday's show.

10 I _____ (call) my dad this morning to wish him a happy birthday.

11 Bill _____ (take) a bath when he heard a knock at the door.

 16.5 MATCH THE PICTURES TO THE CORRECT SENTENCES

1

2

3

| I was sleeping soundly when my alarm clock rang. | We were hiking in the countryside when it started to rain. | I've been dreaming of going abroad all year. | After we'd eaten, Marco helped me clear the table. |

16.6 REWRITE THE SENTENCES, CORRECTING THE ERRORS

> Where **did** you **went** on vacation last year?
> *Where did you go on vacation last year?*

1 It **has been** my gran's birthday yesterday.

_____

2 I **use to** like mathematics, but now I prefer chemistry.

_____

3 When I walked into the room, Juan **talked** on the phone.

_____

4 We were sailing to Crete when I **was seeing** a dolphin.

_____

5 You look hot, Karen. **Have** you **be running**?

_____

6 When Dan **has finished** the cleaning, he went to the park.

_____

7 We **have been** lost for three weeks before the helicopter spotted us.

_____

8 **Are** you **lived** in this house for a long time?

_____

9 I **have cycled** all the way to London yesterday.

_____

10 We **walked** through the woods when we saw a bear.

_____

11 When Ben was a child, he **was wanting** to be an astronaut.

_____

12 **Were** you **enjoying** your vacation last week?

_____

17 The future with "going to"

Future forms in English are formed using auxiliary verbs.
One of the most commonly used constructions is
"going to" plus the base form of the main verb.

17.1 MARK WHETHER EACH SENTENCE IS A FUTURE PLAN OR A PREDICTION

I'm going to go see a play this weekend.
Future plan ☑
Prediction ☐

❶ Kirsty's going to fail her exams again.
Future plan ☐
Prediction ☐

❷ I'm not going to eat any more cake today.
Future plan ☐
Prediction ☐

❸ That child's going to fall off the wall.
Future plan ☐
Prediction ☐

❹ I'm going to cook a pizza for dinner tonight.
Future plan ☐
Prediction ☐

❺ We're going to get married in April.
Future plan ☐
Prediction ☐

❻ Marlon is going to win the race tonight.
Future plan ☐
Prediction ☐

❼ Martin's going to travel around Morocco this summer.
Future plan ☐
Prediction ☐

17.2 MATCH THE PICTURES TO THE CORRECT SENTENCES

Ben's brought his guitar. I think he's going to sing.

The forecast says it's going to rain tomorrow.

I think Angela is going to fall off the ladder!

Ted told me he's going to travel around Egypt next year.

Cal has the ball. Is he going to score?

Look at those clouds. I think it's going to rain.

Oh dear! The waiter's going to drop all the plates.

Sam's writing on the wall. His dad's going to be furious.

17.3 REWRITE THE SENTENCES AS QUESTIONS

Emma is going to start her own business.
Is Emma going to start her own business?

❶ Gerald is going to win the race.

_____

❷ Aziz is going to sail to Ireland.

_____

❸ Fiona is going to teach us about statistics.

_____

❹ We're going to run out of milk soon.

_____

17.4 FILL IN THE GAPS BY PUTTING THE VERBS IN THE FUTURE WITH "GOING TO"

We _____*are going to buy*_____ (buy) a new television.

❶ My son _____ (cook) for us tonight.

❷ _____ Jess _____ (study) French at college?

❸ Katie _____ (not teach) us next year.

❹ It looks like it _____ (rain) again.

❺ _____ they _____ (sing) another song for us?

❻ I _____ (sell) my bike. I never use it.

❼ Emily _____ (fix) the shower for us.

❽ Pete _____ (not play) rugby with us today.

❾ Dad _____ (get) perfume for Mom's birthday again.

18 The future with "will"

"Will" is used to form some future tenses in English.
It can be used in several different ways, which are all
different from the future with "going to."

18.1 FILL IN THE GAPS, PUTTING THE VERBS IN THE FUTURE WITH "WILL"

Alice _____ will pass _____ (pass) her exams this summer.

1 Ronaldo _____ (not go) to bed before midnight.

2 The kids _____ (have) a great time in Florida next summer.

3 You _____ (love) the new coat I just bought for the winter.

4 Mia _____ (not eat) anything with meat in it.

5 My car broke down, so I _____ (take) the train to work today.

6 Eric _____ (want) to eat steak and fries for his dinner.

7 Noah _____ (win) the 400m race at the track competition.

8 My children _____ (not like) that flavor of ice cream.

9 Charlotte _____ (marry) her boyfriend this year.

10 I _____ (stay) at home and watch TV tonight.

11 Arnie _____ (go) swimming with Bob and Sue.

18.2 MARK WHETHER EACH SENTENCE IS A PREDICTION, OFFER, PROMISE, OR DECISION

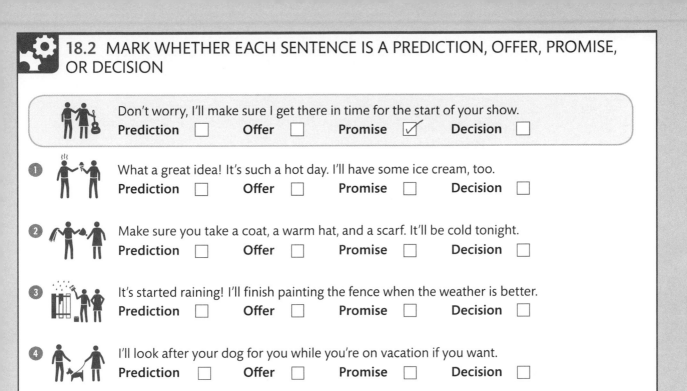

Don't worry, I'll make sure I get there in time for the start of your show.
Prediction ☐ **Offer** ☐ **Promise** ☑ **Decision** ☐

1. What a great idea! It's such a hot day. I'll have some ice cream, too.
Prediction ☐ **Offer** ☐ **Promise** ☐ **Decision** ☐

2. Make sure you take a coat, a warm hat, and a scarf. It'll be cold tonight.
Prediction ☐ **Offer** ☐ **Promise** ☐ **Decision** ☐

3. It's started raining! I'll finish painting the fence when the weather is better.
Prediction ☐ **Offer** ☐ **Promise** ☐ **Decision** ☐

4. I'll look after your dog for you while you're on vacation if you want.
Prediction ☐ **Offer** ☐ **Promise** ☐ **Decision** ☐

18.3 REWRITE THE SENTENCES, PUTTING THE WORDS IN THE CORRECT ORDER

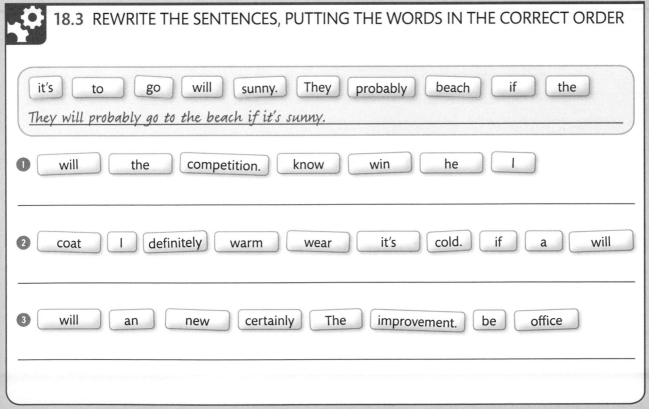

it's | to | go | will | sunny. | They | probably | beach | if | the

They will probably go to the beach if it's sunny.

1. will | the | competition. | know | win | he | I

_____

2. coat | I | definitely | warm | wear | it's | cold. | if | a | will

_____

3. will | an | new | certainly | The | improvement. | be | office

_____

55

19 The present for future events

The present simple and present continuous can be used to talk about future events that are already planned. They are usually used with a future time word or time phrase.

19.1 MARK WHETHER EACH SENTENCE REFERS TO THE PRESENT OR FUTURE

The next train to Liverpool departs in three hours.
Present ☐   **Future** ☑

❶ Kevin lives in a large house in Dublin.
Present ☐   **Future** ☐

❷ The store closes early tomorrow because it's Sunday.
Present ☐   **Future** ☐

❸ Megan's traveling around India with her brother Joseph.
Present ☐   **Future** ☐

❹ We have two cats and a dog.
Present ☐   **Future** ☐

❺ The next flight to Zurich leaves at 9pm tonight.
Present ☐   **Future** ☐

❻ Chiara is playing tennis with her boyfriend tomorrow afternoon.
Present ☐   **Future** ☐

❼ Vihaan likes watching action movies.
Present ☐   **Future** ☐

❽ I can't come to dinner with you on Friday because I'm seeing Nina.
Present ☐   **Future** ☐

❾ We have a rehearsal after work for the concert on Wednesday.
Present ☐   **Future** ☐

❿ Janet is dancing with one of her friends.
Present ☐   **Future** ☐

19.2 CROSS OUT THE INCORRECT WORDS IN EACH SENTENCE

 Bharti ~~sees~~ / **is seeing** a play tomorrow evening.

1 The exam **is** / **is being** next week. I'm nervous!

2 The bus to London usually **departs** / **is departing** at 5pm.

3 Phil **takes** / **is taking** his children to the library tomorrow.

4 Lech won't be at work tomorrow. He **travels** / **is traveling** to Berlin.

5 I can't come to the meeting tomorrow; I **have** / **am having** a doctor's appointment.

6 Mel and Phil **get** / **are getting** married this weekend.

19.3 REWRITE THE SENTENCES, CORRECTING THE ERRORS

Polly **is having** an exam next week.
Polly has an exam next week.

1 We **go** to a party later if you want to join us.
_____

2 The train from Glasgow **arrive** at 10:15pm.
_____

3 I **go** fishing with my father this afternoon.
_____

4 Terry **works** all next weekend to earn a bit of extra money.
_____

20 The future continuous

The future continuous can be formed using "will" or "going to." It describes an event or situation that will be in progress at some point in the future.

 20.1 MATCH THE BEGINNINGS OF THE SENTENCES TO THE CORRECT ENDINGS

I'd love to go to the theater tomorrow,

people will be living on the moon.

1 Will you be coming into college later?

driving past the library anyway.

2 In the year 3000, I think

but I'm going to be doing my homework.

3 I can give you a lift. I'll be

I'll be living in a nice house in the country.

4 Will we be having a meeting

he'll be working as a translator in a few years.

5 I'm sure people won't be driving

I need some help with my project.

6 Mia is going to be bringing her

about the new company logo?

7 I'm working as a waiter now, but I hope

new boyfriend to the party tonight.

8 Will you be playing soccer

as an actor in a few years' time.

9 Enzo's studying French. He hopes

with us this weekend?

10 I can post your letter. I'll be going

today. She looked terrible yesterday.

11 In 10 years' time, I hope

Thursday to see her mother.

12 Tomorrow evening, Femi's band

I'll be running my own restaurant in 10 years.

13 I guess Liz won't be coming to work

flying cars in 20 years' time.

14 Marco hopes that he'll be working

to the post office this afternoon anyway.

15 Sophie will be traveling to Paris next

are going to be performing at Funky Joe's.

20.2 MARK WHETHER EACH SENTENCE IS A NEUTRAL QUESTION OR A REQUEST

Will you be walking past a post office on your way home?
Neutral question ☑   **Request** ☐

❶ Will you go to the supermarket later, please?
Neutral question ☐   **Request** ☐

❷ Will you be going to Anastasia's party later?
Neutral question ☐   **Request** ☐

❸ Will you be taking the train to Colin's wedding?
Neutral question ☐   **Request** ☐

❹ Will we be having a meeting about the new company logo?
Neutral question ☐   **Request** ☐

❺ Will you help me with my project, please?
Neutral question ☐   **Request** ☐

20.3 REWRITE THE SENTENCES, CORRECTING THE ERRORS

Everyone is going to be watch the World Cup.
Everyone is going to be watching the World Cup.

❶ I'll be live in a mansion by the time I'm 40.
_____

❷ Marie is going to talking about the sales figures.
_____

❸ We'll all relaxing on the beach next week!
_____

❹ Cas will probably earning lots of money before too long.
_____

❺ Is Martin going to be play any of his new songs?
_____

❻ I think humans be exploring other planets by 2050.
_____

21 The future perfect

The future perfect is used to talk about an event that will
overlap with, or finish before, another event in the
future. It can be used in simple or continuous forms.

21.1 FILL IN THE GAPS BY PUTTING THE VERBS IN THE FUTURE PERFECT OR FUTURE PERFECT CONTINUOUS

By this time next week, I _____ *will have been traveling* _____ (travel) for a month.

1. Amelia _____ (move) to Cairo by the end of September.

2. By the end of the year, we _____ (live) here for 25 years.

3. _____ Pedro _____ (finish) the painting by the time we return?

4. The paint _____ (dry) by tomorrow morning.

5. By four o'clock, we _____ (wait) here for two hours.

6. I'm sure he _____ (win) more than 10 medals by the end of the year.

7. I think by the end of the year Rio _____ (ask) Yukio to marry him.

8. By the time she's 22, Suzy _____ (finish) college.

9. We _____ (complete) the project by the end of May.

10. Sam _____ (graduate) by this time next year.

11. _____ you _____ (finish) the assignment by early October?

12. How many countries _____ (visit) by the time you're 40?

13. By the time I'm 25, I _____ (study) for six years.

14. They _____ (leave) the country by the time you get here.

15. Dan _____ (retire) by the time he's 60.

16. By this time next week, we _____ (be) married for a year!

17. Sam _____ (cook) all day by the time the dinner's ready.

18. By the end of tonight, I _____ (write) this essay.

21.2 MATCH THE PICTURES TO THE CORRECT SENTENCES

Will Dan have made that chair by the time we come back?

1

I will have finished this book by tomorrow morning.

2

It looks like they won't have finished the building by next month.

3

Don't worry. I'm sure we'll have put up the tent by sunset.

21.3 FILL IN THE GAPS USING THE WORDS IN THE PANEL

I _____*will have cleaned*_____ the whole house by the time the guests arrive.

1 Anika _____ for 10 years by the end of the year.

2 I'm afraid I _____ the kitchen by the time you return.

3 By December, I _____ the piano for six months.

4 The guests _____ all the food by the time Tom arrives.

5 Leroy _____ 18 by the end of next month.

6 In a year's time, Katie _____ in Rome for 20 years.

will have been acting   will have turned   will have been learning   will have eaten

will have cleaned   will have been living   won't have painted

22 The future in the past

There are a number of constructions in English that can be used to describe thoughts about the future that someone had at some point in the past.

22.1 MATCH THE FUTURE SENTENCES TO THE EQUIVALENT SENTENCES THAT USE THE FUTURE IN THE PAST

We think we will have enough money to go on vacation this year.

I thought Hugo would have been promoted by the end of the year.

We thought we would have enough money to go on vacation this year.

① I think Hugo will have been promoted by the end of the year.

I thought Sam would pass the final English exam.

② Pari is going to buy a kitten for her daughter.

Pari was going to buy a kitten for her daughter.

③ Do you think you'll still be working here in 2021?

I knew Michelle would become a successful singer one day.

④ I think Sam will pass the final English exam.

Did you think you'd still be working here in 2021?

⑤ Penny is going to clean her house if she has time.

Beccy wasn't going to do the English course, was she?

⑥ I know Michelle will become a successful singer one day.

Penny was going to clean her house if she had time.

⑦ Beccy isn't going to do the English course, is she?

22.2 REWRITE THE SENTENCES USING THE FUTURE IN THE PAST

> **I'm going to become** a doctor if I **get** the grades.
> _I was going to become a doctor if I got the grades._

1 Christopher **thinks he'll go** traveling when he **finishes** college.

_____

2 Farouk **is going to start** cycling to work in the new year.

_____

3 I **am going to cook** dinner when I **get** home from work.

_____

4 Pablo **has** the ball. I **think he's going to** score.

_____

5 I'm sure Danny **will finish** the wall soon.

_____

6 I **think** Ania **will win** the athletics competition.

_____

7 My sister **is going** to get a cat when she **moves** house.

_____

8 The radio **says it's going to snow** tonight.

_____

9 Craig **thinks he'll visit** Japan in the summer.

_____

10 **We're going to see** a new band playing at Club 9000.

_____

11 I'm sure **he's going to talk** about the company's problems.

_____

12 Kelly **is** sure she **is going to see** some dolphins on vacation.

_____

23 Future review

English uses different constructions to talk about the future. These are mostly formed with the auxiliary verb "will" or a form of "be" with "going to."

23.1 REWRITE THE SENTENCES, PUTTING THE WORDS IN THE CORRECT ORDER

| knew | late. | Irene | going | to | was | she | be |

Irene knew she was going to be late.

---

① | you | sister | Are | for | meeting | this | my | evening? | dinner |

_____

② | will | finished | by | end | They | the | year. | the | have | stadium | the | of |

_____

③ | here | I | for | working | one | have | August, | been | will | By | year. |

_____

④ | clear | Petra | win. | that | going | It's | isn't | to |

_____

⑤ | Derek | thought | at | study | he | college. | would | engineering |

_____

⑥ | lesson | Does | at | past | the | begin | half | three? |

_____

⑦ | in | 10 | I'll | time, | be | In | living | Spain. | years' |

_____

23.2 MATCH THE BEGINNINGS OF THE SENTENCES TO THE CORRECT ENDINGS

The next train to Pasadena	but I made it to work just on time.
1 I thought I was going to be late	volcanoes will be very interesting.
2 Tomorrow's lecture about	leaves the station at 4pm.
3 Tim thought the meeting	I will have finished in 10 minutes.
4 Sorry, I'm busy at the moment, but	would have started by now.

The next train to Pasadena → leaves the station at 4pm.

23.3 CROSS OUT THE INCORRECT WORDS IN EACH SENTENCE

Oh no! He **is going to** / ~~will~~ drop those glasses!

1 Sue tells me she **is going to** / will start learning Spanish next year.

2 You look tired. **I'm going to** / I'll get you some coffee.

3 Look at those clouds. **It's going to** / It will rain soon.

4 **I'm going to** / I'll help you with those bags, Edith.

5 Look! He **is going to** / will ask his girlfriend to marry him.

6 I **am going to** / will see a play at the theater. I've already got the tickets.

7 In the future I think people **are going to** / will travel to other planets.

8 **I'm going to** / I'll have the chocolate cake on the right, please.

23.4 MATCH THE PICTURES TO THE CORRECT SENTENCES

I hope Silvia's going to sing all her hits tonight.

I'm going to be working all weekend.

The forecast said it was going to rain later.

If you're not careful, you'll smash a window.

23.5 REWRITE THE SENTENCES, CORRECTING THE ERRORS

They thought **they will finish** the housework by 6pm.
They thought they would finish the housework by 6pm.

1 Our company **not going to make** a profit this year.
_____

2 I don't think my son **will to be** an artist when he grows up.
_____

3 I can't meet you tommorow. **I'll play** tennis with Antoine.
_____

4 **We going to be miss** the beginning of the play. Let's hurry!
_____

5 Sal **will have be working** at the diner for 10 years in August.
_____

6 **I was going eat** another piece of cake, but I remembered I was on a diet.
_____

23.6 MARK THE SENTENCES THAT ARE CORRECT

In November, I will have finished my degree. ☑
In November, I will have been finishing my degree. ☐

1 My son thinks we will be driving flying cars in the future. ☐
My son thinks we will have driven flying cars in the future. ☐

2 Seb won't have finished the decorating by the time you get back. ☐
Seb won't finish the decorating by the time you get back. ☐

3 Look! That child will fall off that wall. ☐
Look! That child's going to fall off that wall. ☐

4 It's Angie's party tonight. I'll to bring some snacks and cakes. ☐
It's Angie's party tonight. I'll bring some snacks and cakes. ☐

5 The train had broken down, so I knew I am going to be late. ☐
The train had broken down, so I knew I was going to be late. ☐

6 I'm going to buy that house I saw a couple of times last week. ☐
I will buy that house I saw a couple of times last week. ☐

7 Suki joins us for dinner at the Hotel Bristol. ☐
Suki is joining us for dinner at the Hotel Bristol. ☐

8 When I turn 40, I will be living in Lisbon for 20 years. ☐
When I turn 40, I will have been living in Lisbon for 20 years. ☐

9 I travel to Paris by train this afternoon. ☐
I am traveling to Paris by train this afternoon. ☐

10 I know! I'll buy my grandmother a new scarf. ☐
I know! I'm going to buy my grandmother a new scarf. ☐

11 John knew there were going be bad delays on the trains. ☐
John knew there were going to be bad delays on the trains. ☐

12 Do you think you'll have finished the essay by the time I arrive? ☐
Do you think you'll being finished the essay by the time I arrive? ☐

13 This time next year, I hope I'll have been studying medicine at college. ☐
This time next year, I hope I'll be studying medicine at college. ☐

24 The passive

In most sentences, the subject carries out an action and the object receives it, or the result of it. In passive sentences, this is reversed: the subject receives the action.

 24.1 LOOK AT THE PICTURES AND COMPLETE THE SENTENCES USING THE PHRASES IN THE PANEL

The course _____is taught_____ online.

❸ The Eiffel Tower _____ by millions of tourists each year.

❶ The alarm _____ once a month at my workplace.

❹ Lunch _____ in the college cafeteria.

❷ The sculpture _____ in the main hall.

❺ The band _____ to perform its greatest hits.

is expected	is visited	is tested
~~is taught~~	is displayed	is eaten

24.2 MATCH THE ACTIVE SENTENCES TO THE EQUIVALENT PASSIVE SENTENCES

A plumber is fixing the leak in my roof.

This program is used by many students.

1 Many students use this program.

The leak in my roof is being fixed.

2 A famous designer is making her new dress.

The train is usually driven by Martin.

3 Someone cleans our apartment every Thursday.

Her new dress is being made by a famous designer.

4 Martin usually drives the train.

Our apartment is cleaned every Thursday.

24.3 MATCH THE PICTURES TO THE CORRECT SENTENCES

The play is being performed on stage later tonight.

A new apartment buiding is being built near my house.

Solar panels are being used by an increasing number of people.

The game is usually played in Central Park each September.

24.4 FILL IN THE GAPS BY PUTTING THE VERBS INTO THE PRESENT SIMPLE OR PRESENT CONTINUOUS PASSIVE

The newspaper _____ *is delivered* _____ (deliver) every morning at 7am.

1 English _____ (not understand) by many people here.

2 A new shopping mall _____ (build) near the park.

3 Some shows _____ (watch) by millions of people each day.

4 The food _____ (prepare) at home today.

5 The castle _____ (surround) by dense forests.

6 Our products _____ usually _____ (dispatch) within two days.

7 Latin _____ (not study) by many young people.

8 Guests _____ always _____ (provide) with a complimentary lunch.

9 My computer _____ (repair) at the moment.

10 Kelvin _____ (teach) how to juggle today.

11 The children _____ always _____ (supervise) by two adults.

12 A lot of old factories _____ (knock down).

13 The crime _____ (investigate) by the police.

14 Students _____ (expect) to be punctual at all times.

15 I'm staying with Claire while my house _____ (decorate).

16 The play _____ (perform) in French tonight.

17 That course _____ usually _____ (teach) by Eduardo.

18 All our plastic and glass _____ (recycle) by the council.

19 Ron _____ (investigate) for fraud.

20 My hair _____ (cut) by a stylist from Ecuador.

21 The car _____ (wash) right now.

22 Karim's performance _____ (record) tonight.

25 The passive in the past

English uses the passive voice in the past to stress the effect of an action that happened in the past, rather than the cause of that action.

25.1 MATCH THE PICTURES TO THE CORRECT SENTENCES

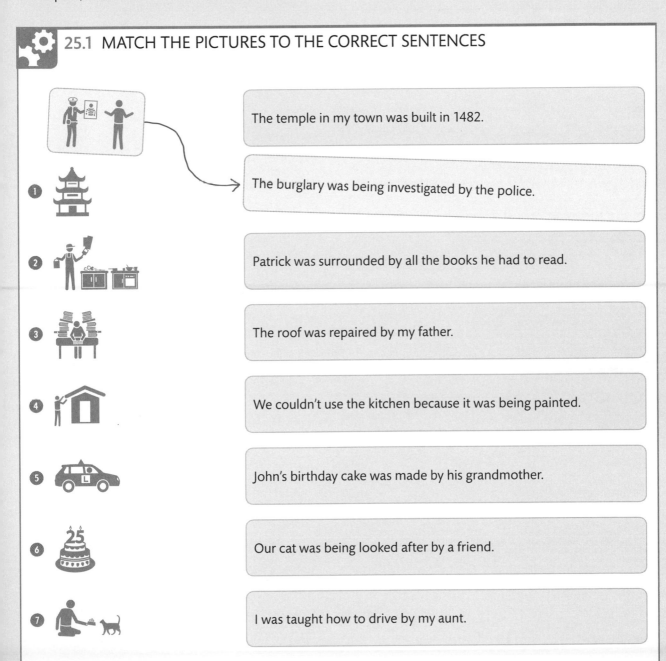

The temple in my town was built in 1482.

The burglary was being investigated by the police.

Patrick was surrounded by all the books he had to read.

The roof was repaired by my father.

We couldn't use the kitchen because it was being painted.

John's birthday cake was made by his grandmother.

Our cat was being looked after by a friend.

I was taught how to drive by my aunt.

25.2 MATCH THE BEGINNINGS OF THE SENTENCES TO THE CORRECT ENDINGS

The lecture had been canceled → because the professor was sick.

❶ When we got home, → we discovered the house had been broken into.

❷ Karen was so upset → because she hadn't been invited to the party.

❸ I hadn't been told it was Rajiv's birthday, → so I didn't have a present for him.

❹ Many houses have been damaged → by the recent hurricane.

❺ Have all the staff been informed → about tomorrow's meeting?

❻ Has your car been fixed yet? → It's been in the auto repair shop for ages!

25.3 FILL IN THE GAPS USING THE PHRASES IN THE PANEL

The puppies ___*have been given*___ to families with big yards.

❶ The play _____ by the smoke alarm. We had to evacuate the theater.

❷ Dan's room was filthy. It _____ in weeks.

❸ That old factory near my house _____.

❹ All of the plants on the balcony _____.

❺ The mail _____ yet. I'm still waiting.

❻ Most of the forest _____ last year.

❼ The spy _____ by two men in hats.

❽ Malcolm _____. He was so lazy!

| has been demolished | was being followed | hadn't been cleaned | hasn't been delivered |
| have been watered | ~~have been given~~ | was cut down | has been fired | was interrupted |

72

> The chefs were cooking lots of food for the party.
> _Lots of food was being cooked for the party._

1 People ate all of the cake that Jemima had made.

_____

2 The thieves stole all the money from the bank's safe.

_____

3 Someone injured my brother in a car accident yesterday.

_____

4 People have booked all the tables in the restaurant.

_____

5 They were building lots of tower blocks in the suburbs.

_____

6 Nobody had explored that part of the country before.

_____

7 They were so happy that someone had found their cat.

_____

8 They didn't inform me that the office was closed on Friday.

_____

9 We have sold all the tickets for tonight's movie.

_____

10 People have never climbed that mountain before.

_____

11 The earthquake has destroyed a lot of buildings.

_____

12 It's cold. Someone has left the window open.

_____

26 The passive in the future

English uses the passive voice in the future to stress the effect of an action that will happen in the future, rather than the cause of that action.

26.1 FILL IN THE GAPS BY PUTTING THE VERBS IN THE FUTURE SIMPLE PASSIVE

The letter _____ *will be sent* _____ (send) to you this afternoon.

1. The new stadium _____ (open) by the president.

2. All the food _____ (cook) by our new chef, Luigi.

3. Our house _____ (not finish) by the end of the year.

4. The prisoner _____ (release) after 30 years.

5. _____ the show _____ (present) by a new DJ?

6. My latest novel _____ (publish) in January.

7. The water _____ (turn off) on Thursday morning.

8. The lecture _____ (give) by Professor O'Brien.

9. Dinner _____ (serve) in the dining room between 7 and 9pm.

10. All the laundry _____ (do) by the time you get back.

11. _____ the students _____ (give) a test at the end of the course?

26.2 MATCH THE PICTURES TO THE CORRECT SENTENCES

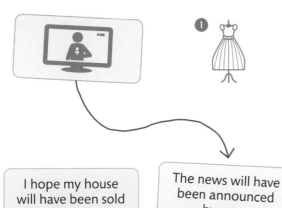

I hope my house will have been sold by next month.

The news will have been announced by now.

I'm sure we'll have been visited by aliens by 2100.

Will the dress have been altered before the wedding day?

 ## 26.3 FILL IN THE GAPS BY PUTTING THE VERBS IN THE FUTURE PERFECT PASSIVE

By tomorrow evening, everyone _____ *will have been notified* _____ (notify) of the changes.

1 By 2030, intelligent robots _____ (develop).

2 I'm sure our car _____ (repair) by the beginning of next week.

3 The computer _____ (replace) before you start work.

4 I think Jane _____ (fire) by this time next year.

5 By 2050, many more galaxies _____ (discover).

6 Do you think the criminals _____ (catch) by then?

7 All our staff _____ (train) by the end of the week.

8 _____ the project _____ (complete) by the time we return?

9 All the issues _____ (resolve) before we release the product.

10 I hope the kitchen _____ (paint) by the time we move in.

11 Our new bed _____ (deliver) by the end of the month.

12 The decision _____ (make) by Friday evening.

27 The passive with modals

Modal verbs in English can be used in passive forms.
As with other passive constructions, the emphasis
changes to the object that receives the action.

27.1 REWRITE THE SENTENCES, PUTTING THE WORDS IN THE CORRECT ORDER

| box | kept | should | place. | a | This | in | be | safe |

This box should be kept in a safe place.

1. turned / off / should / All / before / the / leaving / computers / office. / be

_____

2. at / must / Protective / all / worn / glasses / be / times.

_____

3. have / exam. / about / been / We / the / told / should

_____

4. meeting / until / be / week? / the / postponed / in / Can / later / the

_____

5. tourists / should / a / guidebook. / All / given / the / be

_____

6. have / You / running / could / across / been / that / street! / killed

_____

7. car / been / weeks / have / Our / repaired / should / ago.

_____

27.2 MARK THE SENTENCES THAT ARE CORRECT

They should have been told that the class was canceled. ☑
They should have told that the class was canceled. ☐

1. All the floors must have be mopped at the end of the day. ☐
   All the floors must be mopped at the end of the day. ☐

2. That ugly building should have been demolish years ago. ☐
   That ugly building should have been demolished years ago. ☐

3. The mountain can be climbed with the help of ropes. ☐
   The mountain can been climbed with the help of ropes. ☐

4. Our forests must be protected from destruction. ☐
   Our forests must be protect from destruction. ☐

5. You wouldn't have been stung if you'd remained calm. ☐
   You wouldn't been stung if you'd remained calm. ☐

27.3 MATCH THE BEGINNINGS OF THE SENTENCES TO THE CORRECT ENDINGS

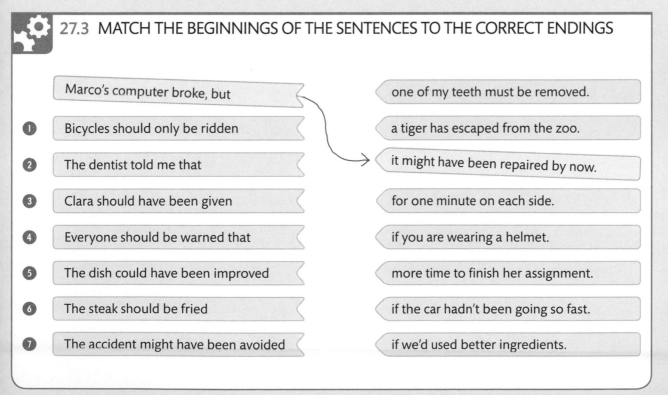

Marco's computer broke, but — it might have been repaired by now.

1. Bicycles should only be ridden — one of my teeth must be removed.

2. The dentist told me that — a tiger has escaped from the zoo.

3. Clara should have been given — for one minute on each side.

4. Everyone should be warned that — if you are wearing a helmet.

5. The dish could have been improved — more time to finish her assignment.

6. The steak should be fried — if the car hadn't been going so fast.

7. The accident might have been avoided — if we'd used better ingredients.

77

28 Other passive constructions

Many idioms in English use passive forms.
Some idioms use standard rules for passive
forms, while others are slightly different.

28.1 MATCH THE PICTURES TO THE CORRECT SENTENCES

That old house across the road is said to be haunted.

1

There is said to be a problem with crime in the local area.

2

The mountain is known to be dangerous to climb.

3

It has been revealed that the company is losing a lot of money.

4

It has been reported that many houses have been destroyed.

5

There are said to be many beautiful temples in Japan.

6

The movie star is rumored to be in a relationship with her co-star.

7

The new gallery is reported to contain a lot of modern art.

28.2 FILL IN THE GAPS USING THE WORDS IN THE PANEL

It's freezing! I hope that the heating will _____ *get fixed* _____ soon.

1 I'm hoping that I will _____ to senior manager soon.

2 My colleague often _____ for the quality of her work.

3 The bedroom's _____ next week.

4 My aunt's car _____ from the parking lot at work.

5 Samantha _____ by a dog in the local park.

gets criticized	got stolen	got bitten
getting redecorated	~~get fixed~~	get promoted

28.3 REWRITE THE SENTENCES, CORRECTING THE ERRORS

My new dress **got deliver** yesterday. It's beautiful!
My new dress got delivered yesterday. It's beautiful!

1 This store **is know** to sell high-quality shoes.
_____

2 It **been reported** that Ella is going to start performing again.
_____

3 The grass **get cut** once a month by our gardener.
_____

4 It **is rumor** that we are going to have an exam today.
_____

5 All the dishes **got wash** by Danny.
_____

79

29 Conditional sentences

Conditional sentences are used to describe real or hypothetical results of real or hypothetical situations. They can use many different verb forms.

29.1 MATCH THE PICTURES TO THE CORRECT SENTENCES

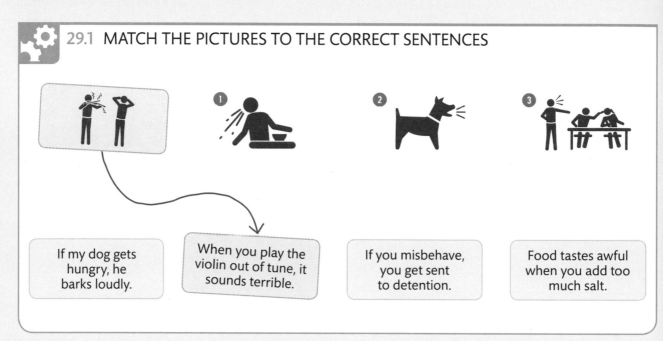

If my dog gets hungry, he barks loudly.

When you play the violin out of tune, it sounds terrible.

If you misbehave, you get sent to detention.

Food tastes awful when you add too much salt.

29.2 MATCH THE BEGINNINGS OF THE SENTENCES TO THE CORRECT ENDINGS

If you don't water plants enough,

① When it gets too cold,

② If you squeeze a balloon hard enough,

③ Water boils if you

④ Eggs usually break when

⑤ If you keep cooling water,

⑥ If you don't pay your bills on time,

we light the fire.

heat it long enough.

they die.

you get fined.

it explodes.

you drop them.

it eventually freezes.

29.3 FILL IN THE GAPS USING THE WORDS IN THE PANEL

If it starts to rain, _____*put on*_____ your coat.

1 If the phone rings, please _____ it.

2 _____ if you have any problems at all.

3 _____ it if you don't like it.

4 When you buy something expensive, always _____ the receipt.

5 If it's sunny tomorrow, _____ to use sunscreen.

Let me know

make sure

answer   ~~put on~~

Don't eat   keep

 29.4 CROSS OUT THE INCORRECT WORDS IN EACH SENTENCE

If they don't hurry up, they will / ~~won't~~ miss their flight.

1 If it stops / will stop raining, I'll finish painting the fence.

2 If Janine works very hard, she passes / will pass her exams.

3 If I don't get / won't get the job, I'll be very upset.

4 Sally loses / will lose her job if she keeps missing deadlines.

5 If it doesn't rain tomorrow, we have / will have a picnic.

6 If I get / don't get a raise, I'll definitely go on an expensive vacation.

7 Sarah will go fishing on Saturday if she has / doesn't have time.

8 If we take this path, we get / will get there more quickly.

29.5 MARK THE SENTENCES THAT ARE CORRECT

If I owned a television, I will watch the football game. ☐
If I owned a television, I would watch the football game. ☑

① Phil would buy a new television if he had more money. ☐
Phil would buy a new television if he would have more money. ☐

② If I didn't have a headache, I'd definitely come to the party. ☐
If I wouldn't have a headache, I'd definitely come to the party. ☐

③ I'd visit you more often if I'd had more time. ☐
I'd visit you more often if I had more time. ☐

④ If I was young again, I will go traveling around the world. ☐
If I was young again, I would go traveling around the world. ☐

29.6 REWRITE THE SENTENCES, PUTTING THE WORDS IN THE CORRECT ORDER

they | money, | buy | more | bigger | a | house. | If | would | had | they

If they had more money, they would buy a bigger house.

① a | lottery. | buy | if | would | he | Tony | villa | won | the

_____

② we | money, | If | more | own | we | would | had | start | business. | our

_____

③ sure | would | if | I'm | you | David | him. | you | help | asked

_____

④ went | If | she'd | Ania | go | traveling, | Vietnam. | to

_____

29.7 FILL IN THE GAPS BY PUTTING THE VERBS IN THE THIRD CONDITIONAL

If Carlos _had studied_ (study) harder, he _would have passed_ (pass) his exams.

1 If Fleur _____ (go) to bed earlier, she _____ (not feel) tired all day.

2 Simon _____ (go) to jail if the police _____ (catch) him.

3 If Marco _____ (know) there was a test, he _____ (study) for it.

4 I _____ (bring) an umbrella if I _____ (know) it was going to rain.

5 If Chris _____ (not score), we _____ (not win) the championship.

6 If I _____ (know) you were coming, I _____ (clean) the apartment.

7 I _____ (buy) you a present if I _____ (know) it was your birthday.

8 Dom _____ (not be) alone on his birthday if he _____ (invite) his friends.

9 If I _____ (not sleep) through my alarm, I _____ (not arrive) late for work.

10 Abbie _____ (study) art if she _____ (go) to college.

11 If we _____ (arrive) early, we _____ (not miss) the train.

12 Libby _____ (win) the race if she _____ (be) faster than George.

13 We _____ (not go) camping if _____ (know) it was going to be so hot.

14 If Lou _____ (not work) so hard, the project _____ (not be) such a success.

29.8 MATCH THE BEGINNINGS OF THE SENTENCES TO THE CORRECT ENDINGS

If she hadn't forgotten her phone,
if she'd remembered her key this morning.

1 If I hadn't brought the umbrella
he'd be going to a good college now.

2 If Ed had scored higher on his tests,
she would be able to call someone for help.

3 I'd be at work now
if he hadn't stolen the painting from the gallery.

4 Chloe wouldn't be sitting outside now
if I hadn't missed the 7am train.

5 Gordon wouldn't be in prison
I'd be very wet now.

 29.9 FILL IN THE GAPS USING THE PHRASES IN THE PANEL

If I had done this work earlier, I _____ *could be relaxing* _____ this evening.

1 Jemma _____ so tired now if she'd gone to bed earlier.

2 If they _____ the decorating, we wouldn't be sleeping in a camper.

3 If Emma _____ to our advice, she would be more successful now.

4 I wouldn't be such a good athlete if I _____ so hard.

5 If Len had fixed my car, I _____ to work today.

6 Tim _____ it here if he had decided to join us.

7 Karen wouldn't have to stand if she _____ a seat.

8 If I hadn't lost my job, I _____ with my sister.

9 If you _____ practicing, I'm sure you'd be a famous singer today.

had reserved   wouldn't be   had listened   wouldn't be walking   had kept

wouldn't be living   ~~could be relaxing~~   would love   had finished   hadn't trained

84

29.10 REWRITE THE SENTENCES, CORRECTING THE ERRORS

> If Fiona won more races, she will enjoy running more.
> *If Fiona won more races, she would enjoy running more.*

1 If I have to make a choice, I would say I prefer dogs.

_____

2 I would graduated by now if I'd continued with my studies.

_____

3 If you won't hurry up, you're going to be late for school.

_____

4 You would have had a great time at the party if you will come.

_____

5 We'd be on vacation now if we haven't missed the flight.

_____

6 When water will get hot enough, it boils.

_____

7 I go to the doctor if my leg still hurts tomorrow.

_____

8 The soup tastes better if I had added more salt.

_____

9 I always drink plenty of water if I got too hot.

_____

10 It would have be a perfect party if the dog hadn't eaten the cake.

_____

11 I repair the roof this afternoon if the weather's good.

_____

12 I will be very scared if I ever saw a UFO.

_____

30 Other conditional sentences

English allows for some variations in conditional sentence structures. These give more information about the context of the conditional.

 30.1 LOOK AT THE PICTURES AND COMPLETE THE SENTENCES USING THE PHRASES IN THE PANEL

If you entered the competition, you _____ *could win* _____ some money!

❸ We _____ camping if I take a few days off work.

❶ You _____ an ice cream if you're really good.

❹ If she had practiced more, Helena _____ a great singer.

❷ If you'd asked her to marry you, she _____ yes.

❺ If I have some free time later, I _____ some gardening.

could have been	might have said	can have
could go	~~could win~~	might do

86

30.2 MATCH THE BEGINNINGS OF THE SENTENCES TO THE CORRECT ENDINGS

Your infection will get worse → unless you go to the doctor today.

1. Unless you get up now, — unless we start paying her more.
2. She'll leave the firm — the neighbors will complain.
3. Unless you turn the music down, — unless you go to the doctor today.
4. You'll get sunburned — you're going to be late.
5. Unless you start working harder, — you're not going to graduate on time.
6. Angelica will get annoyed — unless you wear sun protection.
7. Unless there's bad weather, — we'll reach the summit before noon.

unless you reply to her email.

30.3 REWRITE THE THIRD CONDITIONAL SENTENCES USING FORMAL INVERSION

If Simon had ordered his sofa sooner, it would be here by now.
Had Simon ordered his sofa sooner, it would be here by now.

1. If business had been better, the company wouldn't have gone bankrupt.

_____

2. If Pamela had been richer, she would have bought a larger house.

_____

3. If you had studied harder, the exam wouldn't have been so difficult.

_____

4. If Paul had attended the meeting, he would have known about the new project.

_____

5. If the weather had been better, their trip would have been more enjoyable.

31 Conditional sentences review

There are four types of conditional sentences. The zero conditional refers to real situations, but the first, second, and third conditionals all refer to hypothetical situations.

31.1 MARK WHETHER EACH SENTENCE USES THE ZERO, FIRST, SECOND, OR THIRD CONDITIONAL

If she had more money, she would buy a new phone.
Zero ☐   **First** ☐   **Second** ☑   **Third** ☐

❶ If I didn't feel so tired, I would go to Jake's party.
Zero ☐   **First** ☐   **Second** ☐   **Third** ☐

❷ If you eat another cupcake, you will feel ill.
Zero ☐   **First** ☐   **Second** ☐   **Third** ☐

❸ Plants die if you don't give them water.
Zero ☐   **First** ☐   **Second** ☐   **Third** ☐

❹ If Juan had studied harder, he could have been a doctor.
Zero ☐   **First** ☐   **Second** ☐   **Third** ☐

❺ If the weather is nice tomorrow, we will go to the beach.
Zero ☐   **First** ☐   **Second** ☐   **Third** ☐

❻ We will miss the train if you don't hurry up.
Zero ☐   **First** ☐   **Second** ☐   **Third** ☐

❼ If you mix red and yellow, you get orange.
Zero ☐   **First** ☐   **Second** ☐   **Third** ☐

❽ I'd study mathematics at college if I were you.
Zero ☐   **First** ☐   **Second** ☐   **Third** ☐

❾ I would have returned this suit if I hadn't lost the receipt.
Zero ☐   **First** ☐   **Second** ☐   **Third** ☐

❿ If I had a lot of money, I'd buy a sports car.
Zero ☐   **First** ☐   **Second** ☐   **Third** ☐

31.2 REWRITE THE SENTENCES ADDING COMMAS WHERE NECESSARY

> If David finishes his homework he can play with his toys.
> *If David finishes his homework, he can play with his toys.*

1 If I had more money I'd go on vacation to Rome.

_____

2 We would have packed warmer clothes if we'd known it was so cold here.

_____

3 They could play baseball if it stopped raining.

_____

4 If you keep practicing you will win the championship.

_____

31.3 MARK THE SENTENCES THAT ARE CORRECT

> If you will win the race, you'll get a medal. ☐
> If you win the race, you'll get a medal. ☑

1 I would have passed the test if I'd studied. ☐
I would passed the test if I'd studied. ☐

2 If Mia had more time, she'd start a hobby. ☐
If Mia has more time, she'd start a hobby. ☐

3 If it's sunny tomorrow, I go swimming. ☐
If it's sunny tomorrow, I'll go swimming. ☐

4 If you heat ice, it turns into water. ☐
If you will heat ice, it turns into water. ☐

5 I'd have caught the bus if I hadn't overslept. ☐
I'd have catch the bus if I hadn't overslept. ☐

6 If my team won't win, I'll be disappointed. ☐
If my team doesn't win, I'll be disappointed. ☐

7 If Mel won the lottery, she'd buy a villa. ☐
If Mel won the lottery, she'll buy a villa. ☐

8 If I had seen Rob, I would said hello. ☐
If I had seen Rob, I would have said hello. ☐

9 If I'm late again, my boss is so angry. ☐
If I'm late again, my boss will be so angry. ☐

10 If she had asked me, I would have helped her. ☐
If she asked me, I would have helped her. ☐

11 If you go to bed earlier, you'd feel less tired. ☐
If you went to bed earlier, you'd feel less tired. ☐

32 Future possibilities

There are many ways to talk about imaginary future situations. Different structures can be used to indicate whether a situation is likely or unlikely.

32.1 MARK WHETHER EACH SENTENCE IS LIKELY, UNLIKELY, OR DIDN'T HAPPEN

> Suppose the factory closed down. Where would we work instead?
> **Likely** ☐   **Unlikely** ☑   **Didn't happen** ☐

① What if we miss the train? We won't get to the wedding on time.
Likely ☐   **Unlikely** ☐   **Didn't happen** ☐

② Suppose I hadn't met Ella. Who would I be with now?
Likely ☐   **Unlikely** ☐   **Didn't happen** ☐

③ What if I hadn't moved to New York? Would I still be living in Chicago?
Likely ☐   **Unlikely** ☐   **Didn't happen** ☐

④ What if you won the election? How would you feel?
Likely ☐   **Unlikely** ☐   **Didn't happen** ☐

⑤ Suppose I'd practiced every day for the recital. Would I have sounded better?
Likely ☐   **Unlikely** ☐   **Didn't happen** ☐

⑥ What if I took piano classes? Do you think I'm too old to start?
Likely ☐   **Unlikely** ☐   **Didn't happen** ☐

⑦ Suppose you saw a tiger. What would you do?
Likely ☐   **Unlikely** ☐   **Didn't happen** ☐

⑧ What if someone doesn't eat meat? We'd better make something vegetarian too.
Likely ☐   **Unlikely** ☐   **Didn't happen** ☐

⑨ Let's take some waterproof jackets in case it rains at the festival.
Likely ☐   **Unlikely** ☐   **Didn't happen** ☐

⑩ What if I got a new job? I'd like to work for a museum.
Likely ☐   **Unlikely** ☐   **Didn't happen** ☐

32.2 MATCH THE SENTENCES TOGETHER

Make sure you lock the doors

Where do you think you'd work?

1 What if Vicky became a famous actress?

We may not be able to find the path.

2 Suppose you lost your job at the café.

in case someone tries to break in.

3 Suppose we get lost in the forest.

She really enjoys drama, after all.

4 Let's prepare some more food

What if the audience don't like me?

5 Take some water with you

in case more people arrive.

6 I'm nervous about going on stage tonight.

in case you get hot while you're jogging.

32.3 MARK THE SENTENCES THAT ARE CORRECT

What if we ran out of money? We won't be able to get home! ☐
What if we run out of money? We won't be able to get home! ☑

1 Check the gallery's website in case it will be closed on Mondays. ☐
CLOSED Check the gallery's website in case it is closed on Mondays. ☐

2 Suppose the factory would close. What would the town do? ☐
Suppose the factory closed. What would the town do? ☐

3 What if we come across a bear? There are lots of them in the mountains. ☐
What if we will come across a bear? There are lots of them in the mountains. ☐

4 Your interview's tomorrow. Set an alarm in case you don't wake up on time. ☐
Your interview's tomorrow. Set an alarm in case you didn't wake up on time. ☐

5 What if we would win the lottery? What would we do with the money? ☐
What if we won the lottery? What would we do with the money? ☐

6 Take a good book in case you got bored waiting. ☐
Take a good book in case you get bored waiting. ☐

33 Wishes and regrets

English uses the verb "wish" to talk about present and past regrets. The tense of the verb that follows "wish" affects the meaning of the sentence.

33.1 MATCH THE PICTURES TO THE CORRECT SENTENCES

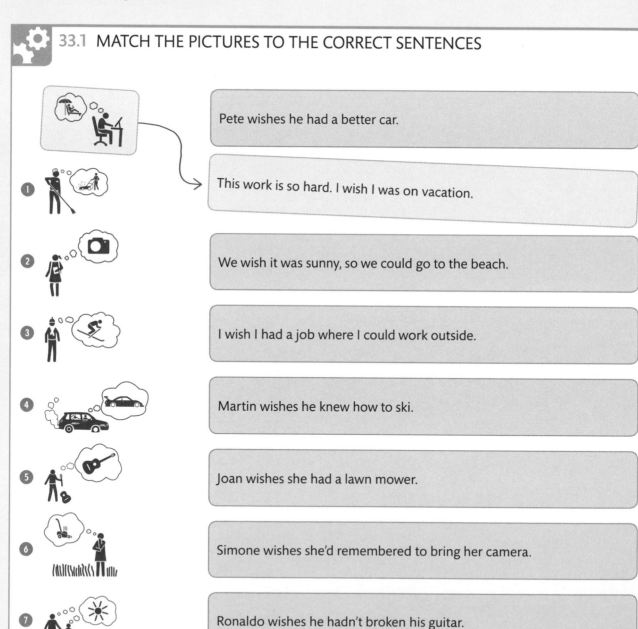

Pete wishes he had a better car.

This work is so hard. I wish I was on vacation.

We wish it was sunny, so we could go to the beach.

I wish I had a job where I could work outside.

Martin wishes he knew how to ski.

Joan wishes she had a lawn mower.

Simone wishes she'd remembered to bring her camera.

Ronaldo wishes he hadn't broken his guitar.

33.2 MARK WHETHER EACH SENTENCE COULD STILL HAPPEN OR CAN NO LONGER HAPPEN

> Brian wishes his sister would call him more often.
> **Could still happen** ☑️ **Can no longer happen** ☐

1 Kasia wishes she had studied harder at school.
Could still happen ☐ **Can no longer happen** ☐

2 Carmen wishes she hadn't eaten so much at dinner.
Could still happen ☐ **Can no longer happen** ☐

3 Bob wishes he lived in a bigger house.
Could still happen ☐ **Can no longer happen** ☐

4 If only you had told me it was your birthday.
Could still happen ☐ **Can no longer happen** ☐

5 I wish you wouldn't interrupt me all the time.
Could still happen ☐ **Can no longer happen** ☐

 ## 33.3 REWRITE THE SENTENCES, CORRECTING THE ERRORS

> Public transportation here is terrible. If only **I know** how to drive.
> _Public transportation here is terrible. If only I knew how to drive._

1 I wish I **don't work** so late all the time. I'm so tired in the evenings.

_____

2 We're lost! We **should planned** our route a little better.

_____

3 Ed, I wish **that you stop** singing out of tune all the time.

_____

4 If only **I can** cook! Everything I make is a disaster.

_____

34 Forming questions

If a statement uses "be" or an auxiliary verb, its question
form is made by inverting that verb and the subject.
Any other question is formed by adding "do" or "does."

34.1 MATCH THE STATEMENTS TO THE CORRECT QUESTIONS

She is a police officer. → Is she a police officer?

Is there a good restaurant on Park Street?

1. The children are waiting.

2. There is a good restaurant on Park Street.

Can Fu speak fluent French?

3. Fu can speak fluent French.

Are the children waiting?

4. Jean is going to win the game.

Should Peter tell Amy about the party?

5. Peter should tell Amy about the party.

Has Kelly bought a gift for her dad?

6. Kelly has bought a gift for her dad.

Is Jean going to win the game?

34.2 MATCH THE STATEMENTS TO THE CORRECT QUESTIONS

He goes swimming on Mondays. → Does he go swimming on Mondays?

Does Wayne want to come to the zoo with us?

1. Anthony started his new job at the bank.

2. Wayne wants to come to the zoo with us.

Did Anthony start his new job at the bank?

3. Harleen worked for us a few years ago.

Do Lara and Michael go to the same school?

4. Henry likes classical music.

Do they own the bookstore by the park?

5. Lara and Michael go to the same school.

Did Harleen work for us a few years ago?

6. They own the bookstore by the park.

Does Henry like classical music?

34.3 MARK THE SENTENCES THAT ARE CORRECT

Do they goes to the cinema often? ☐
Do they go to the cinema often? ☑

1. Does Tina still work at the boutique? ☐
   Does Tina still works at the boutique? ☐

2. Does you prefer cats or dogs? ☐
   Do you prefer cats or dogs? ☐

3. Did the children enjoyed the fair? ☐
   Did the children enjoy the fair? ☐

4. Did you manage to move that box? ☐
   Did manage you to move that box? ☐

5. Does Selma go jogging often? ☐
   Do Selma goes jogging often? ☐

6. Did you helped clean up after the party? ☐
   Did you help clean up after the party? ☐

7. Do you often go abroad on vacation? ☐
   Do go you often abroad on vacation? ☐

8. Doesn't Clara has two large dogs? ☐
   Doesn't Clara have two large dogs? ☐

9. Have you ever read *Little Women*? ☐
   Have read you ever *Little Women*? ☐

10. Don't you like fast food, Phillippe? ☐
    Don't you liking fast food, Phillippe? ☐

11. Have you ever have a driving lesson? ☐
    Have you ever had a driving lesson? ☐

12. Did you enjoyed the art exhibition? ☐
    Did you enjoy the art exhibition? ☐

13. Did you remember to feed the dog? ☐
    Did you remembered to feed the dog? ☐

 34.4 CROSS OUT THE INCORRECT WORD IN EACH SENTENCE

~~Has~~ / Have you set a date for your wedding yet?

1. Do / Does Dora work in a bank?

2. Is / Are your colleagues coming to the party?

3. Do / Does we start work at 10am on Fridays?

4. Do / Does Marlon really live in a mansion?

5. Did Bill work / worked for the government?

6. Was / Were there many animals in the forest?

7. Do / Does Marcel come from Argentina?

8. Did you went / go to the theater last night?

9. Has / Have you seen Anika's new car?

10. Is / Are Tom going to finish the report today?

11. Did Bruce live / lived in Glasgow?

12. Was / Were John at the airport to meet you?

13. Do / Does you take a shower in the evening?

14. Is / Are there any juice left?

15. Has / Have we got enough time left?

16. Is / Are your brother coming later?

17. Do / Does Claire and Sam have any children?

18. Do / Does Tim play soccer on the weekend?

19. Is / Are those your tools on the table?

20. Did Elsa have / had a boyfriend named Gus?

21. Do / Does Ash still work at the café?

22. Is / Are your daughter still in college?

23. Has / Have Sheila seen your new house yet?

34.5 REWRITE THE SENTENCES, PUTTING THE WORDS IN THE CORRECT ORDER

someone? | call | we | Should
Should we call someone?

3 you | the | party | Are | later? | coming | to

_____

1 finished | painting | Has | she | yet? | the

_____

4 teacher? | Is | Jackie | still | a

_____

2 India? | you | Have | to | been

_____

5 remember | door? | Did | the | you | lock | to

_____

 34.6 REWRITE THE SENTENCES AS QUESTIONS

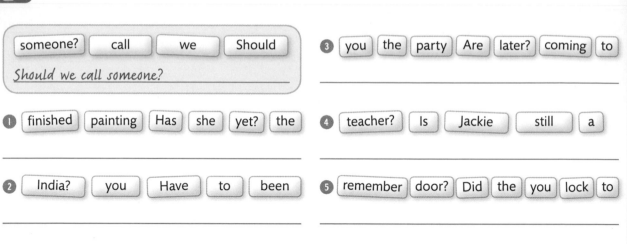

He was snowboarding in Canada last week.
Was he snowboarding in Canada last week?

1 Ed has lived in New York for more than 10 years.

_____

2 Katia and Pavel are getting married in June.

_____

3 Claudia took a flight to Rio de Janeiro.

_____

4 Mia goes swimming every evening after work.

_____

5 You remembered to buy some water.

_____

6 Ron and Lily are playing tennis this afternoon.

_____

35 Question words

Open questions are questions that do not have simple "yes" or "no" answers. In English, they are formed by using question words.

35.1 CROSS OUT THE INCORRECT WORDS IN EACH SENTENCE

Where / ~~Who~~ has your dog gone?

1. **What / Where** did you buy at the market?
2. **Why / Who** is Lena laughing so much?
3. **Where / Which** of these bags is yours?
4. **Why / How** does your dad feel today?
5. **Whose / Who** is going to teach the course?
6. **Whose / Where** car is parked outside?
7. **How / What** quickly can you finish it?
8. **When / Where** does your cousin live?
9. **When / What** does the hardware store close?
10. **Whose / What** diary is on the desk?
11. **How / When** did you last see Maria?
12. **What / How** many times has he been to Kenya?
13. **Why / How** did she quit the course?
14. **Where / What** is the entrance?
15. **When / Who** did you invite to the party?
16. **How / What** long does it take to get there?
17. **Which / Who** car should I buy?
18. **Whose / Where** did I put my glasses?

35.2 PUT THE WORDS IN THE CORRECT ORDER

you | How | are | today?
How are you today?

1. the | is | classroom? | Where
_____

2. this? | Whose | is | phone
_____

3. do | you | Why | that? | did
_____

4. long | wait? | did | How | you
_____

5. earlier? | did | meet | Who | you
_____

6. house | Which | yours? | is
_____

7. movie | the | When | start? | does
_____

35.3 MATCH THE PICTURES TO THE CORRECT SENTENCES

How does the soup taste, Gustav?

Which of these dresses should I buy?

Which way do you think we should go?

When did you start playing the guitar, Tom?

 35.4 MARK THE SENTENCES THAT ARE CORRECT

What is bigger, the moon or the sun? ☐
Which is bigger, the moon or the sun? ☑

1 What is the date today? ☐
Which is the date today? ☐

2 What's the name of your business? ☐
Which is the name of your business? ☐

3 What train are you taking, the 1pm or the 3pm? ☐
Which train are you taking, the 1pm or the 3pm? ☐

4 What do you prefer, skiing or snowboarding? ☐
Which do you prefer, skiing or snowboarding? ☐

5 What time are they arriving? ☐
Which time are they arriving? ☐

6 If you had to choose between dogs and cats, what would you choose? ☐
If you had to choose between dogs and cats, which would you choose? ☐

35.5 MARK THE MOST LIKELY QUESTION IN EACH CONVERSATION

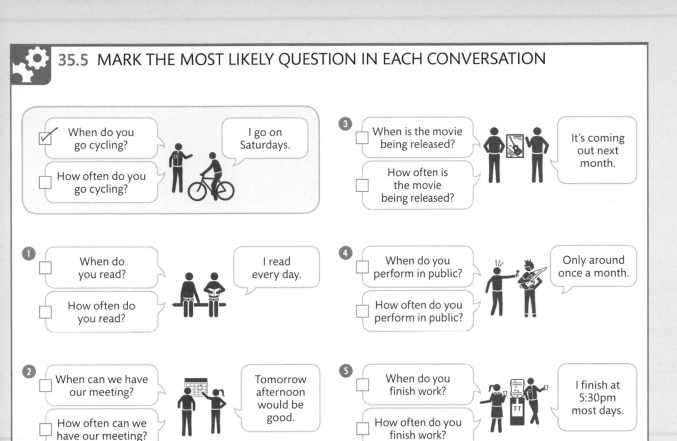

When do you go cycling? ✓

How often do you go cycling?

I go on Saturdays.

3 When is the movie being released?

How often is the movie being released?

It's coming out next month.

1 When do you read?

How often do you read?

I read every day.

4 When do you perform in public?

How often do you perform in public?

Only around once a month.

2 When can we have our meeting?

How often can we have our meeting?

Tomorrow afternoon would be good.

5 When do you finish work?

How often do you finish work?

I finish at 5:30pm most days.

35.6 MATCH THE BEGINNINGS OF THE QUESTIONS TO THE CORRECT ENDINGS

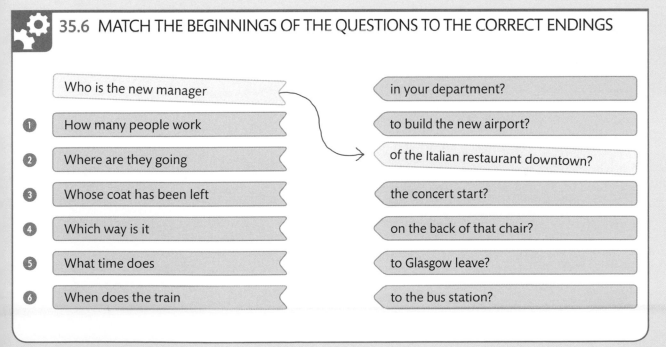

Who is the new manager

1 How many people work

2 Where are they going

3 Whose coat has been left

4 Which way is it

5 What time does

6 When does the train

in your department?

to build the new airport?

of the Italian restaurant downtown?

the concert start?

on the back of that chair?

to Glasgow leave?

to the bus station?

36 Open questions

Open questions can't be answered with "yes" or "no." They are formed differently depending on the main verb of the question.

36.1 LOOK AT THE PICTURES AND COMPLETE THE QUESTIONS USING THE PHRASES IN THE PANEL

_____ *How far is it* _____ to the nearest hotel?

❸ _____ after the race?

❶ _____ if you saw a ghost?

❹ _____ water your plants?

❷ _____ you will finish building the house?

❺ _____ look so happy?

How do you feel	~~How far is it~~	What would you do
Why do you both	How often do you	When do you think

36.2 MARK THE QUESTIONS THAT ARE CORRECT

Who should I talk to about this? ✓
Who I should talk to about this? ☐

1. What time does the train leave? ☐
   What time the train does it leave? ☐

2. What your name is? ☐
   What is your name? ☐

3. How the movie was? ☐
   How was the movie? ☐

4. When did you get this dog? ☐
   When you did get this dog? ☐

5. Why you did phone me earlier? ☐
   Why did you phone me earlier? ☐

6. Who can speak English here? ☐
   Who speak can English here? ☐

7. Who should I call to complain? ☐
   Who I should call to complain? ☐

8. When you start work? ☐
   When do you start work? ☐

9. What is this button for? ☐
   What this button is for? ☐

10. Which dress you prefer? ☐
    Which dress do you prefer? ☐

11. Why aren't you at work today? ☐
    Why you aren't at work today? ☐

12. What do you eat for breakfast? ☐
    What you eat for breakfast? ☐

13. Where do David live? ☐
    Where does David live? ☐

 ## 36.3 REWRITE THE QUESTIONS, CORRECTING THE ERRORS

When **she does finishes** work?
When does she finish work?

1. What **she is going** to sing for us next?
   _____

2. Where **you bought** that lovely dress?
   _____

3. What **did happened** to your leg, Paul?
   _____

4. **Who's** bicycle is that in the yard?
   _____

5. Why **you have** to watch so much TV?
   _____

6. How **feel you** about losing your job?
   _____

7. Where **you do cycle** to on Sundays?
   _____

8. How many times **you visited** New York?
   _____

9. Why **you** so angry, Anthony?
   _____

10. How old **the twins are** today?
    _____

11. What time **you do eat** your lunch?
    _____

12. When **you** last **went** camping, Sam?
    _____

37 Object and subject questions

There are two kinds of question: object questions and subject questions. They are formed in different ways and are used to ask about different things.

37.1 MATCH THE QUESTIONS TO THE CORRECT ANSWERS

Who taught you how to drive? → My dad taught me how to drive.

An artist from Australia painted it.

1. Who did you go to the party with?

I went with an old friend from school.

2. Who painted that amazing picture?

We saw a play by William Shakespeare.

3. Who gave you that lovely necklace?

Angelica. She has so much experience.

4. What did you see at the theater?

It was a present from my boyfriend.

5. What are you going to have for dinner?

There was a terrible storm last week.

6. Who are you going to offer the job to?

I'm going to have fish and chips.

7. What caused all that damage to your house?

37.2 MARK THE CORRECT OPTION FOR EACH QUESTION

What did she have for dinner?
Subject question ☐
Object question ☑

1. Who was performing last night?
Subject question ☐
Object question ☐

2. Who teaches you English?
Subject question ☐
Object question ☐

3. Who did you borrow the money from?
Subject question ☐
Object question ☐

4. What just made that awful noise outside?
Subject question ☐
Object question ☐

5. Who paid for all these drinks?
Subject question ☐
Object question ☐

6. What are you doing tomorrow?
Subject question ☐
Object question ☐

7. Who did the police arrest?
Subject question ☐
Object question ☐

37.3 CROSS OUT THE INCORRECT WORDS IN EACH SENTENCE

> Who **came** / ~~did come~~ into the office today?

1 Who **played** / **did play** golf with you yesterday?

2 What **saw you** / **did you see** at the movies last night?

3 Who **married** / **did marry** Sonia at the end of the movie?

4 What **caught you** / **did you catch** while fishing yesterday?

 37.4 REWRITE THE SENTENCES, CORRECTING THE ERRORS

> What **watched you** on TV last night?
> *What did you watch on TV last night?*

1 Who **I saw** you playing golf with on Sunday?

_____

2 Who **did stole** the money from the bank?

_____

3 Who **did leave** this terrible mess?

_____

4 What **you are going** to wear to the wedding?

_____

5 Who in that huge castle **lives**?

_____

6 What **you did give** the cat to eat?

_____

7 Who the race **won** this afternoon?

_____

38 Indirect questions

Indirect questions are more polite than direct questions.
They are very common in formal spoken English,
particularly when asking for information.

38.1 FILL IN THE GAPS, PUTTING THE WORDS IN THE CORRECT ORDER

| is | library | where | the |

Could you tell me __where__ __the__ __library__ __is__ ?

| the | begins | what | time | lesson |

1 Do you know _____ _____ _____ _____ _____ ?

| bus | where | is | the | station |

2 Do you know _____ _____ _____ _____ _____ ?

| get | to | how | gallery | to | the | national |

3 Could you tell me _____ _____ _____ _____ _____ _____ _____ ?

| costs | ticket | a | Oslo | to | much | how |

4 Do you know _____ _____ _____ _____ _____ _____ _____ ?

| still | if | served | breakfast | being | is |

5 Could you tell me _____ _____ _____ _____ _____ _____ ?

| is | why | so | expensive | this |

6 Could you tell me _____ _____ _____ _____ _____ ?

| train | Swansea | goes | to | the | whether |

7 Do you know _____ _____ _____ _____ _____ _____ ?

38.2 MARK THE SENTENCES THAT ARE CORRECT

> Do you know when does the supermarket open? ☐
> Do you know when the supermarket opens? ☑

❶ Could you tell me where Lizzy lives? ☐
Could you tell me where does Lizzy live? ☐

❷ Do you know why is the school closed? ☐
Do you know why the school is closed? ☐

❸ Do you know has the course begun yet? ☐
Do you know if the course has begun yet? ☐

❹ Could you tell me why you did that? ☐
Could you tell me why did you do that? ☐

38.3 REWRITE THE SENTENCES, CORRECTING THE ERRORS

> Do you know why are you in trouble?
> *Do you know why you are in trouble?*

❶ Do you know has Emma brushed the yard?
_____

❷ Could you tell me whose is that old car?
_____

❸ Do you know will the car be ready by 5pm?
_____

❹ Could you tell me where is the station?
_____

❺ Do you know when will you finish the report?
_____

39 Question tags

In spoken English, small questions are often added to the ends of sentences. These are called question tags, and they are most often used to invite someone to agree.

39.1 MATCH THE BEGINNINGS OF THE SENTENCES TO THE CORRECT QUESTION TAGS

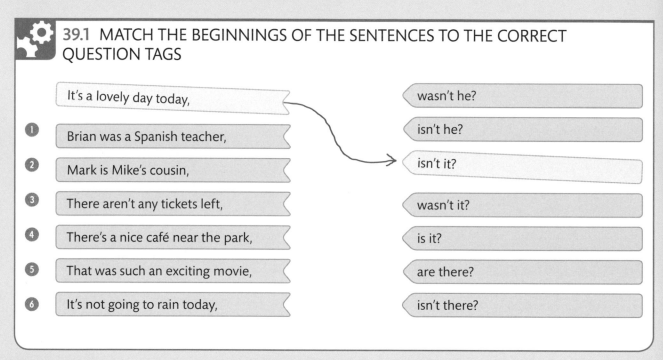

It's a lovely day today,

1 Brian was a Spanish teacher,

2 Mark is Mike's cousin,

3 There aren't any tickets left,

4 There's a nice café near the park,

5 That was such an exciting movie,

6 It's not going to rain today,

wasn't he?

isn't he?

isn't it?

wasn't it?

is it?

are there?

isn't there?

39.2 FILL IN THE GAPS USING THE QUESTION TAGS IN THE PANEL

I could become a lawyer, *couldn't I?*

1 Your grandmother likes tea, _____

2 Gerald has finished the gardening, _____

3 Luca didn't pass the English exam, _____

4 Carla worked in a bakery, _____

5 We should buy a new fridge, _____

6 You haven't seen my glasses, _____

7 Mike can swim, _____

couldn't I?   shouldn't we?   have you?   can't he?

didn't she?   did he?   hasn't he?   doesn't she?

39.3 ADD QUESTION TAGS TO THESE SENTENCES

The photocopier shouldn't do that, _____ *should it* _____ ?

1. The hat on the left is gorgeous, _____ ?

2. That ride was really scary, _____ ?

3. You're Daniel's cousin, _____ ?

4. I think our team's going to win, _____ ?

5. We aren't going to catch our plane, _____ ?

6. You've read that book before, _____ ?

7. The guests don't look very happy, _____ ?

8. Bill plays the guitar really well, _____ ?

9. Chloe will do the shopping for you, _____ ?

10. I should have brought an umbrella, _____ ?

11. Martin doesn't like cooking much, _____ ?

12. Paul looks absolutely exhausted, _____ ?

13. We've been waiting here for 30 minutes, _____ ?

14. You're not listening to anything I say, _____ ?

40 Short questions

Short questions are a way of showing interest during conversation. They're used to keep conversation going, rather than to ask for new information.

40.1 MARK THE BEST REPLY TO EACH STATEMENT

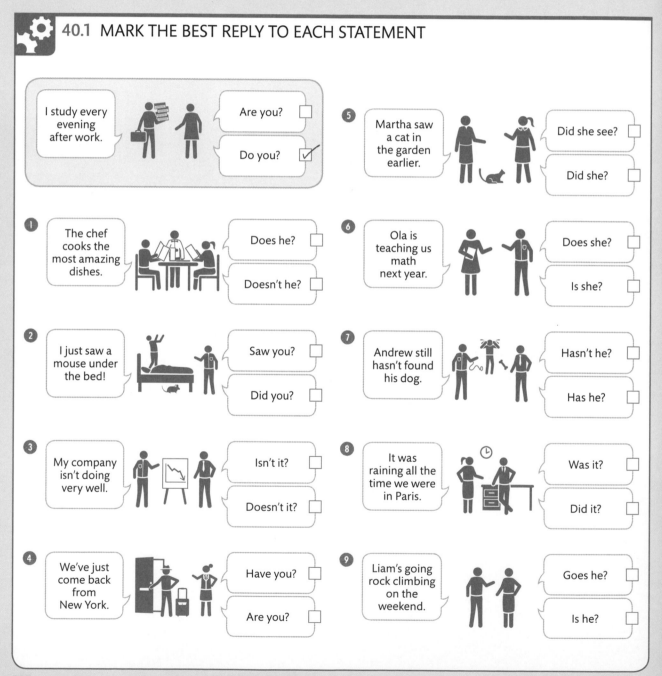

41 Short answers

When answering closed questions in English, some words can often be left out to make responses shorter. These short answers are often used in spoken English.

41.1 MARK THE BEST REPLY TO EACH STATEMENT

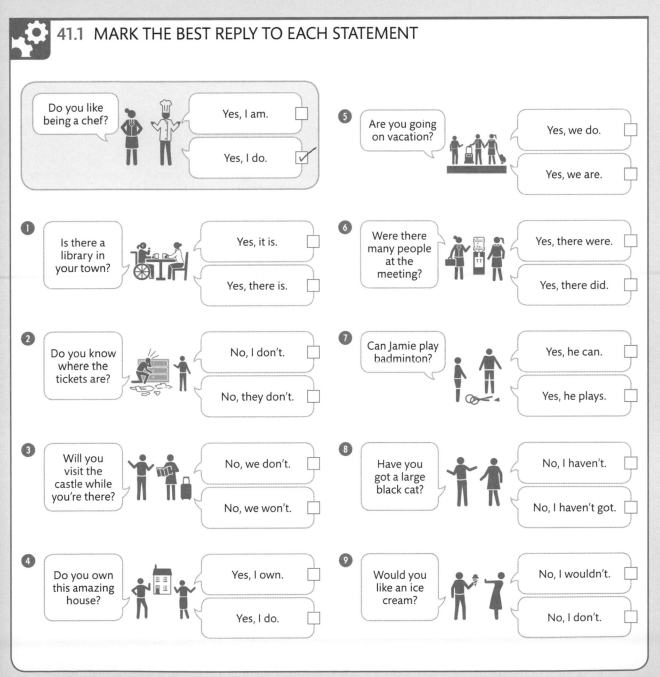

Do you like being a chef?
- Yes, I am. ☐
- Yes, I do. ☑

1 Is there a library in your town?
- Yes, it is. ☐
- Yes, there is. ☐

2 Do you know where the tickets are?
- No, I don't. ☐
- No, they don't. ☐

3 Will you visit the castle while you're there?
- No, we don't. ☐
- No, we won't. ☐

4 Do you own this amazing house?
- Yes, I own. ☐
- Yes, I do. ☐

5 Are you going on vacation?
- Yes, we do. ☐
- Yes, we are. ☐

6 Were there many people at the meeting?
- Yes, there were. ☐
- Yes, there did. ☐

7 Can Jamie play badminton?
- Yes, he can. ☐
- Yes, he plays. ☐

8 Have you got a large black cat?
- No, I haven't. ☐
- No, I haven't got. ☐

9 Would you like an ice cream?
- No, I wouldn't. ☐
- No, I don't. ☐

42 Questions review

Questions in English are formed in different ways depending on the main verb. Open and closed questions are formed differently, and spoken with different intonation.

42.1 REWRITE THE STATEMENTS AS QUESTIONS

Helen went to Sydney last year.
Did Helen go to Sydney last year?

1. Joe's playing tennis on Thursday.
_____

2. They've knocked down the apartment block.
_____

3. Jean-Paul is learning to cook.
_____

4. Rob is going to win the race.
_____

5. Chrissy does exercises each morning.
_____

6. They will play all their greatest hits.
_____

7. Claire and Ben got married last week.
_____

8. Aziz works late every evening.
_____

9. Jessica took the dog for a walk.
_____

42.2 WRITE THE QUESTIONS FROM THE PANEL UNDER THE CORRECT HEADING

SUBJECT QUESTIONS

Who wrote this book?

_____

_____

_____

OBJECT QUESTIONS

_____

_____

_____

_____

Who did you invite?   Who do you live with?   What does John do for work?

What happened next?   What did you buy?

Who wrote this book?   Who called earlier?   Who drove you to work?

42.3 MARK WHETHER EACH QUESTION IS AN OPEN QUESTION OR A CLOSED QUESTION

Where did you put my phone charger?
Open question ☑   **Closed question** ☐

1 What are you going to buy at the supermarket?
Open question ☐   **Closed question** ☐

2 Would you like to go see a jazz concert with me tonight?
Open question ☐   **Closed question** ☐

3 Have you already finished your final assignment?
Open question ☐   **Closed question** ☐

4 Why did you decide to study environmental science at college?
Open question ☐   **Closed question** ☐

5 Did your brother really make that delicious dinner we just ate?
Open question ☐   **Closed question** ☐

6 Shall we go ice skating again tonight? I enjoyed it last time.
Open question ☐   **Closed question** ☐

43 Reported speech

The words that people say are called direct speech.
Reported speech is often used to describe what
someone said at an earlier point in time.

43.1 MATCH THE DIRECT SPEECH SENTENCES TO THE CORRECT REPORTED SPEECH

| You look very happy today! | → | She said her husband was from Alabama. |

1 I want to come to the park with you.   He told me I looked very happy today.

2 My husband is from Alabama.   She told me that she was a lawyer.

3 It is extremely hot in Adelaide.   Our boss told us we had to work harder.

4 I'm a lawyer.   Emilia said she wanted to come to the park with us.

5 I want to quit school.   They told me they owned a villa in Spain.

6 You have to work harder.   He said it was extremely hot in Adelaide.

7 We own a villa in Spain.   My son said he wanted to quit school.

43.2 MARK THE SENTENCES THAT ARE CORRECT

They said that there was a big carnival today. ☑
They said me that there was a big carnival today. ☐

1. She told me she was a Canadian citizen. ☐
   She said me she was a Canadian citizen. ☐

2. Rob said me he had won a huge amount of money. ☐
   Rob said he had won a huge amount of money. ☐

3. Ella said that Phil's 18th birthday party was great fun. ☐
   Ella told that Phil's 18th birthday party was great fun. ☐

4. Ted told me he went backpacking around Europe last year. ☐
   Ted told he went backpacking around Europe last year. ☐

43.3 REWRITE THE SENTENCES USING REPORTED SPEECH, PUTTING THE VERBS IN THE PAST SIMPLE

I want to buy a new basketball.
He _____*told*_____ (tell) me that he _____*wanted*_____ (want) to buy a new basketball.

1. I travel around the world a lot for work.
   She _____ (say) that she _____ (travel) around the world a lot for work.

2. My new boyfriend is from Ethiopia.
   She _____ (tell) me that her new boyfriend _____ (be) from Ethiopia.

3. I live in Milan with my family.
   Silvio _____ (tell) Maria that he _____ (live) in Milan with his family.

4. I feel sick, so I'm going home.
   Mike _____ (say) that he _____ (feel) sick, so he went home.

5. My brother works in a travel agency.
   She _____ (tell) me that her brother _____ (work) in a travel agency.

44 Tenses in reported speech

In reported speech, the reported verb usually
"goes back" a tense. Time and place references
and pronouns sometimes also change.

44.1 MARK THE BEST REPORTED SPEECH EQUIVALENT TO EACH DIRECT SPEECH SENTENCE

It is raining very heavily.
Shaun said it rained very heavily. ☐
Shaun said it was raining very heavily. ☑

1 I'll give you a call later tonight.
Jan said she would give me a call later that evening. ☐
Jan said she gave me a call later that evening. ☐

2 I'm seeing my grandma later today.
Benedict said he saw his grandma later that day. ☐
Benedict said he was seeing his grandma later that day. ☐

3 I arrived at the hotel hours ago.
George told me he'd arrived at the hotel hours earlier. ☐
George told me he would arrive at the hotel hours later. ☐

4 We're going to the movies to see the new thriller.
Matt and Mabel said they had gone to the movies to see a thriller. ☐
Matt and Mabel said they were going to the movies to see a thriller. ☐

5 I can't afford to come on vacation with you this summer.
Danny said he didn't afford to come on vacation with us this summer. ☐
Danny said he couldn't afford to come on vacation with us this summer. ☐

6 Your new dress looks great.
Gemma told me that my new dress looks great. ☐
Gemma told me that my new dress looked great. ☐

7 I'll give the camera back to you tomorrow.
Katie said she had given the camera back to me the next day. ☐
Katie said she'd give the camera back to me the next day. ☐

44.2 MATCH THE PICTURES TO THE CORRECT SENTENCES

1

2

3

| Malcolm told Mel that he works in a salon. | George and Tamsin told me they go on vacation a lot. | Archie told me that his car had broken down. | Betty said she'd seen a wolf in the woods last year. |

44.3 REWRITE THE SENTENCES, CORRECTING THE ERRORS

Christopher told me that he **will** call me yesterday.

Christopher told me that he would call me yesterday.

1 Cath told me she **has** posted the letter a few days ago.

2 The weather forecast said it **is** going to be sunny yesterday.

3 Angela told me she **was** already mowed the lawn.

4 Miles told us that the company **is** losing money before it went bankrupt.

5 In February, Lisa told me that she **has** had a great idea for a vacation.

6 Emil said he **will** visit me in Japan that summer.

44.4 MATCH THE DIRECT SPEECH SENTENCES TO THE CORRECT REPORTED SPEECH

An engineer will come to your house tomorrow.

The shop assistant told me they didn't have a shirt in my size.

They told me an engineer would come to my house the following day.

1 We're going to the zoo on Thursday.

The manager said the hotel was fully booked in July.

2 We don't have a shirt in your size, sorry.

Harry told me they were going to the zoo on Thursday.

3 I don't want to go to the party tonight.

Michelle said she didn't want to go to the party last night.

4 I'm afraid the hotel's fully booked in July.

Billy's mom said he would pass all his exams.

5 I worked on a farm when I was a student.

She said that she lives in a house near the bus station.

6 Billy will pass all his exams this summer.

Jenny told me that she'd worked on a farm when she was a student.

7 I'm writing a novel set in Ancient Rome.

Carlo said he was going to buy a new car that afternoon.

8 I live in a house near the bus station.

Robert told me he was writing a novel set in Ancient Rome.

9 I'm going to buy a new car this afternoon.

45 Reporting verbs

In reported speech, "said" can be replaced
with a wide variety of verbs that give people more
information about how someone said something.

45.1 FILL IN THE GAPS, PUTTING THE WORDS IN THE CORRECT ORDER

| she | that | admitted |

Katrina _admitted_ _that_ _she_ didn't understand the question.

| me | buy | to | reminded |

1 Don _____ _____ _____ _____ some milk on the way home.

| study | me | encouraged | to |

2 My parents _____ _____ _____ _____ medicine in college.

| be | explained | would | that | she |

3 Tina's sister _____ _____ _____ _____ _____ late to the recital.

45.2 MATCH THE PICTURES TO THE CORRECT SENTENCES

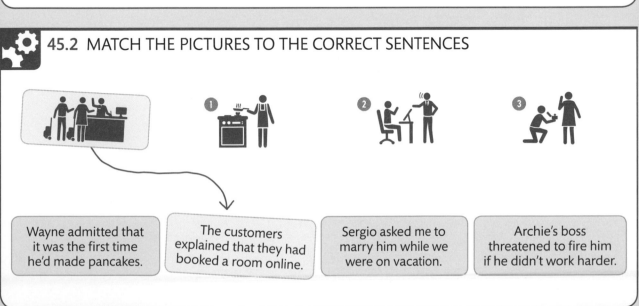

Wayne admitted that
it was the first time
he'd made pancakes.

The customers
explained that they had
booked a room online.

Sergio asked me to
marry him while we
were on vacation.

Archie's boss
threatened to fire him
if he didn't work harder.

46 Reported speech with negatives

Negatives in reported speech are formed in the same way as negatives in direct speech. "Not" is used with the auxiliary, or with the main verb if there is no auxiliary.

46.1 MATCH THE BEGINNINGS OF THE SENTENCES TO THE CORRECT ENDINGS

The weather report advised people	not to draw on the walls.
① Pedro explained that he	not to forget my passport.
② Paul's mom told him	not to travel during the storm.
③ Monika reminded me	didn't work on Fridays.
④ I said that I didn't want	come because I was feeling ill.
⑤ I told my brother I couldn't	to drive to the restaurant.

46.2 MARK THE SENTENCES THAT ARE CORRECT

My husband reminded me to don't be late for dinner. ☐
My husband reminded me not to be late for dinner. ☑

① My colleague mentioned that the printer wasn't working. ☐
My colleague mentioned that the printer not working. ☐

② Mark explained me that he didn't like dogs. ☐
Mark explained that he didn't like dogs. ☐

③ Myra phoned to say that she not to come to the meeting. ☐
Myra phoned to say that she wasn't coming to the meeting. ☐

④ Jon tried to persuade me not to eat any more cake. ☐
Jon tried to persuade me not eating any more cake. ☐

47 Reported questions

Reported questions are used to describe questions that someone has asked. Direct questions and reported questions use different word orders.

47.1 MATCH THE PICTURES TO THE CORRECT SENTENCES

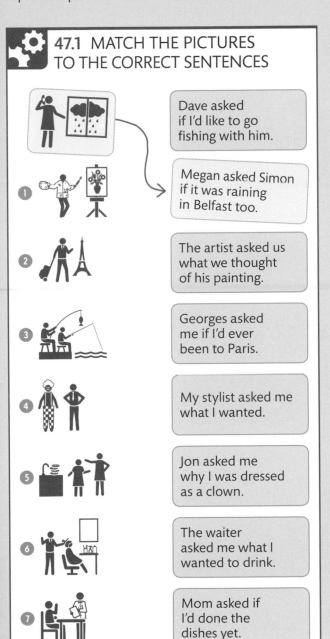

Dave asked if I'd like to go fishing with him.

Megan asked Simon if it was raining in Belfast too.

The artist asked us what we thought of his painting.

Georges asked me if I'd ever been to Paris.

My stylist asked me what I wanted.

Jon asked me why I was dressed as a clown.

The waiter asked me what I wanted to drink.

Mom asked if I'd done the dishes yet.

47.2 REWRITE THE SENTENCES, CORRECTING THE ERRORS

Rick asked me **where I do work.**
Rick asked me where I work.

① He asked me **where do you live.**

_____

② Sue asked me **what did I think.**

_____

③ Amy asked us **should she bring something.**

_____

④ Paul asked **why did I leave.**

_____

⑤ They asked me **where had I been.**

_____

⑥ The girl asked me **where is the station.**

_____

⑦ She asked **where was the exit.**

_____

⑧ Mia asked me **do I own a car.**

_____

⑨ They asked me **who is he.**

_____

47.3 FILL IN THE GAPS, PUTTING THE WORDS IN THE CORRECT ORDER

| me | what | asked |

The officer __asked__ __me__ __what__ my name was.

| to | coming | were | if | you | the |

1 Peter asked _____ _____ _____ _____ _____ _____ performance later.

| to | I'd | if | decided | me | asked |

2 My teacher _____ _____ _____ _____ _____ _____ study math in college.

| I | to | me | go | where | wanted |

3 Lou asked _____ _____ _____ _____ _____ _____ on Saturday.

| if | order | we | wanted | to | asked |

4 The waiter _____ _____ _____ _____ _____ _____ more drinks.

| time | me | we | usually | what | have |

5 Susan asked _____ _____ _____ _____ _____ _____ our lunch break.

| wanted | go | if | to | I | the | to |

6 She asked me _____ _____ _____ _____ _____ _____ movies with her.

| kids | wanted | her | they | if | mint | or |

7 Claire asked _____ _____ _____ _____ _____ _____ strawberry ice cream.

| we | lived | how | had | in | long |

8 Fran asked _____ _____ _____ _____ _____ _____ San Francisco.

| help | could | him | I | house | whether | move |

9 Pete asked _____ _____ _____ _____ _____ _____ this weekend.

47.4 REWRITE THE SENTENCES USING REPORTED SPEECH, PUTTING THE VERBS IN THE CORRECT TENSES

Are you studying physics or chemistry here?

He asked me whether I _____*was studying*_____ (study) physics or chemistry there.

1 Can I borrow your T-shirt?

Paul asked if he _____ (can) borrow my T-shirt.

2 Is it raining where you are?

Danny wanted to know if it _____ (rain) here.

3 Is Tim coming to the lecture later today?

Hiroshi asked whether you _____ (come) to the lecture later today.

4 Will you post this letter for me?

Shona asked me if I _____ (post) this letter for her.

5 How long have you been knitting for, Grandma?

My granddaughter asked me how long I _____ (knit) for.

6 Where is Silvio living at the moment?

Antonia asked me where you _____ (live) at the moment.

7 Who is the singer in this band?

Greg asked me who the singer _____ (be) in the band we saw last night.

8 Do you know when you are going to finish the block?

I asked the architect if he knew when they _____ (finish) the block.

9 Who won the marathon today?

Ella asked me who _____ (win) the marathon yesterday.

10 Do you believe in ghosts, Mom?

My children asked me today if I _____ (believe) in ghosts.

11 Who directed the new comedy?

Patsy wanted to know who _____ (direct) the new comedy.

48 Reported speech review

When forming reported speech from direct speech, some words change in order to keep the meaning consistent. Other words stay the same.

48.1 MATCH THE DIRECT SPEECH SENTENCES TO THE CORRECT REPORTED SPEECH

I am moving house next week. → Sanjay told me that he was moving house the following week.

1 I really miss my friends and family.

2 Christine paid for lunch last week.

3 I really don't want to work this Saturday.

4 My daughter dreams of becoming an actor.

5 I'll be a famous singer by 2015.

6 We're going to the theater tomorrow.

7 I've never been to the Tower of London.

Les told me Christine had paid for lunch the week before.

Sanjay told me that he was moving house the following week.

Jiya once told me she'd be a famous singer by 2015.

Steph told me that she really missed her friends and family.

Angela tells me she's never been to the Tower of London.

Rohan tells me he really doesn't want to work this Saturday.

Mia told Dan that her daughter dreamed of becoming an actor.

Lou told me they were going to the theater the following day.

48.2 MARK THE SENTENCES THAT ARE CORRECT

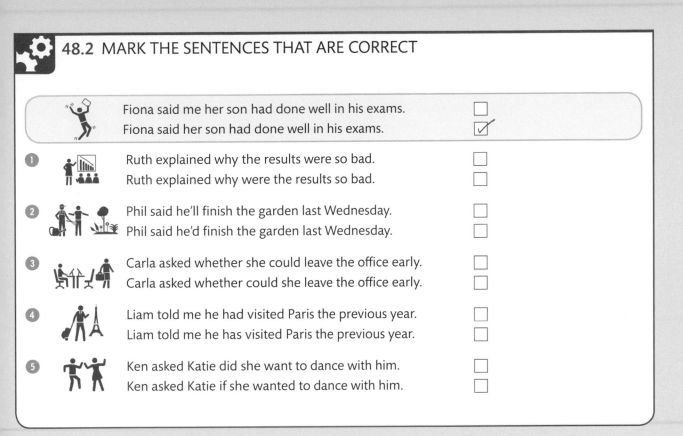

Fiona said me her son had done well in his exams. ☐
Fiona said her son had done well in his exams. ☑

1. Ruth explained why the results were so bad. ☐
   Ruth explained why were the results so bad. ☐

2. Phil said he'll finish the garden last Wednesday. ☐
   Phil said he'd finish the garden last Wednesday. ☐

3. Carla asked whether she could leave the office early. ☐
   Carla asked whether could she leave the office early. ☐

4. Liam told me he had visited Paris the previous year. ☐
   Liam told me he has visited Paris the previous year. ☐

5. Ken asked Katie did she want to dance with him. ☐
   Ken asked Katie if she wanted to dance with him. ☐

48.3 REWRITE THE SENTENCES, PUTTING THE WORDS IN THE CORRECT ORDER

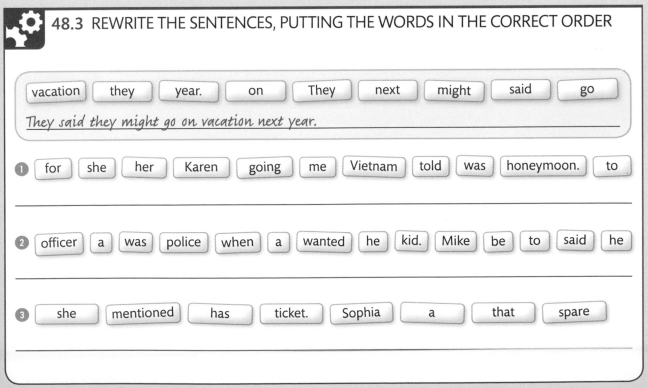

| vacation | they | year. | on | They | next | might | said | go |

They said they might go on vacation next year.

1. for | she | her | Karen | going | me | Vietnam | told | was | honeymoon. | to

_____

2. officer | a | was | police | when | a | wanted | he | kid. | Mike | be | to | said | he

_____

3. she | mentioned | has | ticket. | Sophia | a | that | spare

_____

49 Types of verbs

Verbs can be described as main verbs or auxiliary verbs.
Main verbs describe actions, occurrences, or states of being.
Auxiliary verbs modify the meaning of main verbs.

49.1 MARK WHETHER EACH VERB IS MAIN OR AUXILIARY

Unfortunately, nobody told Harry that the meeting time **had** changed.
Main ☐   Auxiliary ☑

1. Jen **called** a taxi to take her home from the supermarket.
   Main ☐   Auxiliary ☐

2. Sally **had** been studying for her exams all day.
   Main ☐   Auxiliary ☐

3. **Would** you like me to help you with your bag?
   Main ☐   Auxiliary ☐

4. You **should** always do warm-up exercises before running.
   Main ☐   Auxiliary ☐

5. I like to **listen** to the radio early in the morning.
   Main ☐   Auxiliary ☐

6. Julio **plays** baseball with his friends after school.
   Main ☐   Auxiliary ☐

7. They **had** just sold the last tickets for the show.
   Main ☐   Auxiliary ☐

8. Mia **gave** her sister her birthday present.
   Main ☐   Auxiliary ☐

9. Ella and Paul **are** buying an apartment together.
   Main ☐   Auxiliary ☐

10. Ed **works** as a scientist at the university.
    Main ☐   Auxiliary ☐

49.2 FILL IN THE GAPS USING THE VERBS IN THE PANEL

My friends _____ *are* _____ very funny, you'd like them!

1 You _____ call your grandma. It's her birthday.

2 The students _____ all handed in their papers.

3 Sandra _____ coming to the party tonight.

4 My son _____ already swim when he was three.

5 I _____ already left by the time Jim arrived.

6 I _____ like her boyfriend. He was rude.

7 You _____ speak so loudly in the library.

have
didn't
had
isn't
mustn't
~~are~~
should
could

49.3 FIND SIX MORE VERBS IN THE GRID AND WRITE THEM UNDER THE CORRECT HEADING

```
G P N I D R A O B W T N S
C A R R I V E G T A S N V
N D E M J S R D S N M R D
R I N T H R O W U T I U I
S W G T X B A A R D L J G
D G I V E Y D D F A E N X
M Z L O U A O L I O R I Z
P A Q E S N V A N S E S D
T C D H T N D U G J A G I
B R I N G R I G I E O S S
R E Q E P S K H C O M E H
A E C D E F X F I J J L M
```

TRANSITIVE

give

1 _____

2 _____

3 _____

INTRANSITIVE

laugh

4 _____

5 _____

6 _____

50 Action and state verbs

Verbs that describe actions or events are known as "action" or "dynamic" verbs, whereas those that describe states are known as "state" or "stative" verbs.

50.1 MARK WHETHER EACH VERB IS AN ACTION OR STATE VERB

One day, I **want** to be famous.
Action ☐
State ☑

❶ We **play** soccer after school.
Action ☐
State ☐

❷ I **like** your new blouse, Katie.
Action ☐
State ☐

❸ Liam **goes** home at 4:30pm.
Action ☐
State ☐

❹ Fay **cooks** wonderful meals.
Action ☐
State ☐

❺ This cheese **tastes** a bit strange.
Action ☐
State ☐

❻ Chiara **wants** to study art history.
Action ☐
State ☐

❼ Rob **takes** the bus to work.
Action ☐
State ☐

50.2 REWRITE THE SENTENCES, CORRECTING THE ERRORS

I'm **having** a cold at the moment.
I have a cold at the moment.

❶ We **are knowing** Jenny very well.
_____

❷ This soup **is tasting** awful.
_____

❸ Chris **is wanting** an ice cream.
_____

❹ Our vacation **was costing** a lot of money.
_____

❺ Craig **is understanding** Spanish.
_____

❻ I **was recognizing** that man.
_____

❼ My son **is hating** vegetables.
_____

❽ Dom's pie **was smelling** great.
_____

❾ Your book **is sounding** interesting.
_____

50.3 WRITE THE VERBS FROM THE PANEL IN THE CORRECT GROUPS

ACTION VERBS	STATE VERBS
try	

drive	be	contain	hear	own
~~try~~	kick	know	eat	read

50.4 CROSS OUT THE INCORRECT WORDS IN EACH SENTENCE

 Chrissy **doesn't want** / ~~isn't wanting~~ to go to work today.

 ① Fatima **writes** / **is writing** a book about her childhood.

 ② It **rains** / **is raining** outside. Let's watch something on TV.

 ③ Marco **plays** / **is playing** guitar on stage now.

 ④ Rosita **has** / **is having** two sisters, who live in the United States.

 ⑤ Claude **hates** / **is hating** all salad and vegetables.

 ⑥ I **read** / **am reading** a travel guide to Los Angeles.

51 Infinitives and participles

Infinitives and participles are forms of verbs that are rarely used on their own, but are important when making other forms or constructions.

51.1 WRITE EACH VERB IN ITS OTHER FORMS

BASE FORM	PRESENT PARTICIPLE	PAST PARTICIPLE
walk	walking	walked
①	planning	
② play		
③	doing	
④	liking	
⑤		found
⑥		written
⑦ finish		
⑧		bought
⑨ read		
⑩		told
⑪		hoped
⑫ swim		
⑬		gone
⑭	crying	
⑮	beginning	
⑯		said
⑰	loving	

51.2 FILL IN THE GAPS USING THE PARTICIPLES IN THE PANEL

I have been _____*waiting*_____ for a train for ages.

to go	planned
going	finished
~~waiting~~	planning

1. Carla has _____ all of her assignments.
2. Marsha's _____ a surprise party for Ed.
3. Marion is _____ to get married this fall.
4. We hadn't _____ to stay in, but it started raining.
5. We want _____ to the art exhibition tomorrow.

 51.3 REWRITE THE SENTENCES, CORRECTING THE ERRORS

I need help **chooseing** my college major. I can't decide!
I need help choosing my college major. I can't decide!

1. **Writting** new vocabulary in a notebook helps me remember it.

   _____

2. Tim's English teacher asked if he'd **donne** his homework.

   _____

3. My husband keeps **forgeting** his keys. It's so frustrating.

   _____

4. My children don't **want go** to school this morning.

   _____

5. I go **swiming** most weekends with my friends.

   _____

6. Everyone had **sang** Happy Birthday by the time I arrived.

   _____

52 Verb patterns

Some verbs in English can only go with a gerund or an infinitive. Some verbs can go with either. These verbs often describe wishes, plans, or feelings.

 52.1 LOOK AT THE PICTURES AND COMPLETE THE SENTENCES USING THE PHRASES IN THE PANEL

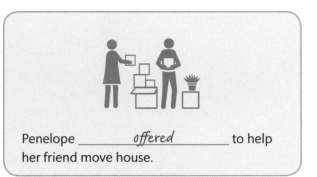

Penelope _____*offered*_____ to help her friend move house.

3 We _____ to meet for a drink after work.

1 I finally _____ to buy a house after saving for years.

4 My brother _____ buying a sports car when he turned 40.

2 Alberto has _____ painting the landscape.

5 I really _____ meeting your friends at the party.

| arranged | managed | considered | enjoyed | ~~offered~~ | finished |

52.2 REWRITE THE SENTENCES, PUTTING THE WORDS IN THE CORRECT ORDER

| don't | too | running; | tiring! | I | like | it's |

I don't like running; it's too tiring!

① | start | Spanish. | decided | dad | studying | My | to | has |

_____

② | colleague | help | the | My | finish | to | report. | me | offered |

_____

③ | really | weekend. | on | enjoy | I | running | the |

_____

52.3 CROSS OUT THE INCORRECT WORDS IN EACH SENTENCE

Brian was considering ~~to buy~~ / **buying** a new surfboard.

① Carlo enjoys **going** / to go to the theater every Friday.

② Rob and Phil intend buying / **to buy** a house this year.

③ Ellie is planning visiting / **to visit** Sydney while she's in Australia.

④ I don't feel like **playing** / to play football this evening.

⑤ Margo refused eating / **to eat** the ice cream Jed offered her.

⑥ My boss agreed letting / **to let** me go home early from work.

52.4 MATCH THE CORRESPONDING SENTENCES

We regret to inform you that you have not got the job.

I was driving home when I decided to stop for a cup of coffee.

We have to tell you that you have not got the job, and we are sorry.

1 I regret telling Jon about my new job. He's told everyone.

2 On the way back home, I stopped to have a cup of coffee.

I will remember to pick Angela up later from the airport.

3 I won't forget to pick Angela up from the airport.

I wish I hadn't told Jon about my job.

4 Do you remember meeting Paul at the conference last year?

The professor thanked the organizers and then talked about the experiment.

5 I stopped drinking coffee ages ago. I only drink tea now.

You were supposed to meet Paul. Did you remember to do that?

6 After thanking the organizers, the professor went on to talk about the experiment.

I used to drink coffee, but I decided to stop a long time ago.

7 Did you remember to meet Paul at the conference?

The professor was talking about the experiment and continued to do so.

8 I'll never forget seeing Angela at the airport for the first time.

Do you remember the time you first met Paul at the conference?

9 The professor went on talking about the experiment for hours.

I'll always remember when I saw Angela for the first time.

53 Verb patterns with objects

Some verbs, known as transitive verbs, have objects. When these verbs are followed by infinitives or gerunds, the object must come between the verb and the infinitive or gerund.

53.1 MARK THE SENTENCES THAT ARE CORRECT

My teacher expects me to do a lot of homework. ☑
My teacher expects me doing a lot of homework. ☐

1. Alfred spends a lot of time playing golf after work. ☐
   Alfred spends a lot of time to play golf after work. ☐

2. Janice watched the kids to play in the park. ☐
   Janice watched the kids playing in the park. ☐

3. Marco tried sold his old car to me. ☐
   Marco tried to sell his old car to me. ☐

4. My boss wants me working more quickly. ☐
   My boss wants me to work more quickly. ☐

5. Helena heard people talking in the room next door. ☐
   Helena heard people to talk in the room next door. ☐

6. My aunt borrowed a lot of money to my dad. ☐
   My aunt borrowed a lot of money from my dad. ☐

7. My mom wants me clean my room immediately. ☐
   My mom wants me to clean my room immediately. ☐

8. Hanif asked me to help him use the new software. ☐
   Hanif asked me helping him use the new software. ☐

9. Yuri bought an ice cream for his girlfriend. ☐
   Yuri bought an ice cream to his girlfriend. ☐

10. Tom reminded Peter buying some tickets for the concert. ☐
    Tom reminded Peter to buy some tickets for the concert. ☐

53.2 REWRITE THE SENTENCES, PUTTING THE WORDS IN THE CORRECT ORDER

> | Caroline | son | advice. | her | gave | some |
>
> *Caroline gave her son some advice.*

1 | keep | parents | room | to | clean. | my | My | expect | me |

_____

2 | Gus's | finish | him | boss | early | allows | Fridays. | on | to |

_____

3 | on | the | children | Danny | lawn. | watched | playing | the |

_____

4 | to | my | Don | reminded | grandmother. | me | phone |

_____

5 | told | walk | The | to | principal | more | slowly. | us |

_____

6 | an | becoming | I | Katie | day. | imagine | actor | can | one |

_____

7 | on | summer | Ravi | beach. | spent | lying | the | his |

_____

8 | friendly. | to | dog | Eleanor | more | wants | be | her |

_____

9 | from | milk | to | Mona | me | the | buy | store. | some | asked |

_____

54 Verb patterns with prepositions

Some verb patterns include prepositions.
Prepositions cannot be followed by infinitives,
so these verb patterns only use gerunds.

 54.1 FILL IN THE GAPS USING THE PREPOSITIONS IN THE PANEL

Stop worrying _____ *about* _____ what might happen tomorrow!

❶ Emma is talking _____ quitting her job.

❷ Ania finally admitted _____ stealing the jewelry.

❸ My dad tried to prevent me _____ studying art in college.

❹ Our company believes _____ doing the best possible job.

❺ Frank apologized _____ forgetting my birthday.

❻ I want to ask my tutor _____ doing the exam again.

❼ We congratulated Sandra _____ winning the competition.

❽ Paul objected _____ Danny eating a burger in the office.

❾ We decided _____ buying a house in the country.

❿ We're all looking forward _____ visiting you soon.

⓫ I need to concentrate _____ passing all my exams this spring.

⓬ Peter is worrying _____ his interview tomorrow.

⓭ The council banned people _____ taking dogs onto the beach.

⓮ Chloe accused me _____ stealing her idea for the presentation.

⓯ Leo's parents tried to stop him _____ marrying the girl he loved.

about	from	to	about	to	in	about	on
of	~~about~~	on	against	from	to	for	from

55 Phrasal verbs

Some verbs in English have two or more words in them, and usually have a new meaning when they are used together. These are called phrasal verbs.

55.1 MATCH THE PICTURES TO THE CORRECT SENTENCES

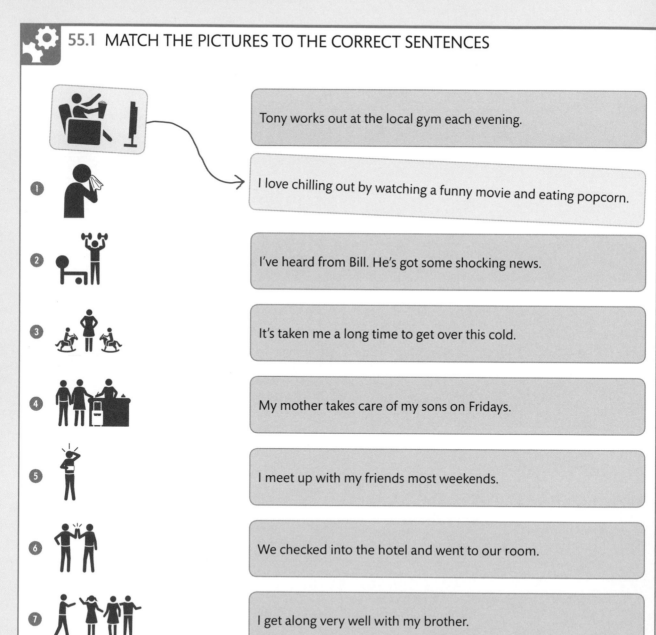

Tony works out at the local gym each evening.

I love chilling out by watching a funny movie and eating popcorn.

I've heard from Bill. He's got some shocking news.

It's taken me a long time to get over this cold.

My mother takes care of my sons on Fridays.

I meet up with my friends most weekends.

We checked into the hotel and went to our room.

I get along very well with my brother.

55.2 MARK THE SENTENCES THAT ARE CORRECT

I've dress upped for the party. ☐
I've dressed up for the party. ☑

1. Jen and Hugo eat out very often. ☐
   Jen and Hugo eat very often out. ☐

2. You should try it on before buying it. ☐
   You should try on it before buying it. ☐

3. The music was loud so I turned it down. ☐
   The music was loud so I turned down it. ☐

4. I've always looked up to my brother. ☐
   I've always up to my brother looked. ☐

5. We've run out milk of. ☐
   We've run out of milk. ☐

6. We checked into the hotel at noon. ☐
   We checked the hotel into at noon. ☐

7. Rob meets up with Nina on Fridays. ☐
   Rob meet ups with Nina on Fridays. ☐

8. Does Pete always shows up on time? ☐
   Does Pete always show up on time? ☐

9. I was annoyed because he woke up me. ☐
   I was annoyed because he woke me up. ☐

10. I'm staying in to watch the game tonight. ☐
    I'm in staying to watch the game tonight. ☐

11. Sharon hand inned her essay early. ☐
    Sharon handed in her essay early. ☐

12. The caterpillar turned into a butterfly. ☐
    The caterpillar turned a butterfly into. ☐

13. It's heavy. Please help me pick it up. ☐
    It's heavy. Please help me pick up it. ☐

 ## 55.3 REWRITE THE SENTENCES, CORRECTING THE ERRORS

If you drop litter, pick up it.
If you drop litter, pick it up.

1. Ramon is getting the flu over.
   _____

2. It was lovely from you to hear.
   _____

3. She told the children to down sit.
   _____

4. Here's your coat. Put on it please.
   _____

5. We need to check the hotel into.
   _____

6. I spotted a coin and picked up it.
   _____

7. Riku up gets at 9:30am on Saturdays.
   _____

8. The baby's crying. You woke up him.
   _____

9. I love cooking so I don't out eat often.
   _____

10. The café has out run of coffee.
    _____

11. Femi up grew in New York.
    _____

12. The airplane take offs in one hour.
    _____

55.4 REWRITE THE SENTENCES, PUTTING THE WORDS IN THE CORRECT ORDER

| forward | I'm | seeing | tomorrow. | you | looking | to |

I'm looking forward to seeing you tomorrow.

1 | most | work | I | gym | in | evenings. | the | out |

_____

2 | up | Camila | to | teacher. | really | her | looks | English |

_____

3 | after | father. | Rachel | her | takes |

_____

4 | to | It's | so | up | hard | Libby. | keep | with |

_____

5 | more. | some | We | I | ran | of | out | so | made | food |

_____

6 | were | I | when | on | didn't | with | get | we | brother | young. | my |

_____

7 | got | trip | We | to | from | Wales | our | Thursday. | on | back |

_____

8 | I | up | the | get | later | usually | on | weekend. |

_____

9 | down. | car | My | breaking | is | dad's | always |

_____

55.5 WRITE THE PHRASAL VERBS FROM THE PANEL IN THE CORRECT GROUPS

SEPARABLE

_____
_____
_____
_____

INSEPARABLE

_____ do without _____
_____
_____
_____

get through   turn on   fill up   come across   go over   do without   throw away   wake up

55.6 FILL IN THE GAPS USING THE WORDS IN THE PANEL

Our business is not doing well, so we have had to make a lot of _____ cutbacks _____ .

1 A break on the coast sounds like the ideal _____ .

2 There has been another _____ of the disease in the city.

3 The café was a _____ ! We paid $20 for a bowl of soup.

4 After the _____ , the sun came out again.

5 It's important to make a _____ of any work you do.

6 There have been so many _____ from the course this year.

7 All the students were given a _____ with important information.

8 Following her _____ with Charlie, Ola was very unhappy.

9 We haven't had _____ like this for years. There's snow and ice everywhere.

downpour   snowfall   getaway   break-up   rip-off

handout   cutbacks   dropouts   outbreak   backup

139

56 Modal verbs

Modal verbs are very common in English. They are used to talk about a variety of things, particularly possibilities, obligations, and deductions.

56.1 REWRITE THE SENTENCES, PUTTING THE WORDS IN THE CORRECT ORDER

you	me	Could	where	is?	library	tell	the

Could you tell me where the library is?

1. | learn | computer. | You | a | should | to | how | use |

_____

2. | cake? | Could | piece | have | another | I | of |

_____

3. | run | corridor. | the | You | not | in | must |

_____

4. | languages | My | fluently. | sister | four | can | speak |

_____

5. | I | Can | with | give | you | shopping? | a | hand | your |

_____

6. | moment? | your | lend | Could | pen | you | me | a | for |

_____

7. | be | from | That | must | letter | college. | Ken's |

_____

| Can I get you a drink? | Maybe I should call my mother. | Can I help you with your bag? | You mustn't be late for work again. |

 ## 56.3 REWRITE THE SENTENCES AS QUESTIONS

Simon can speak Irish fluently.
Can Simon speak Irish fluently?

1 I can help you clean up.

_____

2 Phil should study math in college.

_____

3 Graham can play the violin.

_____

4 Peter has to go to the meeting.

_____

5 She can have another chocolate.

_____

6 Angela could drive us to the party.

_____

 ## 56.4 REWRITE THE SENTENCES USING THE NEGATIVE

Students must bring a calculator.
Students must not bring a calculator.

1 Leroy can repair your oven.

_____

2 My grandma could speak Welsh.

_____

3 You should eat more red meat.

_____

4 Louisa can swim well.

_____

5 Students have to wear uniforms.

_____

6 You can have another piece of cake.

_____

57 Ability

"Can" is a modal verb that describes what someone is able to do. It is used in different forms to describe past and present abilities.

57.1 MATCH THE PICTURES TO THE CORRECT SENTENCES

Emma can make beautiful dresses.

Tina can dance really well.

Chris can repair your car.

Jamie can't lift that box. I'll help him.

I can't solve this. It's too difficult.

Rita can cook the most amazing dishes.

Chloe can speak three languages.

I can't climb that mountain.

57.2 REWRITE THE SENTENCES IN THE CORRECT ORDER

box. | can't | I | that | reach

I can't reach that box.

1. the | Jonathan | can | guitar. | play

2. can't | We | door. | open | the

3. well. | really | can | Amy | sing

4. Lizzie | car. | cannot | a | drive

5. can | trees. | Femi | climb

6. languages. | can | five | speak | Marion

7. that | piano. | Derek | can't | move

57.3 MATCH THE BEGINNINGS OF THE SENTENCES TO THE CORRECT ENDINGS

I couldn't buy a new laptop

make wonderful cakes.

1 My grandmother could

You need a new one.

2 I couldn't fix your phone.

because they were too expensive.

3 When I was a child,

because I felt ill.

4 Martha could play the piano

I could run much faster.

5 I couldn't come to the party

Jen could already speak six languages.

6 When she was six,

when she was four years old.

 57.4 MATCH THE PRESENT SENTENCES TO THE CORRECT FUTURE SENTENCES

I can play most of this piece now.

I'll be able to speak it fluently by the summer.

1 I can already speak some Spanish.

I'll be able to play the whole thing by next week.

2 I can't find my passport.

In the future, we'll be able to travel to other planets.

3 We can already travel to the moon.

I'm hoping I will be able to fix it soon.

4 I still haven't been able to repair your old clock.

I won't be able to take my flight without it.

58 Permission, requests, and offers

"Can," "could," and "may" are used to ask permission to do something or to ask someone to do something for you. They can also be used to offer to help someone.

58.1 MARK WHETHER EACH SENTENCE IS FORMAL OR INFORMAL

Could you be quiet, please?
Formal ☑
Informal ☐

① Could you tell me where the bank is, please?
Formal ☐
Informal ☐

② Can I play outside now?
Formal ☐
Informal ☐

③ May I introduce my sister, Kay?
Formal ☐
Informal ☐

④ Can I have some more cake?
Formal ☐
Informal ☐

⑤ Could you turn down the radio, please?
Formal ☐
Informal ☐

⑥ May I go home earlier today?
Formal ☐
Informal ☐

⑦ Can I sit here?
Formal ☐
Informal ☐

58.2 MARK WHETHER EACH SENTENCE IS A REQUEST OR AN OFFER

Can I help you at all?
Request ☐
Offer ☑

① May I make a reservation for 8pm?
Request ☐
Offer ☐

② Can I offer you something to eat?
Request ☐
Offer ☐

③ Can you lend me 10 dollars?
Request ☐
Offer ☐

④ Can I get you something to drink?
Request ☐
Offer ☐

⑤ Can you help me with this report?
Request ☐
Offer ☐

⑥ May I leave the table, please?
Request ☐
Offer ☐

⑦ Shall I take your coat for you?
Request ☐
Offer ☐

58.3 MATCH THE PICTURES TO THE CORRECT SENTENCES

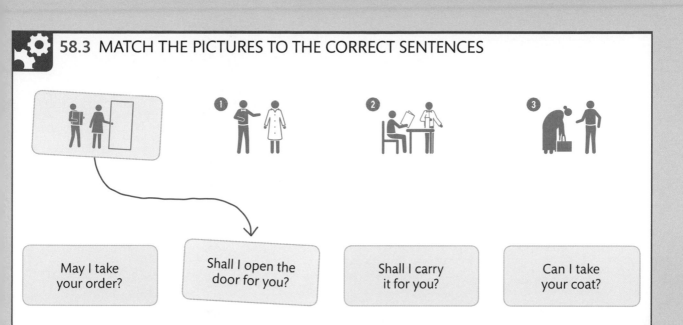

May I take your order?

Shall I open the door for you?

Shall I carry it for you?

Can I take your coat?

58.4 REWRITE THE SENTENCES, CORRECTING THE ERRORS

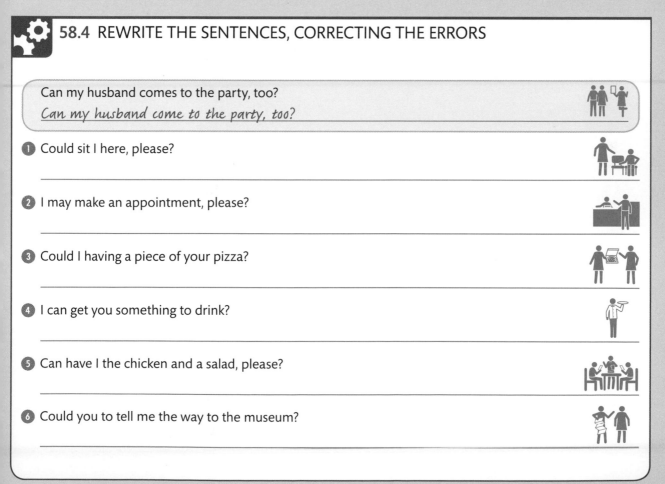

Can my husband comes to the party, too?
Can my husband come to the party, too?

1 Could sit I here, please?

2 I may make an appointment, please?

3 Could I having a piece of your pizza?

4 I can get you something to drink?

5 Can have I the chicken and a salad, please?

6 Could you to tell me the way to the museum?

145

59 Suggestions and advice

The modal verb "could" can be used to offer suggestions. "Could" is not as strong as "should." It communicates gentle advice.

59.1 MATCH THE SITUATIONS TO THE CORRECT ADVICE

It looks like it's very cold outside. ——→ You should wear a coat and some gloves.

You should take it out for a walk.

1. My dog keeps barking. It's so irritating.

2. It's really hot and sunny outside.

3. I want to learn how to speak good English. — You should try talking to a native speaker.

4. My son doesn't have many friends. — You should put on some sunscreen.

5. My wife can't sleep at night. — She should try to relax before bed.

6. I don't know what to buy my girlfriend. — He should join a club or take up a hobby.

7. My cousin wants to lose some weight. — You should go home and get some sleep.

8. I'm not feeling well at all. — You could make a little card for her as a gift.

9. I can't afford to go on vacation this summer. — You should try to save money regularly.

He should eat less cake and exercise more.

59.2 REWRITE THE ADVICE USING "HAD BETTER" OR "HAD BETTER NOT"

> You ought to leave now, or you'll miss the bus.
> _You had better leave now, or you'll miss the bus._

1. It's going to rain. You should take an umbrella.

   _____

2. The train's been canceled. We ought to take a taxi.

   _____

3. It's icy outside. You shouldn't drive tonight.

   _____

4. I'm late for the meeting. I should call my boss.

   _____

59.3 MARK THE BEST ADVICE TO EACH SITUATION

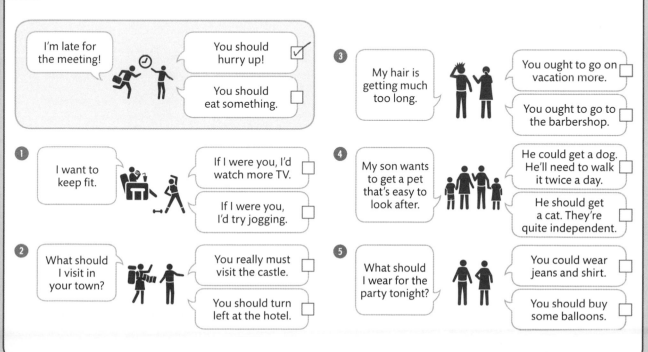

60 Obligations

In English, "have to" or "must" are used when talking about obligations or things that are necessary.
They are often used to give important instructions.

60.1 MATCH THE SITUATIONS TO THE CORRECT OBLIGATIONS

My eyesight is absolutely terrible. → You really must go to the optician.

You have to go. It's about the new IT system.

1 There's a meeting in 10 minutes, but I'm too busy.

2 I've just remembered it's my grandmother's birthday today.

Yes. All our workers must wear a helmet at all times.

3 I've got too much homework to do.

The council must do something to stop people from littering.

4 I'm feeling much better now. The pain has gone.

You must call her right away!

5 There's so much litter in town.

He had to go home because his daughter's unwell.

6 Why are you driving so slowly here?

You won't have to do any when the summer break comes!

7 I forgot to bring my helmet. Does it matter?

You must not lift anything heavy for two weeks.

8 Why isn't Juan at the meeting today?

In that case, you don't have to take your medication any longer.

9 I hurt my back while I was moving house.

I have to keep to the speed limit.

60.2 COMPLETE THE SENTENCES USING "MUST NOT" OR "DON'T HAVE TO"

 You ___*don't have to*___ come swimming, but you are invited.

1 I _____ wear a suit for work, but I wear one anyway.

2 I'm staying in bed because I _____ go to work today.

3 You _____ stay in the sun too long. You'll get burned.

4 You _____ touch that pan. It's hot.

5 You _____ be great at tennis to enjoy it.

6 I have a secret, but you _____ tell anyone else.

60.3 REWRITE THE SENTENCES IN THE FUTURE

Students must use a laptop.
Students will have to use a laptop.

1 Everyone must leave before 5pm.

_____

2 You must inform your manager.

_____

3 Brenda has to go home early today.

_____

4 She must pay for the damage.

_____

60.4 REWRITE THE SENTENCES IN THE PAST

Joe must come in early.
Joe had to come in early.

1 The managers must apologize.

_____

2 Greg must eat all the broccoli.

_____

3 Joe has to work very hard today.

_____

4 I must rest all this week.

_____

61 Making deductions

Modal verbs can also be used to talk about how likely or unlikely something is. They can be used to guess and make deductions about what has happened or is happening now.

61.1 MATCH THE PICTURES TO THE CORRECT SENTENCES

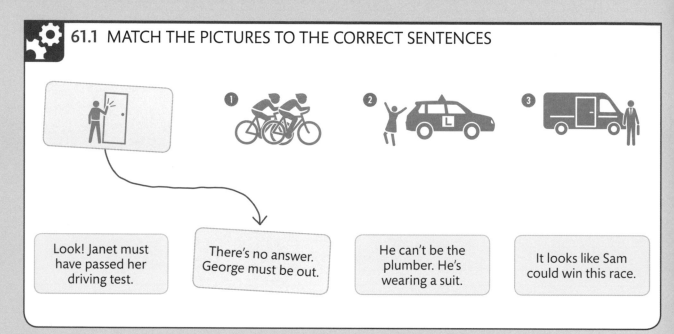

Look! Janet must have passed her driving test.

There's no answer. George must be out.

He can't be the plumber. He's wearing a suit.

It looks like Sam could win this race.

61.2 CROSS OUT THE INCORRECT WORDS IN EACH SENTENCE

Dan has been off work for days. He **must** / ~~cannot~~ be sick.

1 Alina drank all the water. She **must** / **can** have been really thirsty.

2 I can't read this. I **could not** / **might** need new glasses.

3 Ben **can't** / **might** have stolen the vase. He was with me last night.

4 The journey home takes ages. The children **must** / **can** be so bored.

5 I can't find my wallet. I **must** / **can't** have dropped it somewhere.

61.3 FILL IN THE GAPS, PUTTING THE WORDS IN THE CORRECT ORDER

broken	have	must

It's freezing in this house! The heating ___must___ ___have___ ___broken___ .

on	have	it	might	left

1 I can't find my purse. I _____ _____ _____ _____ _____ the bus.

a	have	I	might

2 I keep sneezing. I think _____ _____ _____ _____ cold.

failed	have	her	must

3 Veronika is crying. She _____ _____ _____ _____ test.

bear	be	could	a

4 What's that animal with brown fur? It _____ _____ _____ _____ .

61.4 MATCH THE CORRESPONDING SENTENCES TOGETHER

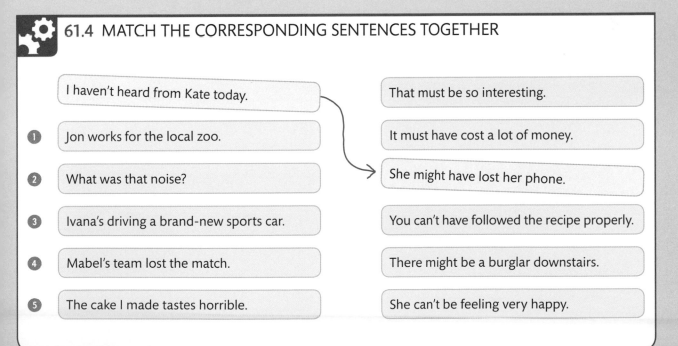

I haven't heard from Kate today.   That must be so interesting.

1 Jon works for the local zoo.   It must have cost a lot of money.

2 What was that noise?   She might have lost her phone.

3 Ivana's driving a brand-new sports car.   You can't have followed the recipe properly.

4 Mabel's team lost the match.   There might be a burglar downstairs.

5 The cake I made tastes horrible.   She can't be feeling very happy.

62 Possibility

Modal verbs can be used to talk about possibility, or to express uncertainty. "Might" is the most common modal verb used for this purpose.

 62.1 LOOK AT THE PICTURES AND COMPLETE THE SENTENCES USING THE PHRASES IN THE PANEL

The weather forecast said it ___*might rain*___ on Saturday.

❶ It looks like my team _____ tonight's game!

❷ I _____ some driving lessons if I can afford them.

❸ I think the train _____ canceled.

❹ I can't find my keys. I _____ them at work.

❺ If you don't hurry, you _____ the deadline!

❻ I think we _____ lost. We'd better ask someone.

❼ I _____ the building by the end of the year.

might take	might not finish	might win	might have left
might be	~~might rain~~	might have been	might miss

62.2 MARK THE SENTENCES THAT ARE CORRECT

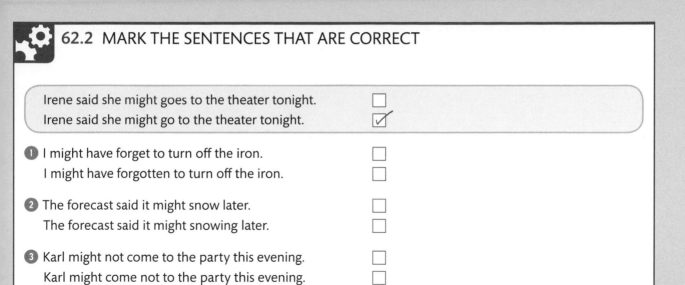

Irene said she might goes to the theater tonight. ☐
Irene said she might go to the theater tonight. ☑

1. I might have forget to turn off the iron. ☐
   I might have forgotten to turn off the iron. ☐

2. The forecast said it might snow later. ☐
   The forecast said it might snowing later. ☐

3. Karl might not come to the party this evening. ☐
   Karl might come not to the party this evening. ☐

4. Jon may have gone away for the weekend. ☐
   Jon can have gone away for the weekend. ☐

62.3 REWRITE THE SENTENCES, PUTTING THE WORDS IN THE CORRECT ORDER

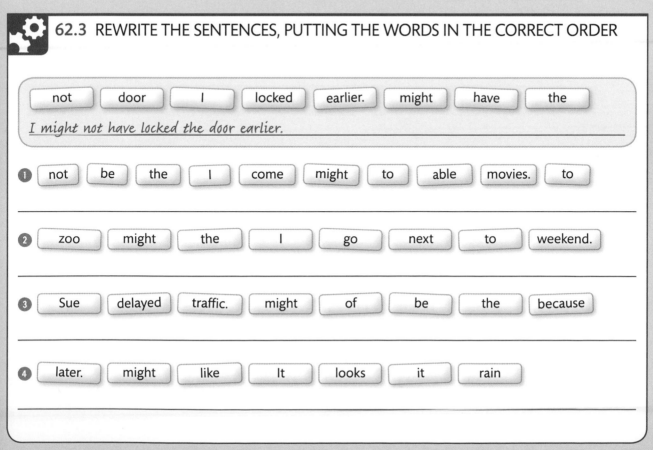

| not | door | I | locked | earlier. | might | have | the |

I might not have locked the door earlier.

1. | not | be | the | I | come | might | to | able | movies. | to |

2. | zoo | might | the | I | go | next | to | weekend. |

3. | Sue | delayed | traffic. | might | of | be | the | because |

4. | later. | might | like | It | looks | it | rain |

153

63 Articles

Articles are short words which come before nouns to show whether they refer to a general or a specific object. There are several rules telling which article, if any, should be used.

63.1 CROSS OUT THE INCORRECT WORDS IN EACH SENTENCE

> There is a / ~~an~~ / ~~the~~ black cat in the garden. I wonder whose it is.

1. Russia is a / an / the huge country. It took me seven days to cross it by train.

2. While hiking in Scotland, I spotted a / an / the eagle soaring above us.

3. Bill took me on a / an / the date to a / an / the most expensive bar in town.

4. Where can you get a / an / the good cup of coffee in a / an / the evening?

5. A / An / The food in Italy was absolutely delicious.

6. When I was a / an / the child, I wanted to be a / an / the actor.

7. A / An / The first train to Madrid leaves at 4:30 from platform 4.

8. It's going to rain this evening. Don't forget to take a / an / the umbrella.

9. Do you live in a / an / the house or a / an / the apartment?

10. I saw a / an / the wolf and a / an / the bear in Canada. A / An / The bear was catching fish.

11. Neil Armstrong was a / an / the first man to set foot on a / an / the moon.

12. Last week, I went to see a / an / the show with my cousin.

13. My brother used to be a / an / the chef. He's a / an / the optician now.

14. While I was in Rome, I visited a / an / the Colosseum.

15. A / An / The cakes in that bakery are a / an / the best in town.

16. I had a / an / the cup of coffee and a / an / the croissant. A / An / The coffee was cold, though.

17. Is there a / an / the good hotel where I can stay in your town?

18. A / An / The book that I just finished was really interesting.

63.2 REWRITE THE SENTENCES USING PLURALS

> There is a book on the table.
> *There are some books on the table.*

1 There's a mug in the dishwasher.

_____

2 I have a pencil here.

_____

3 There's a sandwich for you.

_____

4 Mary has a beautiful dress.

_____

5 Hassan caught a big fish.

_____

6 There's a café in town.

_____

7 There is a watch on the counter.

_____

8 Marco climbed a high mountain.

_____

9 There's a bag in the kitchen.

_____

10 There's a person running outside.

_____

11 There is a big hotel by the shore.

_____

12 Ola sang a beautiful song.

_____

 ## 63.3 REWRITE THE SENTENCES CORRECTING THE ERRORS

> I don't have some pets.
> *I don't have any pets.*

1 Clara works in a office.

_____

2 Do you have some brothers or sisters?

_____

3 There are any banks on my street.

_____

4 There aren't some cookies in the cupboard.

_____

5 Is there the hospital near here?

_____

6 We visited a interesting exhibition today.

_____

7 Are there some good restaurants nearby?

_____

8 London is the very big city.

_____

9 Is there any swimming pool in your town?

_____

10 There aren't some students in the classroom.

_____

11 There are any nice cafés near my house.

_____

12 I tasted a best pasta while I was on vacation.

_____

63.4 MATCH THE BEGINNINGS OF THE SENTENCES TO THE CORRECT ENDINGS

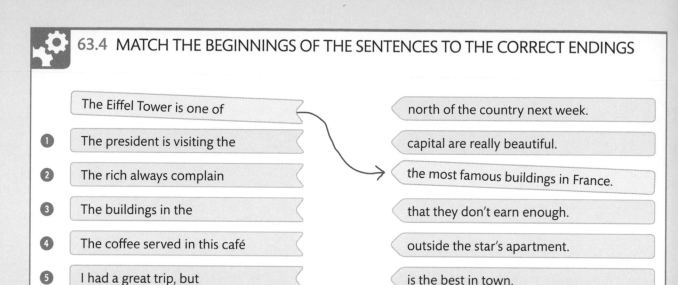

The Eiffel Tower is one of — the most famous buildings in France.

1. The president is visiting the — north of the country next week.

2. The rich always complain — capital are really beautiful.

3. The buildings in the — that they don't earn enough.

4. The coffee served in this café — outside the star's apartment.

5. I had a great trip, but — is the best in town.

6. The press were waiting — the weather was disappointing.

63.5 REWRITE THE SENTENCES, PUTTING THE WORDS IN THE CORRECT ORDER

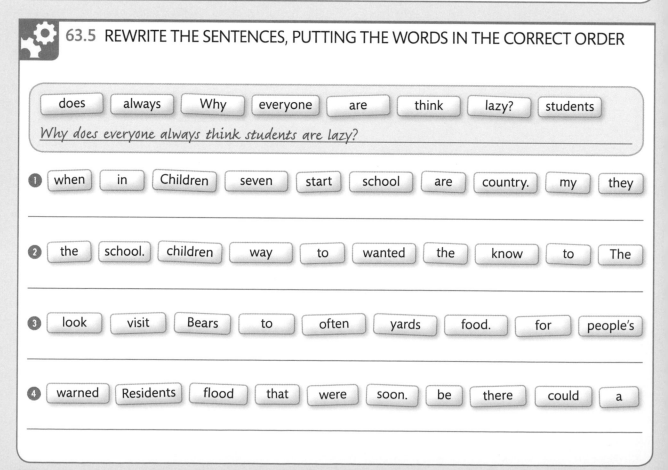

does · always · Why · everyone · are · think · lazy? · students

Why does everyone always think students are lazy?

1. when · in · Children · seven · start · school · are · country. · my · they

_____

2. the · school. · children · way · to · wanted · the · know · to · The

_____

3. look · visit · Bears · to · often · yards · food. · for · people's

_____

4. warned · Residents · flood · that · were · soon. · be · there · could · a

_____

156

63.6 MARK THE SENTENCES THAT ARE CORRECT

Did you see letter that arrived for you this morning? ☐
Did you see the letter that arrived for you this morning? ☑

1. My sister-in-law is doctor at local hospital. ☐
My sister-in-law is a doctor at the local hospital. ☐

2. Perfume you bought for your wife is in my bag. ☐
The perfume you bought for your wife is in my bag. ☐

3. Try not to get water all over the bathroom floor. ☐
Try not to get the water all over a bathroom floor. ☐

4. I'm going to climb the highest mountain in my country. ☐
I'm going to climb a highest mountain in my country. ☐

5. You really should go to the bed. You're exhausted. ☐
You really should go to bed. You're exhausted. ☐

6. The food was excellent during our trip to Morocco. ☐
Food was excellent during our trip to the Morocco. ☐

7. Phone has been ringing all the morning. ☐
The phone has been ringing all morning. ☐

8. Is there the museum I can visit in your town? ☐
Is there a museum I can visit in your town? ☐

9. I rode an elephant when I visited India last year. ☐
I rode the elephant when I visited India last year. ☐

10. You might see lions while you're on safari. ☐
You might see the lions while you're on safari. ☐

11. Christopher has hot dog for the lunch every day. ☐
Christopher has a hot dog for lunch every day. ☐

12. I ride my bike to the office each morning. ☐
I ride my bike to office each morning. ☐

13. Only rich people can afford to go to that restaurant. ☐
Only the rich people can afford to go to that restaurant. ☐

64 Articles review

The definite and indefinite articles are used in different situations, and this can depend on whether they are being used with a singular, plural, or uncountable noun.

 64.1 CROSS OUT THE INCORRECT WORDS IN EACH SENTENCE

I'm sorry, but we don't have a reservation for a / ~~the~~ Peter Radley. Did you book the right dates?

1. It's so warm outside. I'm going to invite some / the friends over for a barbecue.

2. The / A new secretary seems good but doesn't have much experience.

3. I read some / the really good books during my last vacation.

4. What happened in a / the kitchen? It's such a mess.

5. A / The shirt Liam bought for a / the party cost more than $80.

6. My cousin has a / the really friendly dog.

7. While walking in the park, I spotted a / the rare bird.

8. I have a / the lot of friends who still live with their parents.

9. Paula has left a / some money on a / the kitchen table for you.

10. I think Brazil would be a / the fascinating country to visit.

11. I've just baked the / some cupcakes. Would you like to try one?

12. The / Some cake you made for the fair was absolutely delicious.

13. My family's big. I have three brothers and a / the sister.

14. A / The blue whale is a / the biggest animal that has ever existed.

15. I asked an / the waiter for a / the large cup of coffee.

16. A / The saxophone is a / the difficult instrument to play.

17. India is a / the country I'd most like to visit.

18. We saw a / the bear on our trip through a / the mountains.

64.2 FILL IN THE GAPS USING THE CORRECT ARTICLES, LEAVING A BLANK FOR THE ZERO ARTICLE

 I'm lost! I was supposed to get the bus to _____*the*_____ Taj Mahal.

① I don't go to _____ work on Fridays. I look after my daughter.

② My son rides _____ bike to _____ school each day.

③ In my country, _____ people usually retire when they're about 60.

④ Colm works as _____ scientist at a large research center.

⑤ You should make sure you get plenty of _____ sleep before _____ exam tomorrow.

⑥ Irma buys her paint from the store by _____ café.

⑦ Bill got married to _____ woman he met at work.

⑧ _____ band I went to see last night was awful.

⑨ I'm still in touch with _____ friends I made while on _____ vacation.

⑩ My aunt thought she saw _____ wolf in the woods today.

⑪ _____ shoes I bought yesterday are far too big.

⑫ My mom says that _____ cats are much cleaner than _____ dogs.

⑬ While I was traveling in Australia, I saw _____ kangaroo.

⑭ _____ president gave _____ long speech at the conference.

65 "This / that / these / those"

"This," "that," "these," and "those" can be used as determiners before a noun to specify which noun is being talked about. They can also be used as pronouns to replace a noun in a sentence.

 65.1 CROSS OUT THE INCORRECT WORD IN EACH SENTENCE

I really like ~~that~~ / those shoes.

❶ **This** / These is my new boyfriend, Dan.

❷ **That** / Those book is so interesting.

❸ **That** / Those was such a tasty pizza!

❹ I'd like **that** / those grapes, please.

❺ Do you like **this** / these shirt?

❻ I want to see **that** / those movie tonight.

❼ This / **These** are your glasses right here.

❽ Where did you buy **that** / those jeans?

❾ Is **this** / these my cup of coffee?

❿ That / **Those** shoes look great on you!

⓫ **This** / These is the perfect car for a family.

⓬ Is **that** / those your new motorcycle, Andy?

⓭ Who made **this** / these cakes?

⓮ This / **These** are my parents, Anna and Charles.

⓯ **This** / These wardrobe's so heavy!

 65.2 MATCH THE PICTURES TO THE CORRECT SENTENCES

That is my new house. It's just by the ocean.

That is a very nice painting. It looks great!

That was an amazing goal. You should have seen it!

This is your desk and computer.

65.3 REWRITE THE SENTENCES, PUTTING THE WORDS IN THE CORRECT ORDER

| delicious. | apples | absolutely | red | These | taste |

These red apples taste absolutely delicious.

① | boots | suit | you. | really | Those |

_____

② | of | is | best | the | one | I've | This | read. | books |

_____

③ | I've | I'm | this | seen | sure | before. | movie |

_____

④ | this | don't | is | meat | I | properly. | think | cooked |

_____

 65.4 MATCH THE BEGINNINGS OF THE SENTENCES TO THE CORRECT ENDINGS

These new computers are much faster ——→ than those we used to have here.

① That is one of the most beautiful / and a bag of these apricots, please.

② I'll have a half kilo of those potatoes / that of spokesperson for our company.

③ Your most important role is / castles that I've ever seen.

④ The cars we drive today are safer / ever had. It's absolutely delicious.

⑤ I like these jeans here, but I prefer / than those our parents used to drive.

⑥ This is the best coffee I've / those with the stripe on them over there.

66 "No / none"

"No" and "none" both show the absence or lack of something. "No" is always used with a noun, whereas "none" replaces a noun in a sentence.

66.1 MATCH THE PICTURES TO THE CORRECT SENTENCES

> I've missed the train again. I'm having no luck this week!

1

> I'm sorry! I was going to make you a cup of coffee, but there's no milk left!

2

> We wanted a room with a view, but the receptionist said that there were none available.

3

> I wanted to order apple pie, but there was none left.

4

> We had no time to make lunch, so we went out for burgers instead.

5

> None of my friends believed I saw a ghost.

6

> None of the clothes I tried on suited me.

7

> I couldn't call you because there was no reception where I was.

66.2 WRITE EACH SENTENCE IN ITS OTHER FORM

I don't have any time for this.	I have no time for this.
❶	There **are no** free seats.
❷ I don't **have any** money left.	
❸	There **were no** more tickets.
❹	Kinga **has no** friends at work.
❺ It **doesn't take any** time to get there.	
❻ There **wasn't any** doubt that he did it.	

66.3 CROSS OUT THE INCORRECT WORDS IN EACH SENTENCE

I wanted some orange juice, but there was ~~no~~ / none in the fridge.

❶ No / None vegetarian food had been ordered for the convention.

❷ There are **no** / **any** places left on the English course.

❸ No / None of the staff wanted to work on Saturdays.

❹ Amelia wanted to buy salad, but there wasn't **any** / **none** in the store.

❺ There was **no** / **none** time to think about the exam questions.

❻ I called five hotels, but **no** / **none** had a free room for tonight.

❼ There wasn't **no** / **any** milk left, so I went to the shops.

❽ I had **no** / **none** energy left after work, so I watched some TV.

❾ No / None of my friends wanted to see a movie with me.

❿ There weren't **no** / **any** seats free on the train home.

⓫ I wanted to try one of Sarah's cakes, but there were **no** / **none** left.

⓬ No / None dentists were available to see me, so I went home.

67 "Each / every"

"Each" and "every" are words that go before singular nouns to refer to all members of a group of people or things.

67.1 REWRITE THE SENTENCES, PUTTING THE WORDS IN THE CORRECT ORDER

| in | pyramids | I | Egypt. | time | every | I | the | visit | am |

I visit the pyramids every time I am in Egypt.

1. | and | wife | the | David | Poconos | his | every | visit | March. |

_____

2. | the | go | Indian | every | I | Monday. | in | to | restaurant | town |

_____

3. | us | a | of | was | sandwich | given | Each | and | a | drink. |

_____

4. | Luis | buys | Every | a | coffee | morning, | before | work. |

_____

5. | for | type | shampoo | works | This | of | every | hair. |

_____

6. | member | the | was | Each | team | given | of | a | prize. |

_____

7. | gave | of | Maddy | dollars. | each | thousand | a | her | children |

_____

67.2 MATCH THE PICTURES TO THE CORRECT SENTENCES

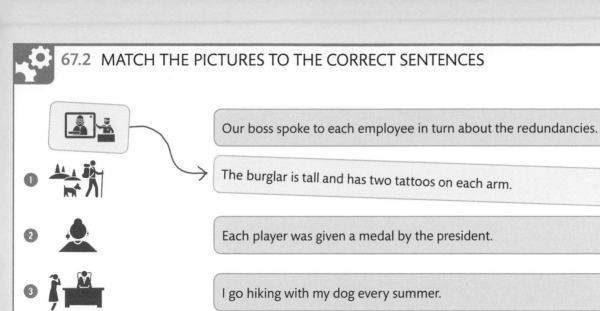

Our boss spoke to each employee in turn about the redundancies.

The burglar is tall and has two tattoos on each arm.

Each player was given a medal by the president.

I go hiking with my dog every summer.

Mona has a different type of earring in each ear.

67.3 MATCH THE BEGINNINGS OF THE SENTENCES TO THE CORRECT ENDINGS

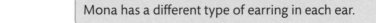

The concert was incredible,

a present and some cake.

1. Our manager has spoken to

with one of my work colleagues.

2. We gave every child at the party

and each singer was extremely talented.

3. My sister loves jewelry and

each employee about the factory closing.

4. Every Thursday, I play golf

every kind of bread you can think of.

5. Oscar makes sure he does

had incredibly beautiful architecture.

6. The bakery near my house sells

wears a bracelet on each wrist.

7. Each city we visited in Spain

every one of her books.

8. Every time I hear that song, I

some exercise every morning.

9. I love that author. I've read

remember the first time I heard it.

68 "Either / neither / both"

"Either," "neither," and "both" are used in situations where two options are being described. They indicate that one, two, or none of the options are possible.

 68.1 CROSS OUT THE INCORRECT WORDS IN EACH SENTENCE

I couldn't decide which suit I preferred, so I bought ~~either~~ / **both** of them.

① **Neither** / Either Dan nor Belinda could remember the way to the theater.

② **Both** / Either of my brothers go hiking in the hills on the weekend.

③ Either / **Neither** of us could resist another piece of cake.

④ Janet could afford to buy **neither** / either the skirt or the dress.

⑤ I invited **both** / either Sheila and Bill to my apartment in Paris.

⑥ Either / **Both** Steve and Louis work really hard in their English class.

⑦ Let's eat out **neither** / either on Wednesday or Thursday.

⑧ Either / **Neither** of the managers were at the meeting, unfortunately.

⑨ I had to take either / **both** the cat and the dog to the veterinarian.

⑩ Ramon can play either / **both** the electric and acoustic guitar.

⑪ Chetana didn't really like either / **neither** of the paintings on sale.

68.2 MATCH THE BEGINNINGS OF THE SENTENCES TO THE CORRECT ENDINGS

Everything looks delicious. I'm going → to have either the steak or the fish.

1 Neither Gabriela nor Carlos came

2 My niece wants to be either an

3 Lisa wants both a puppy

4 Neither the apple pie nor

5 I want to see either an action film

6 Both my brother and sister

7 Neither the electricity nor the water

to the party last night.

the cheesecake appealed to my aunt.

still live with our parents.

actress or an accountant.

works properly in my new house.

and a laptop for her birthday.

or a comedy tonight.

68.3 CROSS OUT THE INCORRECT WORDS IN EACH SENTENCE

Neither the soup nor the other appetizers ~~is~~ / are ready yet.

1 Either my cousin or my parents is / are going to pick you up from the airport.

2 Neither Paula's car nor her bike is / are working properly.

3 I hope either the steak or the fish is / are on the menu today.

4 Both the food and the drink was / were really overpriced.

5 Neither my brother nor my sister is / are coming tomorrow.

6 Either a cat or a dog makes / make a great pet for a family.

7 Neither of us wants / want to go to the conference.

8 I don't really like either of the dress / dresses she bought.

9 Neither the boss nor the workers was / were pleased about the deal.

10 We're thinking about adopting both of the puppy / puppies we saw.

69 Singular and plural nouns

Nouns in English do not have a gender. They change form depending on whether they are singular, meaning there is one, or plural, meaning there is more than one.

69.1 MARK THE NOUN FROM EACH SENTENCE

It's a lovely day today, so let's go out.
lovely ☐ **day** ☑ **so** ☐

① Jim has just bought a second-hand car.
bought ☐ **second-hand** ☐ **car** ☐

② That castle looks like it's really old.
castle ☐ **like** ☐ **really** ☐

③ Andrea asked me if I wanted to play chess.
asked ☐ **wanted** ☐ **chess** ☐

④ I've just had the strangest thought.
just ☐ **strangest** ☐ **thought** ☐

⑤ We walked past an incredible waterfall earlier.
walked ☐ **past** ☐ **waterfall** ☐

69.2 FIND SIX MORE NOUNS IN THE GRID AND WRITE THEM UNDER THE CORRECT HEADING

```
H O P E D R A O B W O N S
N S C I S S O R S Q E N V
N E F M C T U N R Y O R F
R P N T E R T I Y T C U L
J T A O E O R A N G E N O
U E W W R Y A D F A E S W
P M L N L A O G E O R G E
I B V E S T M Q E R I A R
T E D H T N D E G J A K I
E R I J F R A N C E O E S
R E C E P Y F O I F G Y D
```

COMMON NOUNS

town

① _____
② _____
③ _____

PROPER NOUNS

France

④ _____
⑤ _____
⑥ _____

69.3 CROSS OUT THE INCORRECT NOUNS IN EACH SENTENCE

 This is an excellent book / ~~books~~ / ~~bookes~~.

 ① When I finished my dinner, I washed all the dish / dishes / dishs.

 ② I bought my new watch / watchs / watche in Switzerland.

 ③ A lot of persons / peoples / people were waiting on the platform.

 ④ We need to protect endangered species / specieses / speciess.

 69.4 WRITE EACH SENTENCE IN ITS OTHER FORM

The **child likes** ice cream.	*The children like ice cream.*
① _____	Tim asked to borrow the **dictionaries**.
② The **train** always **leaves** on time.	_____
③ The **woman was** talking about the past.	_____
④ _____	The mayor visited the **factories** in our city.
⑤ _____	I think there **are some mice** in the kitchen.
⑥ **That story was** wonderful.	_____
⑦ _____	The **sheep were** standing in the road.
⑧ The **box is** full. We need to buy more.	_____
⑨ _____	Carla rested her **feet** on a cushion.
⑩ _____	Ellie asked the **men** for directions.
⑪ Maria put her **baby** into the **cot**.	_____

169

70 Countable and uncountable nouns

In English, nouns can be countable or uncountable.
Countable nouns can be individually counted. Objects
that aren't counted are uncountable.

70.1 WRITE THE NOUNS FROM THE PANEL IN THE CORRECT GROUPS

COUNTABLE	UNCOUNTABLE
question	

money   city   apple   ~~question~~   knowledge   sugar

70.2 MATCH THE PICTURES TO THE CORRECT SENTENCES

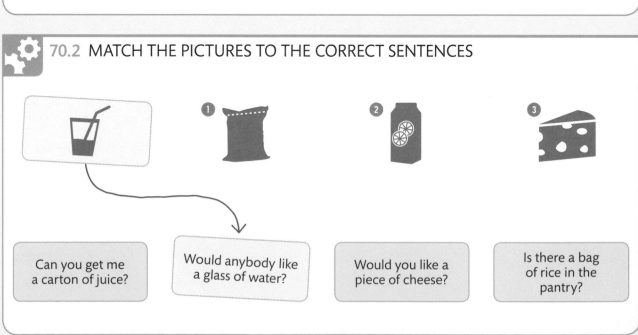

Can you get me
a carton of juice?

Would anybody like
a glass of water?

Would you like a
piece of cheese?

Is there a bag
of rice in the
pantry?

70.3 WRITE EACH SENTENCE IN ITS OTHER FORM

I **have some** paper here.	I don't have any paper here.
1	There **isn't any** milk in the fridge.
2 I **bought some** eggs at the store.	
3 We **saw some** bears in the mountains.	
4	There **isn't any** juice left.
5	I **didn't get any** gifts for my birthday.
6 I **have some** fruit in my bag.	
7	We **don't have any** important information.
8 There's **some** rice in the cupboard.	
9	I **don't have any** money saved for the vacation.

70.4 MARK THE SENTENCES THAT ARE CORRECT

How many bread do you need? ☐
How much bread do you need? ☑

1 How much meat is there? ☐
How many meat is there? ☐

2 How many cups of tea are there? ☐
How much cups of tea are there? ☐

3 How many coffee have you made? ☐
How much coffee have you made? ☐

4 How much bars of chocolate do we have? ☐
How many bars of chocolate do we have? ☐

5 How many jars of jam are there? ☐
How much jars of jam are there? ☐

6 How many juice will we need? ☐
How much juice will we need? ☐

7 How much milk is there? ☐
How many milk is there? ☐

8 How many bowls of cereal are there? ☐
How much bowls of cereal are there? ☐

9 How much bananas do you have? ☐
How many bananas do you have? ☐

10 How much bags of flour did you buy? ☐
How many bags of flour did you buy? ☐

11 How many cartons of milk are there? ☐
How much cartons of milk are there? ☐

71 Subject-verb agreement

One of the basic principles of English is that subjects and verbs must agree in number. Some subjects, however, can act like singular or plural nouns depending on the context.

 71.1 LOOK AT THE PICTURES AND COMPLETE THE SENTENCES USING THE PHRASES IN THE PANEL

Physics _is an extremely interesting_ subject in my opinion.

3 The United States _____ of more than 300 million people.

1 Athletics _____, such as running and the high jump.

4 Measles _____ that usually affects children rather than adults.

2 I think the news _____, but my parents always watch it.

5 _The Adventures of Sherlock Holmes_ _____ _____. I read it every summer.

---

is an illness	consists of a number of sports	is my favorite book
~~is an extremely interesting~~	is really boring	has a population

71.2 REWRITE THE SENTENCES, CORRECTING THE ERRORS

> Darts are a very popular game in some countries.
> *Darts is a very popular game in some countries.*

1 The Netherlands are one of the world's biggest exporters of fresh flowers.

_____

2 Gymnastics weren't my first choice of sport.

_____

3 *The Three Musketeers* have remained a popular novel since its publication in 1844.

_____

4 Mathematics were my favorite subject when I was at school.

_____

 ## 71.3 REWRITE THE SENTENCES, PUTTING THE WORDS IN THE CORRECT ORDER

> is | in | The | this | band | summer. | Rome | performing
>
> *The band is performing in Rome this summer.*

1 gets | each | Christmas. | My | together | family | usually

_____

2 hired | The | of | company | managers. | couple | have | new | a

_____

3 refusing | details. | any | The | reveal | is | to | government

_____

4 are | work. | staff | after | going | meal | All | out | the | a | for

_____

72 Abstract and concrete nouns

Most abstract nouns are uncountable. Some, however,
can be either countable or uncountable, and the two
forms often mean slightly different things.

72.1 MATCH THE BEGINNINGS OF THE SENTENCES TO THE CORRECT ENDINGS

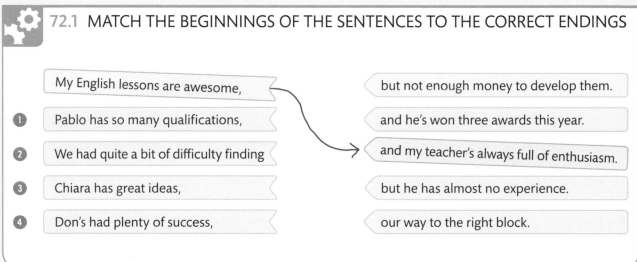

My English lessons are awesome,

but not enough money to develop them.

1 Pablo has so many qualifications,

and he's won three awards this year.

2 We had quite a bit of difficulty finding

and my teacher's always full of enthusiasm.

3 Chiara has great ideas,

but he has almost no experience.

4 Don's had plenty of success,

our way to the right block.

72.2 FIND SIX MORE NOUNS IN THE GRID AND WRITE THEM UNDER THE CORRECT HEADING

```
G  G  N  I  D  A  R  B  Y  W  O  Q  H
N  S  E  F  L  O  V  E  T  Q  E  N  A
N  D  E  V  J  S  M  L  S  M  A  R  P
R  I  N  T  E  R  T  I  U  T  C  L  P
S  B  T  A  O  K  R  E  D  N  A  J  I
E  D  I  S  R  Y  E  F  F  T  R  N  N
M  Z  L  O  L  A  E  Z  I  O  H  I  E
P  E  N  C  I  L  V  O  N  S  E  N  S
T  I  M  E  T  N  D  X  G  J  A  G  S
E  H  I  O  A  Y  T  A  B  L  E  H  G
```

CONCRETE NOUNS

pencil

1 _____

2 _____

3 _____

ABSTRACT NOUNS

happiness

4 _____

5 _____

6 _____

This office is much too small! There isn't enough **room** / ~~rooms~~ for everyone.

1 I met people from many different **cultures** / **culture** at college.

2  After a lot of **thoughts** / **thought**, I've decided to quit my job.

3 Being able to play an instrument is a great **skill** / **skills** to have.

4 I've visited the museum a few **times** / **time** this year.

5 Don't give up **hopes** / **hope**! Your team might win.

6 I have a terrible **memory** / **memories** for people's names.

7 It takes a lot of **times** / **time** to learn a foreign language.

8  Venice is famous for its **culture** / **cultures** and history.

9 Trisha loves to share her **memory** / **memories** of the past.

10  There's a lot of **space** / **spaces** in my new apartment.

11  My uncle is always driving everywhere at high **speeds** / **speed**.

12 I made some lasting **friendships** / **friendship** while traveling.

13 There isn't enough **times** / **time** to finish the project.

73 Compound nouns

Compound nouns are two or more nouns that act as a single unit. The first noun(s) modifies the last, in a similar way to an adjective.

73.1 MATCH THE PICTURES TO THE CORRECT SENTENCES

My mother-in-law had her birthday party in the town hall.

1 Two thieves had just carried out a bank robbery, but a policeman caught them before they could make their getaway.

2 I went to pick up my theater tickets from the ticket office.

3 During the heat wave, we kept the air-conditioning switched on all day.

4 Marc looked at the night sky as he relaxed on his camping trip.

5 Alberto stood at the front door, with his suitcase, waiting for the taxi.

6 As Ellie felt the first raindrops fall, she regretted not bringing a raincoat.

7 Sally had a terrible headache, so she asked her boyfriend to get her some painkillers.

73.2 FILL IN THE GAPS USING THE PHRASES IN THE PANEL

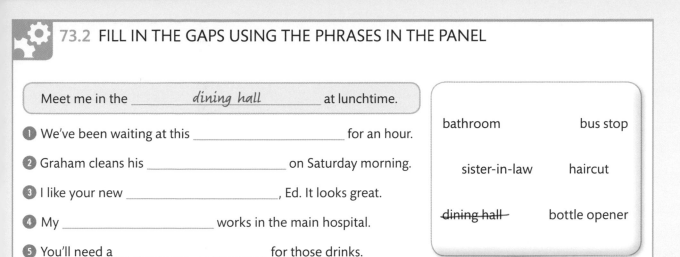

Meet me in the _____ *dining hall* _____ at lunchtime.

1. We've been waiting at this _____ for an hour.

2. Graham cleans his _____ on Saturday morning.

3. I like your new _____, Ed. It looks great.

4. My _____ works in the main hospital.

5. You'll need a _____ for those drinks.

bathroom   bus stop

sister-in-law   haircut

~~dining hall~~   bottle opener

73.3 REWRITE THE SENTENCES, PUTTING THE WORDS IN THE CORRECT ORDER

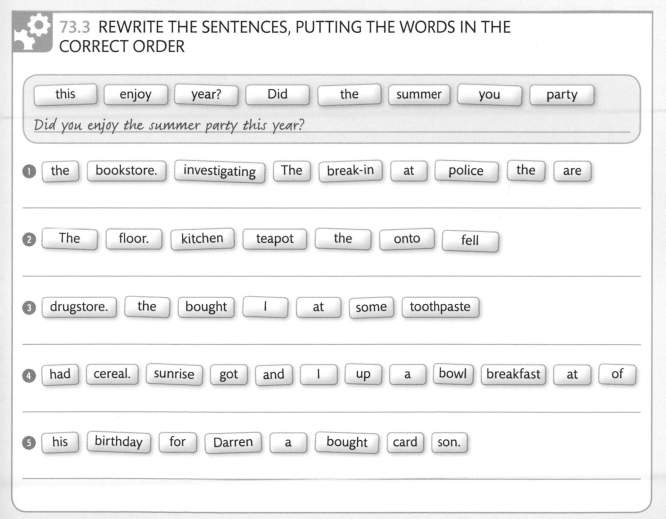

| this | enjoy | year? | Did | the | summer | you | party |

Did you enjoy the summer party this year?

1. the | bookstore. | investigating | The | break-in | at | police | the | are

_____

2. The | floor. | kitchen | teapot | the | onto | fell

_____

3. drugstore. | the | bought | I | at | some | toothpaste

_____

4. had | cereal. | sunrise | got | and | I | up | a | bowl | breakfast | at | of

_____

5. his | birthday | for | Darren | a | bought | card | son.

_____

74 Numbers

Cardinal numbers are used for counting and saying how many of something there are. Ordinal numbers give the position of something in an ordered list.

74.1 MARK WHETHER EACH NUMBER IS CARDINAL OR ORDINAL

sixth
Cardinal ☐
Ordinal ☑

❶ seventy-two
Cardinal ☐
Ordinal ☐

❷ ninety-second
Cardinal ☐
Ordinal ☐

❸ one hundred and five
Cardinal ☐
Ordinal ☐

❹ three thousand
Cardinal ☐
Ordinal ☐

❺ thirty-fourth
Cardinal ☐
Ordinal ☐

❻ one-hundredth
Cardinal ☐
Ordinal ☐

❼ fourteen
Cardinal ☐
Ordinal ☐

74.2 WRITE EACH NUMBER IN ITS OTHER FORM

207	Two hundred and seven
❶ 9,000	
❷	eight hundred and forty-eight
❸	four hundred and seventeen
❹ 6,500	
❺ 958	
❻	ninety-seven
❼ 3,590	
❽ 359	

74.3 MATCH THE FIGURES TO THE CORRECT TEXT

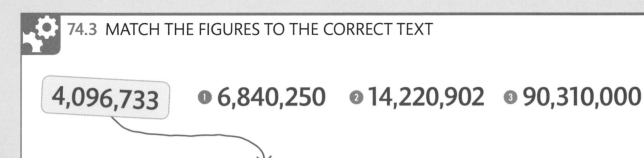

4,096,733   ❶ 6,840,250   ❷ 14,220,902   ❸ 90,310,000

fourteen million, two hundred and twenty thousand, nine hundred and two

four million, ninety-six thousand, seven hundred and thirty-three

ninety million, three hundred and ten thousand

six million, eight hundred and forty thousand, two hundred and fifty

74.4 MATCH THE FRACTIONS, DECIMALS, AND PERCENTAGES TO THE CORRECT TEXT

82%	two-thirds
❶ **12.5**	eighty-two percent
❷ **27.5%**	six and three-quarters
❸ **⅔**	two fifths
❹ **32%**	twelve point five
❺ **6¾**	six point three four
❻ **14.95**	twenty-seven point five percent
❼ **19%**	eight and a third
❽ **⅖**	thirty-two percent
❾ **6.34**	fourteen point nine five
❿ **8⅓**	eight and a half
⓫ **79.4%**	nineteen percent
⓬ **8½**	seventy-nine point four percent

75 Quantity

In English there are many ways to express general or specific quantities, say whether quantities are adequate, and compare different quantities.

 75.1 FILL IN THE GAPS USING THE PHRASES IN THE PANEL

> ___A few people___ in my office work from home on Fridays.

1 _____ also have a part-time job.

2 Only _____ came to my barbecue on Saturday.

3 There are _____ performing tonight.

4 I sent _____ while I was traveling.

5 There is _____ in the fridge if you want some.

---

some good bands

Lots of students   lots of juice

~~A few people~~   a few postcards

a few of my friends

 75.2 CROSS OUT THE INCORRECT WORDS IN EACH SENTENCE

> This essay is due tomorrow; I don't have **enough** / ~~too many~~ time!

1 There **isn't** / **aren't** enough sugar to make a birthday cake.

2 The burger costs six euros? I'm afraid that's **enough** / **too much**.

3 Do we have **enough** / **too much** money to buy a car?

4 There are **too much** / **too many** people on the bus this morning.

5 There **isn't enough** / **is too much** chicken to make dinner for everyone.

6 I bought **too much** / **enough** fruit. Please take some!

7 **Is** / **Are** there enough orange juice in the fridge for breakfast?

8 There are only two seats left. There are **not enough** / **too many** of us here.

75.3 CROSS OUT THE INCORRECT WORDS IN EACH SENTENCE

 I'm going traveling for a year because there are ~~few~~ / a few countries I'd like to visit.

1 **A lot of** / ~~A lot~~ people visit the mountains on the weekend.

2 I'm not rich, but I try to donate **little** / **a little** money to charity every month.

3 Sadly, there are **few** / **a few** Sumatran tigers left in the world today.

4 I met **quite a few** / **quite a bit of** new clients at the conference.

5 I have **little** / **a little** patience for people who are always late. I'm always on time!

6 There's **quite a bit of** / **quite a few** snow. Let's build a snowman!

7 **Lots** / **Lots of** people came to Craig's 40th birthday party.

8 Do you need some help with that report? I have **little** / **a little** time I can spare.

9 Be careful! That vase is worth **quite a bit of** / **quite a few of** money.

10 There are **few** / **a few** paintings in the museum I haven't seen. Can we stay a bit longer?

11 There are very **few** / **a few** people I would lend money to, but my brother is one of them.

12 I don't have lots of friends, but I've got **few** / **a few** who I'm really close to.

75.4 FILL IN THE GAPS USING "FEWER" OR "LESS"

There are much _____fewer_____ entries for the competition than there were last year.

1 I spent _____ time on this essay than I did last time.

2 The lecture was almost empty. There were _____ than 10 students there.

3 I'm earning _____ money with my new job, but the conditions are better.

4 _____ people eat meat today in comparison with a decade ago.

5 The train leaves in _____ than half an hour. We should hurry!

6 There was much _____ traffic than usual on the way to work.

7 There are _____ than 5,000 black rhinos left in the wild.

8 _____ young people are studying languages than in the past.

9 It's _____ than 10 minutes' walk to the historic part of the city.

75.5 MARK THE SENTENCES THAT ARE CORRECT

The brighter the moon is, the fewer stars you can see at night. ☑

The brighter the moon is, the fewer stars than you can see at night. ☐

1 We didn't go shopping because we had enough money. ☐

We didn't go shopping because we didn't have enough money. ☐

2 The weather was awful, but at least I made few friends there. ☐

The weather was awful, but at least I made a few friends there. ☐

3 There is much less traffic in the city than 15 years ago. ☐

There is much fewer traffic in the city than 15 years ago. ☐

4 A male African elephant can weigh more then seven tons. ☐

A male African elephant can weigh more than seven tons. ☐

5 I received lot of presents for my 30th birthday. ☐

I received a lot of presents for my 30th birthday. ☐

You should have **lots of career opportunity** once you graduate.
You should have lots of career opportunities once you graduate.

1 Marco was making **far too many noise**, so Ellie went out to the café.

_____

2 I'm afraid it's bad news. Our company is making **fewer money than** it did last year.

_____

3 Unfortunately, **very a little** can be done about the bad weather.

_____

4 Do we have **pasta enough** to make lunch for all the family?

_____

5 We have **lots things** to pack. Do you think there's room in the box?

_____

6 **A few people** come to the restaurant on a Monday evening. It's almost empty.

_____

7 There are **quite a bit of sandwiches** left. Help yourself to one!

_____

8 There were a **lots of people** waiting on the platform for the train.

_____

9 There were **a quite few clothes** I liked, but I didn't buy any.

_____

10 **Less than 10 people** work for our company. It's very cozy here.

_____

11 The safari park costs **fewer than $5** to visit. It's a real bargain.

_____

12 We have **quite a few time** before we need to leave.

_____

76 Approximate quantity

If specific figures are known, it can be useful to give them. However, more general terms may be needed if figures are not known or to avoid repetition.

76.1 MATCH THE PICTURES TO THE CORRECT INSTRUCTIONS

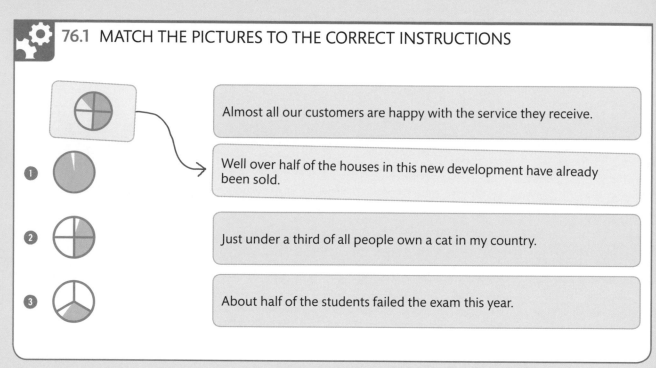

Almost all our customers are happy with the service they receive.

Well over half of the houses in this new development have already been sold.

Just under a third of all people own a cat in my country.

About half of the students failed the exam this year.

76.2 MATCH THE BEGINNINGS OF THE SENTENCES TO THE CORRECT ENDINGS

In many cases, people don't realize

each month on my college course.

① There are as many as two exams

consists of mountains and forests.

② Well over half of the country

what they can and can't recycle.

③ Almost none of the money is left

can speak a second language.

④ Approximately 75% of Earth's

following the expensive carnival.

⑤ As many as 7 out of 10 people

surface is covered in water.

76.3 REWRITE THE SENTENCES, PUTTING THE WORDS IN THE CORRECT ORDER

| will | as | 1,000 | There | as | be | there. | many | people |

There will be as many as 1,000 people there.

---

1 | little | be | could | as | as | months. | You | fluent | two | in | in | English |

---

2 | quickly | poisoning. | In | from | cases, | most | recover | food | people |

---

3 | almost | eaten | cakes. | The | the | children | have | all |

---

4 | students | exam. | About | final | half | failed | the | the |

---

5 | ten | As | applications | in | few | one | are | as | successful. |

---

6 | three-quarters | use | over | of | Well | media. | students | social |

---

7 | cases, | of | to | a | go | minority | In | prison. | people |

---

8 | in | are | my | as | public | There | as | many | 25 | city. | parks |

---

9 | the | away | is | My | from | house | a | just | station. | under | mile |

---

77 Personal pronouns

Personal pronouns are used to replace nouns in a sentence.
They can refer to people or things and have different forms
depending on whether they are a subject or an object.

77.1 WRITE EACH PRONOUN IN ITS OTHER FORM

SUBJECT	OBJECT
I	me
① we	
②	you
③ he	
④	her
⑤ it	
⑥	them

77.2 MARK THE SENTENCES THAT ARE CORRECT

Sonja and me are going shopping. ☐
Sonja and I are going shopping. ☑

① Kelly's so angry with he. ☐
Kelly's so angry with him. ☐

② Paula asked me to marry her. ☐
Paula asked I to marry her. ☐

③ Do you know what happened to them? ☐
Do you know what happened to they? ☐

④ Mike gave she the money. ☐
Mike gave her the money. ☐

77.3 MATCH THE PICTURES TO THE CORRECT SENTENCES

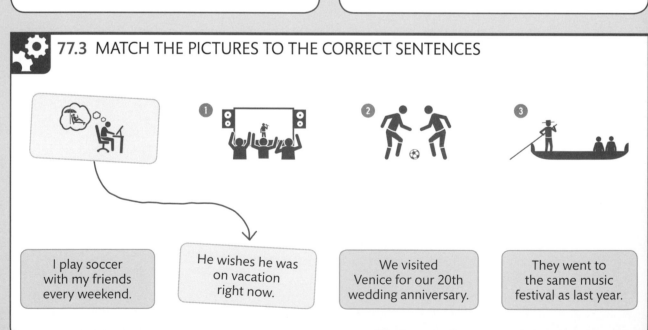

I play soccer
with my friends
every weekend.

He wishes he was
on vacation
right now.

We visited
Venice for our 20th
wedding anniversary.

They went to
the same music
festival as last year.

77.4 MATCH THE CORRESPONDING SENTENCES

Rachel invited Paige and Scott to the heavy metal concert.	She saw him working in a shop in Edinburgh.
1 Jenny saw Andrew working in a shop in Edinburgh.	She invited them to the heavy metal concert.
2 Michael gave Peter and me a ride to the movie theater.	He offered her a flower.
3 Robert offered Angela a flower.	He gave us a ride to the movie theater.

77.5 REWRITE THE SENTENCES, REPLACING THE HIGHLIGHTED WORDS WITH THE CORRECT PRONOUNS

Darren gave Kate a necklace for her birthday, and **Kate** absolutely loved **the necklace**.
Darren gave Kate a necklace for her birthday, and she absolutely loved it.

1 Jane cooked a new dish, but **the dish** tasted awful. **Jane** was so disappointed.

_____

2 Tom asked Roger to water the plants. **Roger** watered **the plants** and went home.

_____

3 The commuters waited for the train. **The commuters** were angry because **the train** was delayed.

_____

4 Mike told his parents he wanted to study drama. **His parents** thought that **drama** was a great choice.

_____

5 Shona bought a coffee for Brian. **Brian** thanked **Shona** for buying **the coffee**.

_____

187

78 Reflexive pronouns

Reflexive pronouns show that the subject of a verb is the same as its object. They can also be used in other situations to add emphasis.

78.1 WRITE EACH PRONOUN IN ITS OTHER FORM

OBJECT	REFLEXIVE
me	myself
① you (singular)	_____
② you (plural)	_____
③ _____	himself
④ _____	herself
⑤ it	_____
⑥ us	_____
⑦ _____	themselves

78.2 FILL IN THE GAPS USING THE PRONOUNS IN THE PANEL

She introduced _____ herself _____ to her new boss.

① I asked _____ if I should leave my job.

② You should pride _____ on your work, Phil.

③ Did Daniel injure _____ when he fell off the wall?

④ Ed and Flora are teaching _____ to cook.

⑤ Sarah is preparing _____ for the interview.

⑥ Did you and Claire enjoy _____ at the party?

> herself   himself
> yourself
> themselves
> ~~herself~~   myself
> yourselves

78.3 CROSS OUT THE INCORRECT WORDS IN EACH SENTENCE

> I really need to pass this test, but I can't **concentrate** / ~~concentrate myself~~!

1. Tim **shaves** / **shaves himself** when he gets up in the morning.

2. Angela **cut** / **cut herself** while she was chopping the onions.

3. The door **opened** / **opened itself**, and my uncle walked into the room.

4. Chan **hurt** / **hurt himself** when he slipped on the ice.

5. Janet **feels** / **feels herself** better after her illness.

 ## 78.4 MARK THE SENTENCES THAT ARE CORRECT

> We were told to take care of us while climbing the dangerous mountain. ☐
> We were told to take care of ourselves while climbing the dangerous mountain. ☑

1. I baked the cake myself. I hope you like it. ☐
   I myself baked the cake. I hope you like it. ☐

2. Most stores close at 5pm in my town. ☐
   Most stores close themselves at 5pm in my town. ☐

3. Did the children behave himself during the class? ☐
   Did the children behave themselves during the class? ☐

4. Annie asked Peter and myself to move the boxes. ☐
   Annie asked Peter and me to move the boxes. ☐

5. The child sat by himself reading a book. ☐
   The child sat with himself reading a book. ☐

6. How was the party? Did you enjoy? ☐
   How was the party? Did you enjoy yourselves? ☐

7. We were talking to each other when the phone rang. ☐
   We were talking to ourselves when the phone rang. ☐

78.5 REWRITE THE SENTENCES, PUTTING THE WORDS IN THE CORRECT ORDER

president | at | will | event. | The | be | the | herself

The president herself will be at the event.

① paint | going | the | My | herself. | wife | house | to | is

_____

② before | Carlos | the | admired | in | himself | leaving. | mirror

_____

③ the | herself | to | The | clean | CEO | offered | office. | help

_____

④ but | evening, | bad. | the | I | the | movie | was | enjoyed | itself

_____

 78.6 MATCH THE CORRESPONDING SENTENCES

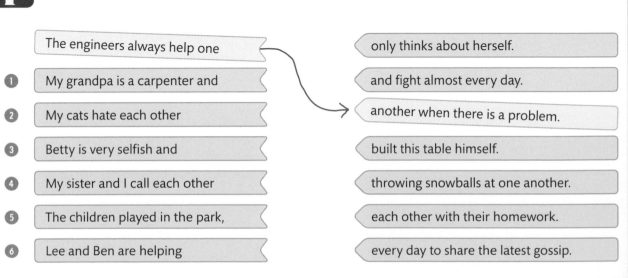

The engineers always help one	only thinks about herself.
① My grandpa is a carpenter and	and fight almost every day.
② My cats hate each other	another when there is a problem.
③ Betty is very selfish and	built this table himself.
④ My sister and I call each other	throwing snowballs at one another.
⑤ The children played in the park,	each other with their homework.
⑥ Lee and Ben are helping	every day to share the latest gossip.

190

78.7 FILL IN THE GAPS USING REFLEXIVE PRONOUNS, LEAVING A BLANK IF ONE IS NOT NEEDED

> Jennifer told _____*herself*_____ that she would start eating more healthy food.

1 Sharon is teaching _____ how to knit.

2 It's hard to tear _____ away from a really good book.

3 Martin shaves _____ each morning when he gets up.

4 I made some tea while the cake baked _____ in the oven.

5 We found _____ in a strange part of town. We were lost.

6 My grandparents have convinced _____ to go swimming each day.

7 How was the fair? Did the children enjoy _____ there?

8 The truck started to reverse _____, so we moved out of the way.

9 I'm familiarizing _____ with the new software.

10 Jim and Ula are decorating their new house _____. It's so much cheaper.

11 My arm really hurts _____. I hope I haven't broken it.

12 Our café prides _____ on its excellent service.

13 I find it so hard to concentrate _____ with all that noise.

14 It looks like the weather is improving _____. Let's go out.

79 Indefinite pronouns

Indefinite pronouns, such as "anyone," "someone," and "everyone," are used to refer to a person or object, or a group of people or objects, without explaining who or what they are.

79.1 MATCH THE QUESTIONS TO THE CORRECT RESPONSES

Does anybody here speak Greek?

What would you prefer? Tea or coffee?

1 Could I have something to drink?

No, nobody here speaks that language.

2 Where's everyone gone?

It was nothing. Probably just the cat playing.

3 Is there anything wrong, Edward?

Yes, it's half past five.

4 Did you hear something downstairs?

There's a meeting in room 10.

5 Does anyone know what time it is?

I'm not feeling very well at all.

6 Can someone help me open this jar?

No one's heard of him, sorry.

7 Does anyone know Bill Jones here?

Of course. Pass it here.

79.2 MATCH THE PICTURES TO THE CORRECT SENTENCES

Did you buy anything when you were at the grocer's?	There's nothing here to eat!	I was exhausted after checking everything.	Everyone's asking why you're not at the party!

79.3 REWRITE THE SENTENCES, CORRECTING THE ERRORS

Michael was bored because he didn't know **nobody** at the party.

Michael was bored because he didn't know anybody at the party.

1 I'm sorry. I know absolutely **anything** about electronics.

_____

2 Libby doesn't want **something** to eat at the moment.

_____

3 I don't get on with my brother. We have **something** in common.

_____

4 I didn't buy **nothing** while I was at the store.

_____

5 There's **anything** to do here. I'm bored!

_____

6 I think I just heard **nothing** downstairs.

_____

80 Possession

Possessive determiners, possessive pronouns, apostrophe with "s," and the verbs "have" and "have got" are all used to express possession in English.

80.1 WRITE EACH WORD IN ITS OTHER FORMS

SUBJECT PRONOUN	POSSESSIVE DETERMINER	POSSESSIVE PRONOUN
I	my	mine
❶	your	
❷ he		
❸		hers
❹	its	
❺ we		
❻		theirs

80.2 MATCH THE PICTURES TO THE CORRECT SENTENCES

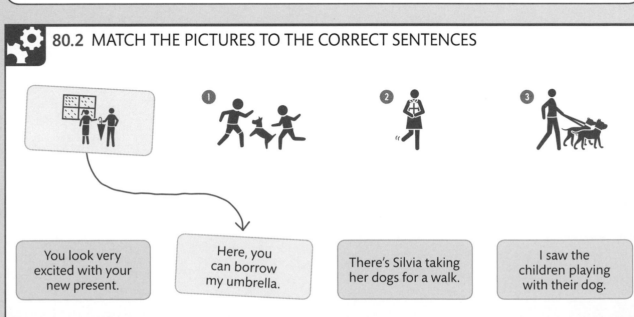

You look very excited with your new present.

Here, you can borrow my umbrella.

There's Silvia taking her dogs for a walk.

I saw the children playing with their dog.

194

80.3 REWRITE THE SENTENCES, PUTTING THE WORDS IN THE CORRECT ORDER

this | Is | phone? | your

Is this your phone?

4 aren't | These | theirs. | books

_____

1 their | Where | house? | is

_____

5 coat. | her | That | is

_____

2 yours. | is | This | desk

_____

6 Are | glasses? | these | his

_____

3 my | that | there? | charger | Is

_____

7 these | mine? | of | Which | cups | is

_____

80.4 CROSS OUT THE INCORRECT WORDS IN EACH SENTENCE

This is **my** / ~~mine~~ jacket, so this one must be ~~your~~ / **yours**.

1 **Their** / **Theirs** IT system is modern, but **our** / **ours** needs replacing soon.

2 These earrings are **my** / **mine**, but that bracelet is **her** / **hers**.

3 **My** / **Mine** bag is the yellow one. Which one is **your** / **yours**?

4 The large boxes are **their** / **theirs**, but these small ones are **our** / **ours**.

5 **Her** / **hers** parents live in the countryside, while **my** / **mine** live in the city.

6 If this is **your** / **yours**, then I don't know which laptop is **my** / **mine**.

7 Stacey put **her** / **hers** lunch in the fridge. Are these sandwiches **your** / **yours**?

8 Katia parked **her** / **hers** car by the park. Where did your parents park **their** / **theirs**?

9 We drive **our** / **ours** cars on the right, whereas they drive **their** / **theirs** on the left.

10 **Your** / **Yours** father drives a sports car, but **my** / **mine** rides a bike.

80.5 REWRITE THE PHRASES USING THE POSSESSIVE "S"

> The cat of Laura
> _Laura's cat_

1 The uncle of Mary and Don

_____

2 The son of Ben

_____

3 The grades of the students

_____

4 The cat of Sam and Ayshah

_____

5 The house of Debbie

_____

6 The dog of my parents

_____

7 The car of Marco and Kate

_____

8 The house of my grandparents

_____

9 The grandchild of Elsa

_____

10 The parrot of Beth

_____

11 The choice of the people

_____

 ## 80.6 MARK THE SENTENCES THAT ARE CORRECT

> Look at the dog! It's chasing its tail. ✓
> Look at the dog! Its chasing it's tail. ☐

1 The women's clothes are downstairs. ☐
The womens' clothes are downstairs. ☐

2 Pick the babie's toys up, please. ☐
Pick the babies' toys up, please. ☐

3 Your car's new, while my is old. ☐
Your car's new, while mine is old. ☐

4 That book is yours, and this one is mine! ☐
That book is your, and this one is my! ☐

5 Toms' computer is slow. ☐
Tom's computer is slow. ☐

6 Hurry up! Its time you left for work. ☐
Hurry up! It's time you left for work. ☐

7 My town is bigger than yours. ☐
My town is bigger than your. ☐

8 The childrens' food is here. ☐
The children's food is here. ☐

9 That bag over there is your. ☐
That bag over there is yours. ☐

10 These are the ladie's coats. ☐
These are the ladies' coats. ☐

11 My parent's house is small. ☐
My parents' house is small. ☐

12 The mens' changing room is there. ☐
The men's changing room is there. ☐

13 The dog can't find it's home. ☐
The dog can't find its home. ☐

80.7 MATCH THE BEGINNINGS OF THE SENTENCES TO THE CORRECT ENDINGS

Have you got any good		and a bowling alley.
1 I don't have any money		two brothers and two sisters.
2 The nearest town has a swimming pool	→	ideas about what present to buy Dad?
3 Have you got any free time		left to go on vacation this year.
4 My dad hasn't got a phone or		to help me with this project?
5 My wife's from a big family and has		doesn't have any friends at college.
6 Has your brother got		an email account.
7 I'm very worried that my son		red hair and a long beard?

 80.8 MARK THE BEST REPLY TO EACH QUESTION

Have you got some time to look at these files?

Yes, I have, no problem. 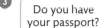 ✓

Yes, I do, no problem. ☐

1 Do you have a moment?

Yes, I have. How can I help? ☐

Yes, I do. How can I help? ☐

2 Has your sister got a boyfriend?

No, she doesn't. Why do you ask? ☐

No, she hasn't. Why do you ask? ☐

3 Do you have your passport?

Yes, I do. It's in my bag. ☐

Yes, I have. It's in my bag. ☐

4 Do we have a meeting today?

No, we don't. There's one tomorrow. ☐

No, we haven't. There's one tomorrow. ☐

5 Has your town got a metro? METRO

Yes, it does. There are two lines. ☐

Yes, it has. There are two lines. ☐

81 Defining relative clauses

A relative clause is a part of a sentence that gives more
information about the subject. A defining, or restrictive,
relative clause identifies the subject being talked about.

81.1 REWRITE THE SENTENCES, PUTTING THE WORDS IN THE CORRECT ORDER

| the | English. | assistant | could | We | speak | hired | who |

We hired the assistant who could speak English.

1. who a I man sailed met around world. has the

_____

2. exciting. you The really book was that me lent

_____

3. that delicious. ordered The Misha looks dessert

_____

4. knows some she invited college. people who Laura from

_____

5. visit to was The hoping palace was that closed. I

_____

6. Sanjay sea. house close that is a moving the to to is

_____

7. performed stage. on I band loved the which

_____

81.2 MARK THE SENTENCES THAT ARE CORRECT

I wish my neighbors had a dog that didn't bark so much. ✓

I wish my neighbors had a dog who didn't bark so much. ☐

1. My son has a camera which takes wonderful photos. ☐
My son has a camera which it takes wonderful photos. ☐

2. The milk what you bought yesterday has turned sour. ☐
The milk that you bought yesterday has turned sour. ☐

3. The woman who was just speaking to you is incredibly rich. ☐
The woman was just speaking to you is incredibly rich. ☐

4. Where did you get the hat you're wearing? ☐
Where did you get the hat who you're wearing? ☐

81.3 MATCH THE BEGINNINGS OF THE SENTENCES TO THE CORRECT ENDINGS

My sister is starting a fashion business → that helps people find clothes that suit them.

1. Ben works for a company — which produces kitchen equipment.

2. Do you like the shirt — who dreams of becoming an astronaut.

3. Fatima showed me the dog — which we're planning to buy.

4. Betty is playing a woman — that I bought at the market today?

5. This is the villa — who lives over the road.

6. There are only two stores — that she wants to adopt.

7. My dad studied with the woman — that she could lend me?

8. Does Mira have an umbrella — that sell that particular part.

82 Non-defining relative clauses

Like defining relative clauses, non-defining relative clauses add extra information about something. However, this simply gives extra detail, rather than changing the sentence's meaning.

 82.1 MATCH THE PICTURES TO THE CORRECT SENTENCES

The Statue of Liberty, which is on a small island, is popular with tourists.

1

Someone crashed into my brand new car, which I only bought last week.

2

Sam has a lovely dog, which he takes for a walk each morning.

3

Den has a new sports car, which he spent all his savings on.

 82.2 CROSS OUT THE INCORRECT WORDS IN EACH SENTENCE

The lecture, which / ~~who~~ had been scheduled for 3pm, was canceled at the last minute.

1 My new sweater, who / which is made of wool, cost $40.

2 I teach many international students, many of that / whom are Indian.

3 David's cat, who / which is usually very calm, just scratched me!

4 My wife, who / that is an optician, enjoys her job very much.

5 He has two daughters, both of who / whom are lawyers.

82.3 REWRITE THE SENTENCES, ADDING COMMAS WHERE NECESSARY

> My rabbit which I haven't seen for days is still missing.
> *My rabbit, which I haven't seen for days, is still missing.*

❶ I've recently bought a house which I'm now decorating.

_____

❷ My nephew who is only seven years old is learning to play the violin.

_____

❸ The singer thanked her fans many of whom were at the event.

_____

❹ My car which I only bought last week has already broken down.

_____

❺ Jill who has worked here for 15 years is extremely reliable.

_____

82.4 MARK WHETHER EACH RELATIVE CLAUSE IS DEFINING OR NON-DEFINING

> The Algarve, which is in Portugal, has some amazing beaches.
> **Defining** ☐   **Non-defining** ☑

❶ I'm working with someone who is always late for work.
Defining ☐   **Non-defining** ☐

❷ The fans, many of whom had traveled far, were delighted.
Defining ☐   **Non-defining** ☐

❸ I own so many books, most of which I've never read.
Defining ☐   **Non-defining** ☐

❹ Sula's wearing the necklace that you bought her.
Defining ☐   **Non-defining** ☐

83 Other relative structures

Relative words introduce phrases that describe a noun in the main part of the sentence. Different relative words are used to refer to different types of nouns.

 ## 83.1 CROSS OUT THE INCORRECT WORD IN EACH SENTENCE

This building is ~~whereby~~ / **where** the local council used to meet before they moved offices.

1 I'll never forget that afternoon **when** / **which** Paula told me she wanted to move to another country.

2 Jane, **who** / **whose** sister you work with, is giving the speech this afternoon.

3 A long break and some sunshine is exactly **which** / **what** Kelly needs right now.

4 Toni's café, **where** / **that** you worked as a student, has closed down.

5 I'm interviewing a woman **whose** / **that** brother used to work here.

6 I'm looking forward to a time **which** / **when** we don't have to work so late.

7 That sofa is just **which** / **what** we need for the living room.

8 The companies have an agreement **whereby** / **which** they share customer data.

83.2 FILL IN THE GAPS USING THE RELATIVE WORDS IN THE PANEL

Sam is a new author _____ *whose* _____ first book has just become a bestseller.

1 I thought it was Monday _____ Manuela was supposed to come.

2 I have no idea _____ he's bought me for my birthday.

3 We visited the part of India _____ my parents grew up.

4 Liam, _____ report you've just read, is an excellent lawyer.

5 Stratford-upon-Avon, _____ Shakespeare was born, is lovely.

whose   where

~~whose~~   when

where   what

83.3 MARK THE SENTENCES THAT ARE CORRECT

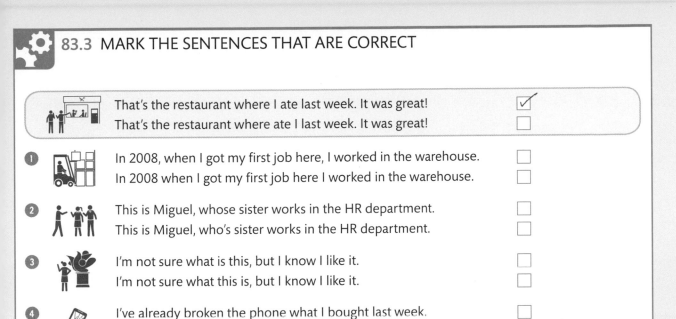

That's the restaurant where I ate last week. It was great! ✓
That's the restaurant where ate I last week. It was great! ☐

① In 2008, when I got my first job here, I worked in the warehouse. ☐
In 2008 when I got my first job here I worked in the warehouse. ☐

② This is Miguel, whose sister works in the HR department. ☐
This is Miguel, who's sister works in the HR department. ☐

③ I'm not sure what is this, but I know I like it. ☐
I'm not sure what this is, but I know I like it. ☐

④ I've already broken the phone what I bought last week. ☐
I've already broken the phone that I bought last week. ☐

83.4 FILL IN THE GAPS, PUTTING THE WORDS IN THE CORRECT ORDER

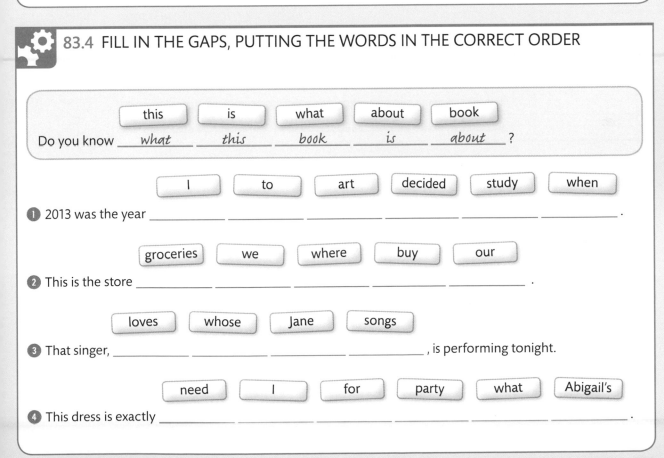

| this | is | what | about | book |

Do you know ___what___ ___this___ ___book___ ___is___ ___about___ ?

| I | to | art | decided | study | when |

① 2013 was the year _____ _____ _____ _____ _____ _____ .

| groceries | we | where | buy | our |

② This is the store _____ _____ _____ _____ _____ .

| loves | whose | Jane | songs |

③ That singer, _____ _____ _____ _____ , is performing tonight.

| need | I | for | party | what | Abigail's |

④ This dress is exactly _____ _____ _____ _____ _____ _____ .

84 Question words with "-ever"

Adding "-ever" to question words changes their meaning.
These words can be adverbs or determiners in their
own clauses, or they can join two clauses together.

84.1 MATCH THE BEGINNINGS OF THE SENTENCES TO THE CORRECT ENDINGS

My son always sends me a postcard → from wherever he is in the world.

① I want to finish this puzzle,

whichever decision I make.

② Catrina said she'd support me,

for John's birthday dinner tonight.

③ You can wear whatever you like

however long it takes.

④ Tony tries to visit his parents

has left a terrible mess.

⑤ Whoever was in the kitchen last

whenever he gets the chance.

84.2 CROSS OUT THE INCORRECT WORD IN EACH SENTENCE

Let's grab a coffee together wherever / whenever you're in London next.

① However / Whatever did Jon do to make you so angry with him?

② We're going to be late, whenever / whichever route we take.

③ Elsie told me that she'd be there to help whenever / however I needed her.

④ The engagement's not a secret. You can tell whoever / whichever you want.

⑤ However / Whoever won first prize must be a really good artist.

⑥ Whenever / Whatever I hear that music, I always think of Paris.

⑦ My new kitten follows me whichever / wherever I go in the house.

84.3 LOOK AT THE PICTURES AND COMPLETE THE SENTENCES USING THE WORDS IN THE PANEL

We think you'll be very happy with your new car, ____*whichever*____ one you choose.

5 I do some gardening _____ I have a spare moment.

1 I'm going to study drama, _____ my parents say.

6 _____ student answers this question will win a prize.

2 John's in front of the TV _____ I go to see him.

7 I'm going to finish writing this novel, _____ long it takes!

3 _____ Andy's gone, he's forgotten his wallet.

8 _____ it is John's cooked, it tastes absolutely terrible.

4 _____ painted this clearly has a vivid imagination.

9 _____ much Anthony earns, he always wants more.

whenever	whatever	wherever	whoever	whatever
however	~~whichever~~	however	whichever	whenever

85 "There"

"There" can be used with a form of "be" to talk about the existence or presence of a person or thing. Sentences with "there" can be used in many different tenses.

85.1 MATCH THE PICTURES TO THE CORRECT SENTENCES

There was such a mess after the party.

This is disgusting! There are rats in this kitchen!

There are some lovely hats for sale in that store.

There's been an explosion at the laboratory.

I'm afraid there isn't any chocolate cake left.

There's going to be a jazz band at the concert hall tonight.

There was some awful pollution on the beach.

85.2 REWRITE THE SENTENCES, CORRECTING THE ERRORS

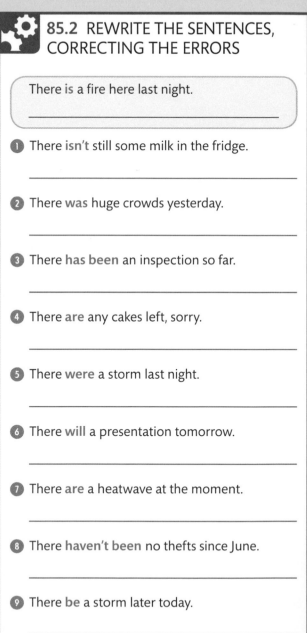

There **is** a fire here last night.

_____

1 There **isn't** still some milk in the fridge.

_____

2 There **was** huge crowds yesterday.

_____

3 There **has been** an inspection so far.

_____

4 There **are** any cakes left, sorry.

_____

5 There **were** a storm last night.

_____

6 There **will** a presentation tomorrow.

_____

7 There **are** a heatwave at the moment.

_____

8 There **haven't been** no thefts since June.

_____

9 There **be** a storm later today.

_____

85.3 MATCH THE BEGINNINGS OF THE SENTENCES TO THE CORRECT ENDINGS

There are going to be lots of people → at the teachers' convention next week.

about the poor service at the restaurant.

1 There have been a lot of complaints

to celebrate our silver wedding anniversary.

2 There will be a meeting to

3 There's going to be a party

seats for all the people here.

4 There weren't many

discuss the forthcoming redundancies.

5 There are not enough

cars in my village when I was a child.

85.4 CROSS OUT THE INCORRECT WORDS IN EACH SENTENCE

Please pay your bill on time. There **is** / ~~are~~ a penalty for late payments.

1 There **are** / **were** a lot of visitors at yesterday's exhibition.

2 There **isn't** / **aren't** any tickets for the show this evening.

3 There **is** / **are** a lot of sugar in the recipe for Cathy's cake.

4 **Is** / **Was** there a party to celebrate Olive's 90th birthday tomorrow?

5 There **is** / **are** going to be a soccer match this afternoon.

6 **Was** / **Were** there enough room for all the guests?

7 Do you know if there **is** / **are** another train tonight?

8 There **has been** / **have been** some terrible weather recently.

9 There **wasn't** / **weren't** many students at the lecture.

10 Bill's so busy at work. There **is** / **was** a deadline soon.

11 There **is** / **are** water all over the floor. What happened?

12 I'm sure there **isn't** / **won't be** another unexpected election this year.

there | at | Will | any | entertainment | party? | the | be

Will there be any entertainment at the party?

1 in | fridge. | food | the | plenty | of | There's

_____

2 a | is | the | street. | in | large | There | dog

_____

3 there | in | town? | good | Are | cafés | any | your

_____

4 and | vegetables. | selling | a | lot | are | of | people | fruit | There

_____

5 bus | won't | another | be | today. | There

_____

6 there | rice | left? | any | you | if | is | Do | know

_____

7 waiting | people | There | are | of | outside. | lots

_____

8 be | course? | the | an | Will | of | end | there | the | exam | at

_____

9 there | a | afternoon? | to | Is | meeting | be | going | this

_____

86 Introductory "it"

"It" is often used when a sentence has no clear subject and is sometimes known as a dummy subject or empty subject.

86.1 MARK THE BEST REPLY TO EACH QUESTION

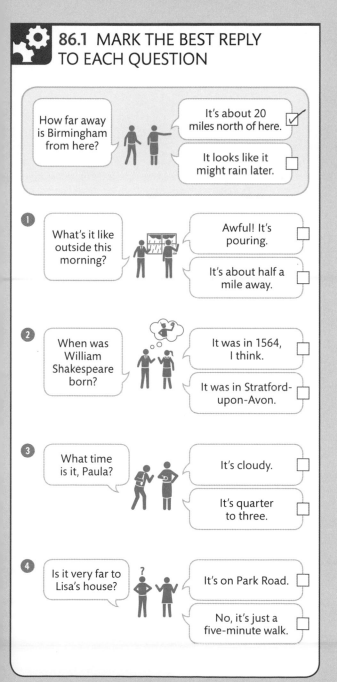

How far away is Birmingham from here?
- It's about 20 miles north of here. ✓
- It looks like it might rain later. ☐

1 What's it like outside this morning?
- Awful! It's pouring. ☐
- It's about half a mile away. ☐

2 When was William Shakespeare born?
- It was in 1564, I think. ☐
- It was in Stratford-upon-Avon. ☐

3 What time is it, Paula?
- It's cloudy. ☐
- It's quarter to three. ☐

4 Is it very far to Lisa's house?
- It's on Park Road. ☐
- No, it's just a five-minute walk. ☐

86.2 MARK WHAT "IT" REFERS TO IN EACH SENTENCE

I've got so much to do, and it's ten past three already!
- Time ✓
- Distance ☐
- Day / Date / Month / Year ☐
- Weather ☐

1 It's about 20 miles to the guest house.
- Time ☐
- Distance ☐
- Day / Date / Month / Year ☐
- Weather ☐

2 It's Monday today, isn't it?
- Time ☐
- Distance ☐
- Day / Date / Month / Year ☐
- Weather ☐

3 It can get really cold in Siberia.
- Time ☐
- Distance ☐
- Day / Date / Month / Year ☐
- Weather ☐

4 It's half past seven.
- Time ☐
- Distance ☐
- Day / Date / Month / Year ☐
- Weather ☐

86.3 MATCH THE BEGINNINGS OF THE SENTENCES TO THE CORRECT ENDINGS

It's easy to forget how difficult → it can be to learn a new language.

absence makes the heart grow fonder.

1. It is essential that all candidates — it's unlikely you'll pass the exam.

2. It's often said that

3. If you don't start working harder, — arrive 15 minutes before the interview.

4. It was so nice to meet — too fast on the highway.

5. It is difficult for foreigners to — you and your husband at the party.

6. It is dangerous to drive — to find a free moment to call you.

7. It would be great if — pronounce some words in my language.

8. It's been impossible for me — rained every day on our vacation.

9. It's such a shame that it — and look up at the stars.

10. It was a surprise to discover — we could meet for coffee next weekend.

11. It is wonderful to lie in a field — like the bus isn't coming.

12. It's been 40 minutes. It looks — that we share the same birthday.

86.4 FILL IN THE GAPS USING "THAT" OR "TO"

It is unlikely _____*that*_____ the house is going to be finished on time.

1. It is true _____ being a doctor involves a lot of hard work.

2. It is important _____ lock all the doors when you go out.

3. It is useful _____ write down important information in a notebook.

4. It is possible _____ Andre forgot that the party is tonight.

87 Shifting focus

"It" clauses, "what" clauses, or moving a noun to the front of a sentence can all be used to put emphasis on a certain word or phrase.

87.1 MATCH THE BEGINNINGS OF THE SENTENCES TO THE CORRECT ENDINGS

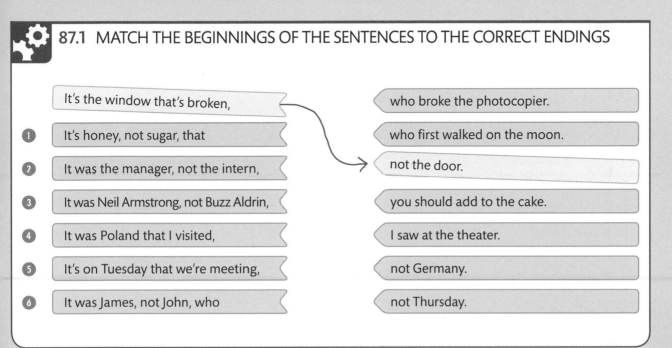

It's the window that's broken, —————→ not the door.

1 It's honey, not sugar, that

2 It was the manager, not the intern,

3 It was Neil Armstrong, not Buzz Aldrin,

4 It was Poland that I visited,

5 It's on Tuesday that we're meeting,

6 It was James, not John, who

who broke the photocopier.

who first walked on the moon.

not the door.

you should add to the cake.

I saw at the theater.

not Germany.

not Thursday.

87.2 MATCH THE PICTURES TO THE CORRECT SENTENCES

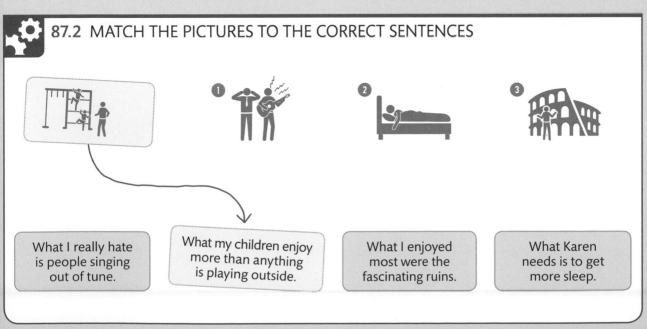

What I really hate is people singing out of tune.

What my children enjoy more than anything is playing outside.

What I enjoyed most were the fascinating ruins.

What Karen needs is to get more sleep.

87.3 FILL IN THE GAPS USING THE PHRASES IN THE PANEL

___The day___ we agreed on for our meeting was Monday, not Tuesday.

The day	
The reason	
The person	
The country	
The one thing	
The subject	

1 _____ I admire most in the world is my grandfather.

2 _____ I'll never forget is when I won the national prize.

3 _____ they gave for firing me was ridiculous.

4 _____ I loved visiting most was Montenegro.

5 _____ I enjoyed most at school was history.

87.4 REWRITE THE SENTENCES, PUTTING THE WORDS IN THE CORRECT ORDER

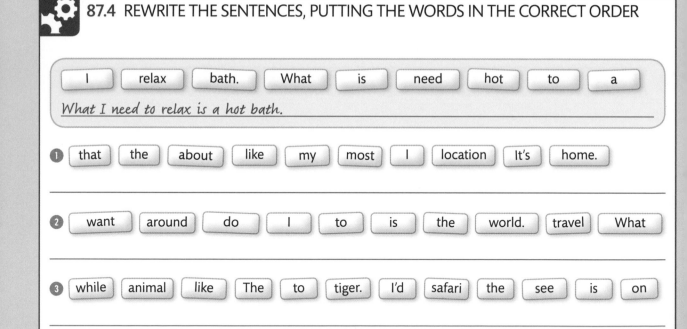

| I | relax | bath. | What | is | need | hot | to | a |

What I need to relax is a hot bath.

1 that | the | about | like | my | most | I | location | It's | home.

_____

2 want | around | do | I | to | is | the | world. | travel | What

_____

3 while | animal | like | The | to | tiger. | I'd | safari | the | see | is | on

_____

4 the | was | Dave | most | acting. | disliked | What | bad

_____

5 about | who | the | was | flood. | neighbor | It | told | my | me

_____

88 Inversion

Reversing the normal order of words, or inversion, can be used for emphasis or a sense of drama. It is common after certain types of adverbials.

88.1 MATCH THE CORRESPONDING SENTENCES

Robert is an excellent writer, and he's also a very confident public speaker.

Only after my departure did I realize that I had forgotten to say goodbye.

1 It had just stopped raining, and the children ran out to play.

Not only is Robert an excellent writer, but he is also a very confident public speaker.

2 I only realized after my departure that I had forgotten to say goodbye.

Never before have we achieved such amazing results.

3 I had just arrived at the airport when I decided I wasn't going to leave the country.

Hardly had it stopped raining when the children ran out to play.

4 We have never achieved such amazing results before.

Rarely have I had such a positive response to a proposal.

5 We did not suspect that the boy would one day become president.

No sooner had I arrived at the airport than I decided I wasn't going to leave the country.

6 I have rarely had such a positive response to a proposal.

Only when I opened the letter did I realize that I was going to college.

7 I only realized that I was going to college when I opened the letter.

Little did we know that the boy would one day become president.

has	Never	book	a	before

Never _before_ _has_ _a_ _book_ sold out so quickly!

since	1980s	such	the	I	Not	known	have

1 _____ _____ _____ _____ _____ _____ _____ a hot summer.

sometimes	such	witness	you	do	Only

2 _____ _____ _____ _____ _____ _____ kindness from strangers.

had	project	sooner	we	the	finished	No

3 _____ _____ _____ _____ _____ _____ _____ than the next one began.

they	Little	expensive	suspect	how	did

4 _____ _____ _____ _____ _____ _____ the vacation would be.

88.3 MARK THE BEST REPLY TO EACH STATEMENT

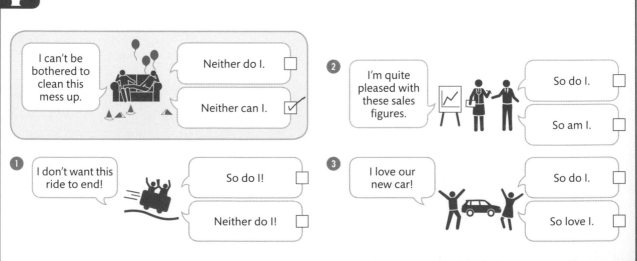

I can't be bothered to clean this mess up.

Neither do I. ☐

Neither can I. ☑

2 I'm quite pleased with these sales figures.

So do I. ☐

So am I. ☐

1 I don't want this ride to end!

So do I! ☐

Neither do I! ☐

3 I love our new car!

So do I. ☐

So love I. ☐

89 Ellipsis

Some words can be left out of a sentence to avoid repetition or when the meaning can be understood without them. This is called ellipsis.

89.1 MATCH THE BEGINNINGS OF THE SENTENCES TO THE CORRECT ENDINGS

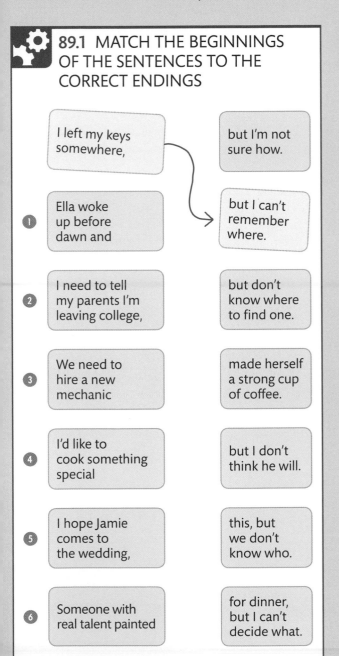

I left my keys somewhere, → but I can't remember where.

but I'm not sure how.

① Ella woke up before dawn and

② I need to tell my parents I'm leaving college, → but don't know where to find one.

③ We need to hire a new mechanic → made herself a strong cup of coffee.

④ I'd like to cook something special → but I don't think he will.

⑤ I hope Jamie comes to the wedding, → this, but we don't know who.

⑥ Someone with real talent painted → for dinner, but I can't decide what.

89.2 MARK THE BEST REPLY TO EACH QUESTION

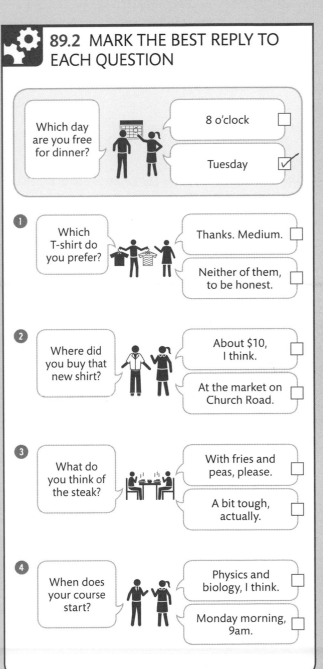

Which day are you free for dinner?
- 8 o'clock ☐
- Tuesday ☑

① Which T-shirt do you prefer?
- Thanks. Medium. ☐
- Neither of them, to be honest. ☐

② Where did you buy that new shirt?
- About $10, I think. ☐
- At the market on Church Road. ☐

③ What do you think of the steak?
- With fries and peas, please. ☐
- A bit tough, actually. ☐

④ When does your course start?
- Physics and biology, I think. ☐
- Monday morning, 9am. ☐

89.3 REWRITE THE SENTENCES, LEAVING OUT THE UNNECESSARY WORDS

> I'm nervous about the exam in case I haven't studied enough for the exam.
> _I'm nervous about the exam in case I haven't studied enough._

① I asked Charlie to stop playing soccer, but he didn't stop playing.
_____

② I'm trying to make an omelet, but I don't know how you make one.
_____

③ I want to move to a new area, but I don't know where to move.
_____

④ I really enjoy skiing, but my brother doesn't enjoy it.
_____

⑤ Someone's left a present, but I'm not sure who left it for me.
_____

⑥ I want to buy one of these laptops, but I'm not sure which one I should buy.
_____

⑦ Catalina said she'd come to the party, but I don't think she will come.
_____

⑧ There is a museum somewhere, but I'm not sure where the museum is.
_____

⑨ I tried to lift the box, but I wasn't strong enough to lift it.
_____

⑩ My wife can swim really well, but I can't swim.
_____

⑪ I want to study something at college, but I'm not sure what I want to study.
_____

⑫ Anne and Si passed the exam, but Matt didn't pass it.
_____

90 Shortening infinitives

Phrases with infinitives can sometimes be reduced or shortened to prevent repetition. This helps language to sound more natural.

90.1 MATCH THE PICTURES TO THE CORRECT SENTENCES

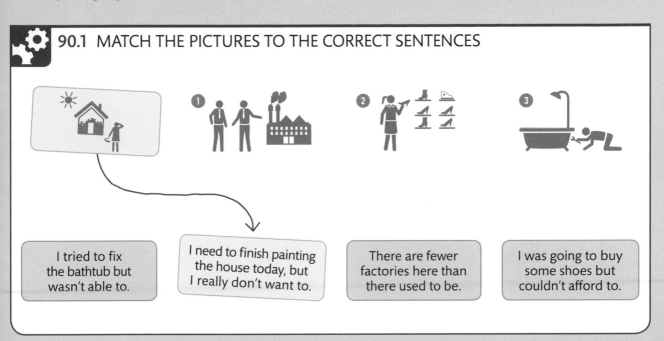

I tried to fix the bathtub but wasn't able to.

I need to finish painting the house today, but I really don't want to.

There are fewer factories here than there used to be.

I was going to buy some shoes but couldn't afford to.

90.2 MATCH THE BEGINNINGS OF THE SENTENCES TO THE CORRECT ENDINGS

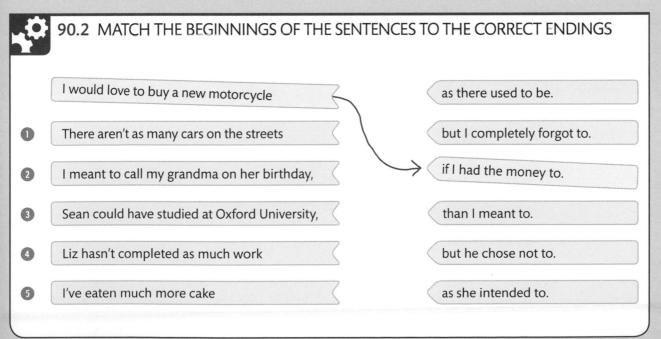

I would love to buy a new motorcycle — if I had the money to.

as there used to be.

1. There aren't as many cars on the streets

but I completely forgot to.

2. I meant to call my grandma on her birthday,

if I had the money to.

3. Sean could have studied at Oxford University,

than I meant to.

4. Liz hasn't completed as much work

but he chose not to.

5. I've eaten much more cake

as she intended to.

90.3 MARK THE BEST REPLY TO EACH STATEMENT

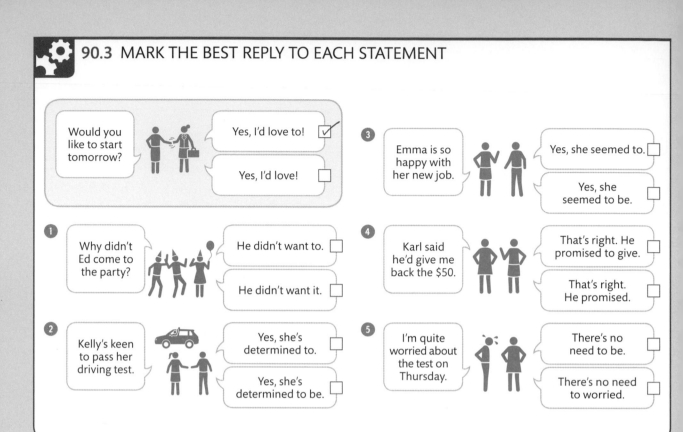

Would you like to start tomorrow?

Yes, I'd love to! ✓

Yes, I'd love!

1 Why didn't Ed come to the party?

He didn't want to.

He didn't want it.

2 Kelly's keen to pass her driving test.

Yes, she's determined to.

Yes, she's determined to be.

3 Emma is so happy with her new job.

Yes, she seemed to.

Yes, she seemed to be.

4 Karl said he'd give me back the $50.

That's right. He promised to give.

That's right. He promised.

5 I'm quite worried about the test on Thursday.

There's no need to be.

There's no need to worried.

90.4 REWRITE THE SENTENCES, PUTTING THE WORDS IN THE CORRECT ORDER

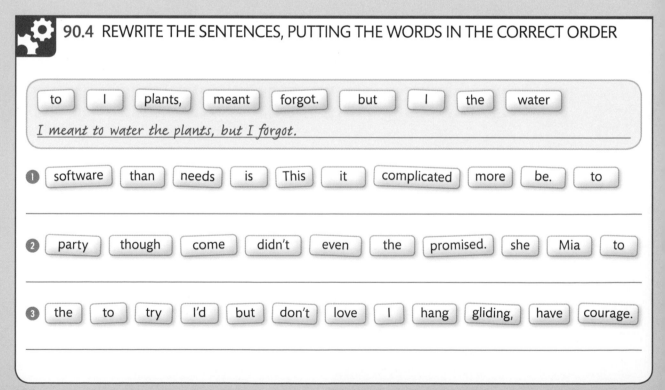

| to | I | plants, | meant | forgot. | but | I | the | water |

I meant to water the plants, but I forgot.

1 software | than | needs | is | This | it | complicated | more | be. | to

_____

2 party | though | come | didn't | even | the | promised. | she | Mia | to

_____

3 the | to | try | I'd | but | don't | love | I | hang | gliding, | have | courage.

_____

90.5 MARK THE SENTENCES THAT ARE CORRECT

There are fewer tigers in the wild these days than there used to. ☐
There are fewer tigers in the wild these days than there used to be. ☑

1. Maurice wasn't at the convention, even though he had hoped to be. ☐
   Maurice wasn't at the convention, even though he had hoped to. ☐

2. I was thinking of studying French at college but decided to not. ☐
   I was thinking of studying French at college but decided not to. ☐

3. Shelly isn't at school today, but she ought to. ☐
   Shelly isn't at school today, but she ought to be. ☐

4. I wasn't able to go on the trip, but I did want to. ☐
   I wasn't able to go on the trip, but I did want be. ☐

5. The dish isn't vegetarian, even though it's supposed to. ☐
   The dish isn't vegetarian, even though it's supposed to be. ☐

90.6 CROSS OUT THE UNNECESSARY WORDS

There's no need to come with us if you don't want to ~~come with us.~~

1. Lisa invited me to visit Spain, and I told her I'd love to visit her country.

2. We asked Mario to play golf with us, but he didn't want to play with us.

3. I wanted to see you this summer, but I won't be able to visit you.

4. We can alter the dress for you. Would you like us to do that?

5. I've never seen the Great Wall of China, but I'd love the chance to see it.

6. Gerard doesn't have a motorcycle now, but he used to have one.

7. Mary was going to buy a dog, but she decided not to buy one.

8. I dream of buying that apartment, but I can't afford to buy it.

91 Substitution

As well as ellipsis (leaving words out), repetition
can be avoided by replacing some phrases
with shorter ones. This is called substitution.

91.1 MATCH THE BEGINNINGS OF THE SENTENCES TO THE CORRECT ENDINGS

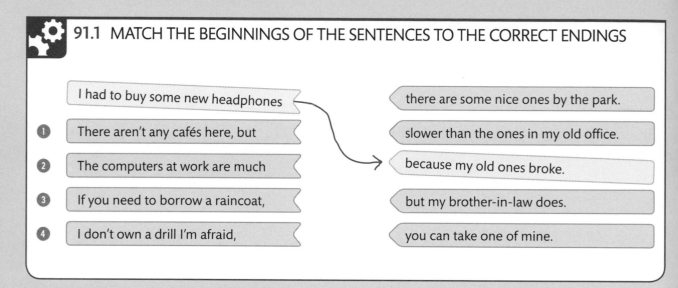

I had to buy some new headphones

there are some nice ones by the park.

1 There aren't any cafés here, but

slower than the ones in my old office.

2 The computers at work are much

because my old ones broke.

3 If you need to borrow a raincoat,

but my brother-in-law does.

4 I don't own a drill I'm afraid,

you can take one of mine.

91.2 FILL IN THE GAPS USING THE PHRASES IN THE PANEL

I thought we'd run out of flour, but I ____*found some*____ in the cupboard.

1 Cathy refuses to get a phone, though her husband _____ .

2 I really don't like this sofa, but I _____ over there.

3 There isn't any juice left, but I think _____ in the fridge.

4 I love your boots. I saw _____ in the boutique by the park.

5 I liked the look of the cakes in the bakery, so I _____ .

has got one	some similar ones	there's some
like the red one	~~found some~~	bought some

91.3 MATCH THE PICTURES TO THE CORRECT SENTENCES

We don't like fishing, but our dad does.

 **1**

I really liked that house, but my husband didn't.

 **2**

My car is ruined. I need to buy a new one.

 **3**

I really like cooking, and so does my husband.

 **4**

If that dress is too expensive, we have cheaper ones, too.

 **5**

We'd like a dessert. Could you recommend one?

 **6**

That looks delicious. Can I try some?

 7

Zhao liked the artwork, but I didn't.

 8

I own few books myself, but there are lots at the library.

91.4 MARK THE BEST REPLY TO EACH STATEMENT

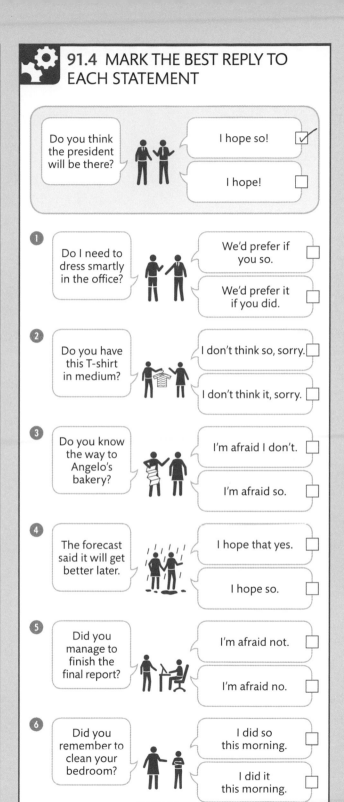

Do you think the president will be there?
- I hope so! ✓
- I hope!

1 Do I need to dress smartly in the office?
- We'd prefer if you so.
- We'd prefer it if you did.

2 Do you have this T-shirt in medium?
- I don't think so, sorry.
- I don't think it, sorry.

3 Do you know the way to Angelo's bakery?
- I'm afraid I don't.
- I'm afraid so.

4 The forecast said it will get better later.
- I hope that yes.
- I hope so.

5 Did you manage to finish the final report?
- I'm afraid not.
- I'm afraid no.

6 Did you remember to clean your bedroom?
- I did so this morning.
- I did it this morning.

92 Adjectives

Adjectives are words that describe nouns. In English, they usually come before the noun that they are describing. There are several categories of adjective.

92.1 FILL IN THE GAPS USING THE PHRASES IN THE PANEL

They're building a _____ *huge luxury* _____ apartment complex there.

1. My boyfriend gave me a _____ necklace for my birthday.

2. My grandma's knitting me a _____ sweater.

3. We went to see the _____ ruins while in Mexico.

4. We adopted a _____ kitten from the shelter.

Panel:
- ~~huge luxury~~
- dark-green woolen
- beautiful gold
- cute friendly
- ancient Aztec

92.2 WRITE THE ADJECTIVES FROM THE PANEL IN THE CORRECT GROUPS

SIZE	SHAPE	AGE
little		

COLOR	NATIONALITY	MATERIAL

Panel:
china   tiny   Argentinian   diamond-shaped   ~~little~~   round   Vietnamese   young   pink
light-blue   red   French   ancient   massive   cotton   steel   old   square

222

92.3 FIND SIX MORE ADJECTIVES IN THE GRID AND WRITE THEM UNDER THE CORRECT HEADING

```
A W F U L R A O B W O N S
N S H I L I N G O O D N V
N D E B E A U T I F U L D
R I N T P R T I U T C U I
A W O Q D U R H H L I J G
E O I S T Y A D F A E N D
M N L O Y A O Z I O R H Z
P D V E C L E V E R E N D
T E F R I E N D L Y A G I
E R I D D E L I C I O U S
R F C E P S R T I E G E D
B U B U T E R R I B L E M
B L T N T Q H W E D L N D
```

GENERAL OPINION

> awful

1 _____

2 _____

3 _____

SPECIFIC OPINION

> clever

4 _____

5 _____

6 _____

92.4 MATCH THE PICTURES TO THE CORRECT SENTENCES

I read this exciting new French novel while on vacation.

Mark's just bought this lovely large detached house.

Ebru made this lovely white silk dress.

That small old brown dog belongs to Harry.

92.5 FILL IN THE GAPS, PUTTING THE ADJECTIVES IN THE CORRECT ORDER

antique   small   vase

Liam bought a ___small___ ___antique___ ___vase___ at the market.

Indian   rug   beautiful   old

❶ Claude has a _____ _____ _____ _____ in his living room.

American   big   red

❷ Nigel's bought himself a _____ _____ _____ sports car.

wooden   small   black

❸ Catalina keeps her jewelry in a _____ _____ _____ box.

tall   charming   young

❹ My granddaughter is engaged to a _____ _____ _____ man.

92.6 CROSS OUT THE INCORRECT ADJECTIVE IN EACH SENTENCE

Sanjay's brother is completely ~~terrifying~~ / terrified of snakes.

❶ Everyone found the presentation extremely boring / bored.

❷ The instructions are so confusing / confused. I don't know what to do.

❸ Selma and Paul are interesting / interested in wildlife.

❹ We were all amazing / amazed when Sharon won the race.

93 Gradable and non-gradable adjectives

Gradable adjectives can be made weaker or stronger by adverbs, whereas non-gradable adjectives describe absolute qualities that cannot usually be graded.

93.1 MATCH THE PICTURES TO THE CORRECT SENTENCES

Ola is a very talented cook.

Turn the TV down! It's really loud!

They were ecstatic when they won the tournament.

It was boiling hot outside.

Marty was really hungry and ordered two hamburgers.

My new shoes are not very comfortable at all.

Our plumber is not particularly reliable.

93.2 MARK WHETHER EACH ADJECTIVE IS EXTREME, ABSOLUTE, OR CLASSIFYING

My grandmother is **Scottish**.
Extreme ☐
Absolute ☐
Classifying ☑

1 I really enjoyed Jessica's presentation; it was **superb**.
Extreme ☐
Absolute ☐
Classifying ☐

2 My wedding day was completely **perfect**.
Extreme ☐
Absolute ☐
Classifying ☐

3 My company now has a **monthly** meeting about taxes.
Extreme ☐
Absolute ☐
Classifying ☐

4 Pete's ideas for the business are always **terrible**.
Extreme ☐
Absolute ☐
Classifying ☐

93.3 FIND SIX MORE ADJECTIVES IN THE GRID AND WRITE THEM UNDER THE CORRECT HEADING

```
I N T E R E S T I N G N S
N S L G A N S G T L E Q V
N D E M J S E D S A A M D
R I N T B R W I L R R R E
X K H W D D A A H G I D G
E I N T E L L I G E N T D
C U U L L A E Z E O R I Z
O A V E S S Q U A R E N D
L C D A W E S O M E A G I
D H I J A R P E R F E C T
R E C E P S K I E N G E D
A W O O D E N H I J J L M
```

GRADABLE

interesting

1 _____

2 _____

3 _____

NON-GRADABLE

awesome

4 _____

5 _____

6 _____

93.4 MATCH THE BEGINNINGS OF THE SENTENCES TO THE CORRECT ENDINGS

The movie was pretty → good. I'd watch it again.

bad. It rained every day.

1 The weather was extremely — were not very tasty.

2 The cookies that Ellie made — good. I'd watch it again.

3 I found the exam almost — unique. There are no others like it.

4 Our business is reasonably — impossible to finish in time.

5 This antique vase is quite — terrified when he saw the bear.

6 Martin was absolutely — successful, but it could do better.

93.5 REWRITE THE SENTENCES, PUTTING THE WORDS IN THE CORRECT ORDER

| found | the | really | lecture | fascinating. | history | Michel |

Michel found the history lecture really fascinating.

① | food | the | wasn't | at | The | particularly | impressive. | wedding |

_____

② | good | she | but | speaks | mistakes. | Hikaru | English, | makes | fairly |

_____

③ | rooms | the | really | were | The | awful. | hotel | in |

_____

④ | reasonably | is | good | in | still | condition. | old | car | Our |

_____

93.6 FILL IN THE GAPS USING THE ADJECTIVES IN THE PANEL

Sonia keeps her jewelry in a _____*wooden*_____ box in her bedroom.

① I can't criticize his cakes. They're absolutely _____ .

② The clothes here are of good quality and _____ priced.

③ The concert was absolutely _____ . She simply can't sing!

④ There's a wonderful _____ castle in my town.

⑤ The software is _____ easy to use and won't cause too many problems.

⑥ It's _____ outside! Make sure you wear a hat.

| reasonably | awful | perfect | ~~wooden~~ | freezing | medieval | fairly |

94 Comparative adjectives

Comparative adjectives are used to compare two things.
They can either be formed by adding the suffix "-er,"
or by putting "more" or "less" before the adjective.

94.1 MATCH THE PICTURES TO THE CORRECT SENTENCES

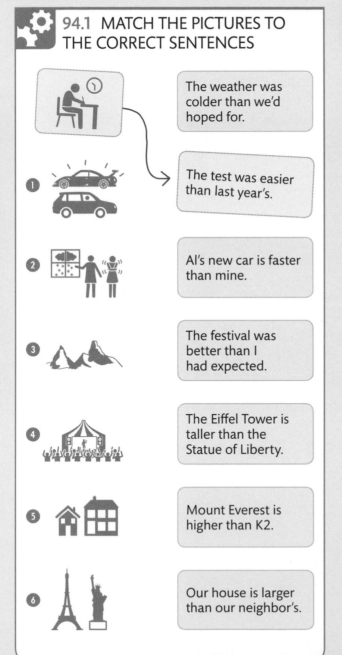

The weather was colder than we'd hoped for.

The test was easier than last year's.

Al's new car is faster than mine.

The festival was better than I had expected.

The Eiffel Tower is taller than the Statue of Liberty.

Mount Everest is higher than K2.

Our house is larger than our neighbor's.

94.2 WRITE THE ADJECTIVES IN THEIR COMPARATIVE FORM

nice	nicer
1 fast	
2 beautiful	
3 happy	
4 hot	
5 young	
6 thin	
7 cold	
8 complicated	
9 early	
10 tiring	
11 bad	
12 popular	
13 big	
14 lazy	
15 good	
16 angry	
17 close	
18 difficult	

94.3 MATCH THE BEGINNINGS OF THE SENTENCES TO THE CORRECT ENDINGS

The castle is far older → than the cathedral.

1 Danny's dog is much — older than her husband.

2 The wedding was more — than the cathedral.

3 Karen is only slightly — larger than mine.

4 Going to work by bike is — common than they were 10 years ago.

5 Electric cars are much more — less stressful than taking a train.

6 I'm less sporty than my — sensible than she used to be.

7 My daughter is much more — elder brother. I prefer reading to football.

extravagant than I'd expected.

94.4 REWRITE THE SENTENCES, PUTTING THE COMPARATIVES INTO THEIR OTHER FORMS

Our new teacher is much **friendlier** than the last.
Our new teacher is much more friendly than the last.

1 The countryside is far **quieter** than the city.

_____

2 The Caspian Sea is **shallower** than the Black Sea.

_____

3 The new software we have to use couldn't be **simpler**.

_____

4 The road was **narrower** than I thought, and I scratched the car.

_____

5 Jane is really mad with you. I've never seen anyone **angrier**.

_____

94.5 MARK THE SENTENCES THAT ARE CORRECT

Jay got up earlyer today because of the test. ☐
Jay got up earlier today because of the test. ☑

1 Lisbon is much more farther away from here than Seville. ☐
Lisbon is much farther away from here than Seville. ☐

2 The Sahara Desert is hotter than the Atacama. ☐
The Sahara Desert is hoter than the Atacama. ☐

3 I feel happier since I moved to Barcelona. ☐
I feel happyer since I moved to Barcelona. ☐

4 The weather in California is much better than in Montana. ☐
The weather in California is more better than in Montana. ☐

5 A cheetah is more faster than a lion. ☐
A cheetah is faster than a lion. ☐

6 Tom is only slightly more tall than his brother, Joe. ☐
Tom is only slightly taller than his brother, Joe. ☐

7 These jeans are much tighter than my old ones. ☐
These jeans are much more tighter than my old ones. ☐

8 The old buildings in my town are beautifuller than the modern ones. ☐
The old buildings in my town are more beautiful than the modern ones. ☐

9 My new apartment is slightly smaller than my old one. ☐
My new apartment is slightly smaller then my old one. ☐

10 My city has a worse transportation system than yours. ☐
My city has a worst transportation system than yours. ☐

11 The staff in this hotel are much more friendly than in the other one. ☐
The staff in this hotel are much more friendlier than in the other one. ☐

12 This book is much interestinger than the last one I read. ☐
This book is much more interesting than the last one I read. ☐

94.6 LOOK AT THE PICTURES AND COMPLETE THE SENTENCES USING THE PHRASES IN THE PANEL

It's ___much cheaper___ to make your own curtains.

4 A salad is _____ than a hamburger.

1 The castle is _____ than the skyscrapers.

5 My colleagues are _____ than me.

2 She was _____ than me in the race.

6 A cruise liner is _____ than a sail boat.

3 The weather was _____ than was forecast.

7 I go to bed _____ on Sunday evenings.

a lot bigger	much more experienced	much better	just a bit quicker
slightly earlier	~~much cheaper~~	quite a bit older	a lot healthier

95 Two comparatives together

Two comparatives can be used together in a sentence to show the effect of an action. They are also used to show that something is changing.

95.1 MATCH THE BEGINNINGS OF THE SENTENCES TO THE CORRECT ENDINGS

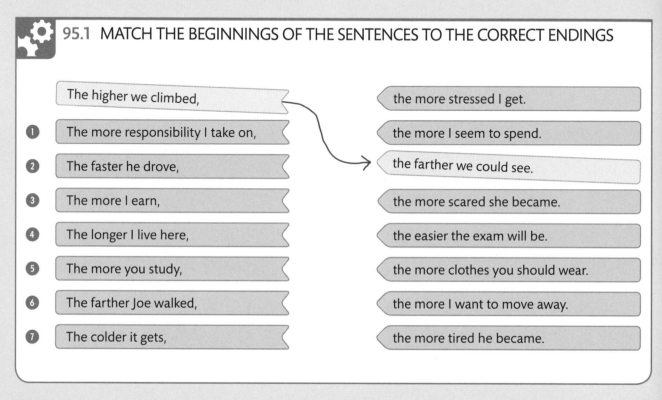

The higher we climbed,

the more stressed I get.

1 The more responsibility I take on,

the more I seem to spend.

2 The faster he drove,

the farther we could see.

3 The more I earn,

the more scared she became.

4 The longer I live here,

the easier the exam will be.

5 The more you study,

the more clothes you should wear.

6 The farther Joe walked,

the more I want to move away.

7 The colder it gets,

the more tired he became.

95.2 FILL IN THE GAPS USING THE COMPARATIVES IN THE PANEL

This book gets _more and more interesting_ with every page.

1 The _____, the more there will be to eat.

2 Ola's getting _____ at the guitar.

3 It's getting _____. Don't forget your scarf!

4 The faster you work, the _____ the project.

5 My nephew gets _____ every time I see him.

earlier you'll finish

more and more skilled

~~more and more interesting~~

colder and colder

taller and taller

bigger the cake

95.3 CROSS OUT THE UNNECESSARY WORDS IN EACH SENTENCE

 The hotter ~~the curry is~~, the better ~~it tastes~~.

① The more people come to the party, the merrier it will be.

② The sooner you finish this, the better it will be for all of us.

③ The stronger the coffee is, the better it tastes.

④ The more glamorous the dress you wear, the better you will look.

95.4 REWRITE THE SENTENCES, PUTTING THE WORDS IN THE CORRECT ORDER

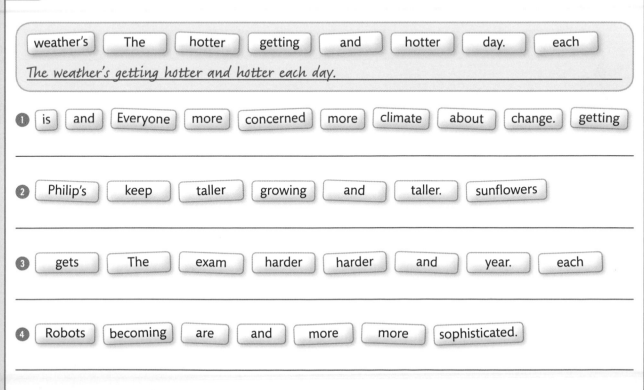

weather's   The   hotter   getting   and   hotter   day.   each

The weather's getting hotter and hotter each day.

① is   and   Everyone   more   concerned   more   climate   about   change.   getting

_____

② Philip's   keep   taller   growing   and   taller.   sunflowers

_____

③ gets   The   exam   harder   harder   and   year.   each

_____

④ Robots   becoming   are   and   more   more   sophisticated.

_____

96 "As... as" comparisons

Comparisons using "as... as" constructions can be used to discuss degrees of similarity and difference. They can be modified with adverbs to make them stronger or weaker.

96.1 MATCH THE PICTURES TO THE CORRECT SENTENCES

I'm sure your pasta will be as tasty as usual.

The other dress isn't as pretty as this one.

This hat is twice as expensive as the other one.

I hope the new chef is as talented as Jean-Louis.

Dogs are not so easy to look after as cats.

I hope the movie is as good as the book.

The results are not as good as we had hoped.

96.2 MARK THE SENTENCES THAT ARE CORRECT

Om can't run as fast so Ravi. ☐
Om can't run as fast as Ravi. ☑

1 I'm not as confident as I was before. ☐
I'm not as confident I was before. ☐

2 The food wasn't half as good as we'd hoped. ☐
The food wasn't as half good as we'd hoped. ☐

3 Rome isn't nowhere near as big as Paris. ☐
Rome is nowhere near as big as Paris. ☐

4 He told us to finish as quickly as possible. ☐
He told us to finish so quickly as possible. ☐

5 It's not quite as cold as last winter. ☐
It's quite not as cold as last winter. ☐

6 Ula doesn't call as much so she used to. ☐
Ula doesn't call as much as she used to. ☐

7 The journey took twice as long as usual. ☐
The journey took as twice as long as usual. ☐

8 Ben was as quiet as a mouse. ☐
Ben was so quiet as a mouse. ☐

9 Ed is as almost old as my aunt. ☐
Ed is almost as old as my aunt. ☐

10 It cost just as much as it did last time. ☐
It cost just as much it did last time. ☐

This dress is **almost** / ~~quite~~ as nice as the skirt.

① The exam was just **so** / **as** hard as I had expected.

② The skyscrapers here are nowhere near as big **as** / **like** in Shanghai.

③ This restaurant is **twice** / **twice as** expensive as the others.

④  The café is **almost as** / **as almost** big as the church.

⑤ The house is **quite not** / **not quite** as easy to find as we thought.

⑥ The singer was nowhere **near** / **close** as good as I hoped.

⑦ The play lasted twice **so** / **as** long as I expected.

⑧ It's **nearly not** / **not nearly** as cold as we'd imagined.

⑨ The supermarket was not **almost** / **quite** as busy as I feared.

⑩  The dress is **twice as** / **twice so** big as I thought it would be.

⑪ The other buildings are nowhere near **so** / **as** tall as the clock tower.

⑫ The company results were not quite **so** / **like** good as last year's.

⑬ The new store will be as popular **as** / **like** the others.

⑭ This was **nearly not** / **not nearly** as easy to make as I expected.

97 Superlative adjectives

Superlative adjectives, such as "the biggest" or "the smallest,"
are used to talk about extremes. Long adjectives
take "most" and "least" to show an extreme.

97.1 MATCH THE PICTURES TO THE CORRECT SENTENCES

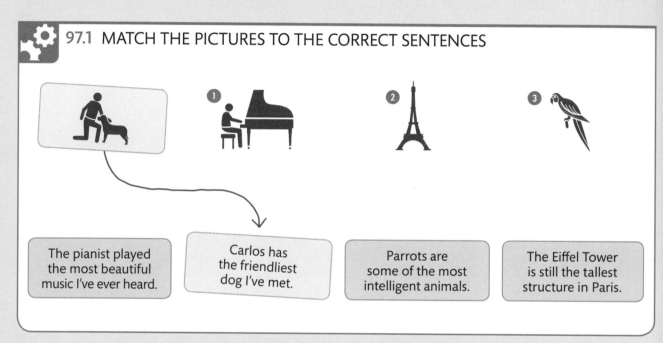

The pianist played
the most beautiful
music I've ever heard.

Carlos has
the friendliest
dog I've met.

Parrots are
some of the most
intelligent animals.

The Eiffel Tower
is still the tallest
structure in Paris.

97.2 MATCH THE BEGINNINGS OF THE SENTENCES TO THE CORRECT ENDINGS

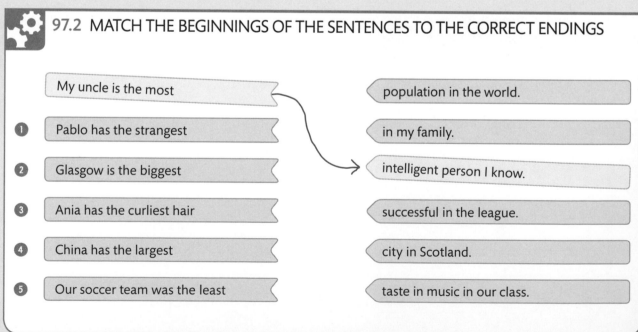

My uncle is the most

population in the world.

1 Pablo has the strangest

in my family.

2 Glasgow is the biggest

intelligent person I know.

3 Ania has the curliest hair

successful in the league.

4 China has the largest

city in Scotland.

5 Our soccer team was the least

taste in music in our class.

97.3 WRITE THE SUPERLATIVE FORM OF EACH ADJECTIVE

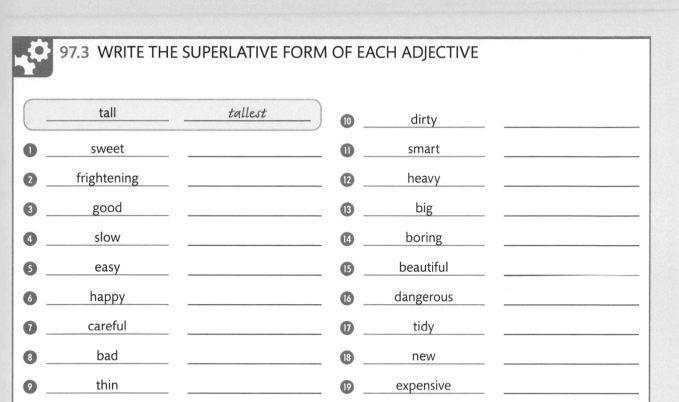

tall	tallest
1 sweet	
2 frightening	
3 good	
4 slow	
5 easy	
6 happy	
7 careful	
8 bad	
9 thin	

10 dirty	
11 smart	
12 heavy	
13 big	
14 boring	
15 beautiful	
16 dangerous	
17 tidy	
18 new	
19 expensive	

97.4 REWRITE THE SENTENCES, PUTTING THE WORDS IN THE CORRECT ORDER

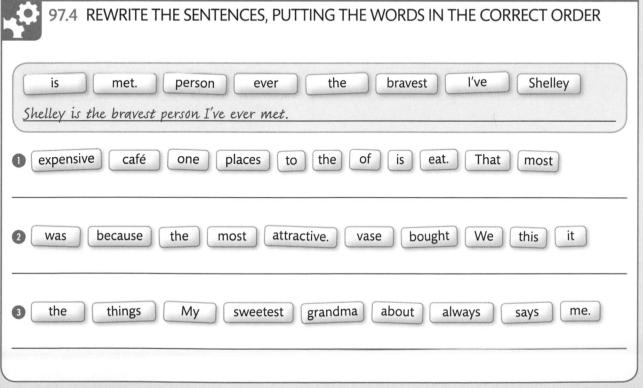

is | met. | person | ever | the | bravest | I've | Shelley

Shelley is the bravest person I've ever met.

1 expensive | café | one | places | to | the | of | is | eat. | That | most

_____

2 was | because | the | most | attractive. | vase | bought | We | this | it

_____

3 the | things | My | sweetest | grandma | about | always | says | me.

_____

237

97.5 FILL IN THE GAPS BY PUTTING THE ADJECTIVES IN THEIR SUPERLATIVE FORM

That was _____ *the most difficult* _____ (difficult) test I've ever done!

1 The Mississippi is _____ (long) river in the United States.

2 The sailfish is _____ (fast) fish in the ocean.

3 Death Valley is _____ (hot) place on earth.

4 Bungee jumping is _____ (exciting) thing I've ever done.

5 Mont Blanc is _____ (high) mountain in France.

6 My sister is _____ (creative) person I know.

7 I felt like _____ (lucky) person alive when I won the lottery.

8 Some of _____ (old) paintings can be found in local caves.

97.6 CROSS OUT THE INCORRECT WORDS IN EACH SENTENCE

We bought ~~a cheapest~~ / the cheapest computer in the store.

1 This is the **worst** / **baddest** coffee I've ever drunk.

2 Daniel is the **most fastest** / **fastest** boy in my class.

3 I think this has been the **hotest** / **hottest** day of the year so far.

4 This feels like the **slowest** / **most slow** train I've ever been on.

5 Ashalata is the **friendliest** / **friendlyest** manager at work.

6 This is the **less** / **least** expensive car we have on sale at the moment.

7 That's the **most exciting** / **excitingest** news I've heard today.

8 Mr. Clarke is the **most strictest** / **strictest** teacher in school.

9 Michael lives the **farest** / **farthest** away from our office.

10 That was one of the **saddest** / **sadest** movies I've ever seen.

> Miguel is **easy the best** artist in my city.
> *Miguel is easily the best artist in my city.*

1 Elvira was the **most fast** cyclist in the race.

_____

2 I chose **least expensive** drink on the menu.

_____

3 This is **of far the tastiest** hamburger I've ever eaten.

_____

4 The Burj Khalifa is one of **the most tallest** buildings in the world.

_____

5 It's **worst** summer I've ever known.

_____

6 This is **the most best book** I've read for ages.

_____

7 Paul **is the happyest** person I know.

_____

8 Anna is **most worried** of us all about tomorrow's inspection.

_____

9 London is **the bigest** city in England.

_____

10 Don is **easiest the tallest** person in our class.

_____

11 Feng is **one the most talented** musicians I know.

_____

12 Claire's is **far the cheapest** salon in town.

_____

98 Adverbs of manner

Words such as "quietly" and "loudly" are adverbs. They describe and give more information about verbs, adjectives, phrases, and other adverbs.

98.1 FILL IN THE GAPS USING THE ADVERBS IN THE PANEL

Paul has arrived _____safely_____.

1 Tim _____ helped Jo with her bags.

2 The kids played _____ with the dog.

3 This bus is moving so _____!

4 Charles _____ ate all the chocolate.

5 It started to rain _____.

6 Carla shouted _____ at her computer.

7 Ed's mom thinks he drives too _____.

8 My doctor told me to eat _____.

9 Kim waited _____ for her results.

safely	nervously	happily
healthily	slowly	heavily
greedily	kindly angrily	quickly

98.2 WRITE EACH ADJECTIVE AS AN ADVERB

powerful	powerfully
1 noisy	
2 reluctant	
3 good	
4 shy	
5 happy	
6 long	
7 calm	
8 straight	
9 easy	
10 hard	
11 soft	
12 dangerous	
13 repeated	
14 clumsy	
15 late	
16 bad	
17 fast	
18 stylish	

98.3 MATCH THE BEGINNINGS OF THE SENTENCES TO THE CORRECT ENDINGS

Liam is in trouble because → he always arrives late for work.

① That child has been waiting | early for the interview tomorrow.

② Anne advised me to arrive | so as not to wake up the baby.

③ George left the room quietly, | patiently for more than an hour.

④ The number of people studying | her operation last week.

⑤ Alina is doing fine after | the questions in the test correctly.

⑥ I think I answered all | fast my daughter rides her bike.

⑦ I worry a lot about how | English has increased rapidly.

 98.4 FILL IN THE GAPS BY WRITING THE ADJECTIVES IN BRACKETS AS ADVERBS

Miguel strolled _____*slowly*_____ (slow) through the forest.

① Ella _____ (gentle) stroked her new kitten.

② Marvin played the piano _____ (beautiful) last night.

③ Louis has worked _____ (hard) to improve his English.

④ An eagle flew _____ (high) above the ruined castle.

⑤ My stapler has _____ (mysterious) disappeared.

⑥ Kathy sang very _____ (good) at the performance.

⑦ Tim shouted _____ (angry) at the TV when his team lost.

⑧ Sangita wasn't _____ (bad) injured in the accident.

⑨ I went _____ (straight) to my boss's office to talk to her.

⑩ Claudio passed the final test _____ (easy).

99 Comparative and superlative adverbs

Adverbs have comparative forms to compare or show differences. They also have superlative forms to talk about extremes.

99.1 MATCH THE BEGINNINGS OF THE SENTENCES TO THE CORRECT ENDINGS

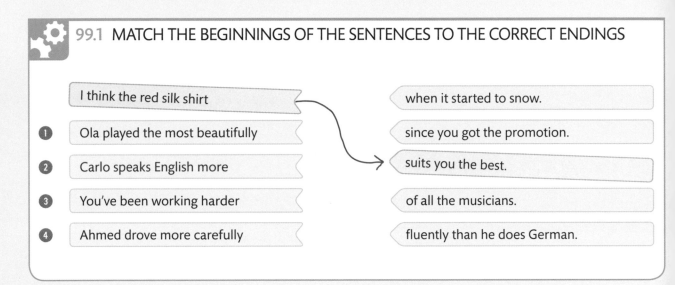

I think the red silk shirt

1 Ola played the most beautifully

2 Carlo speaks English more

3 You've been working harder

4 Ahmed drove more carefully

when it started to snow.

since you got the promotion.

suits you the best.

of all the musicians.

fluently than he does German.

99.2 WRITE EACH ADVERB IN ITS COMPARATIVE AND SUPERLATIVE FORMS

ADVERB	COMPARATIVE	SUPERLATIVE
badly	worse	worst
1 early		
2 fast		
3 regularly		
4 hard		
5 well		
6 stylishly		

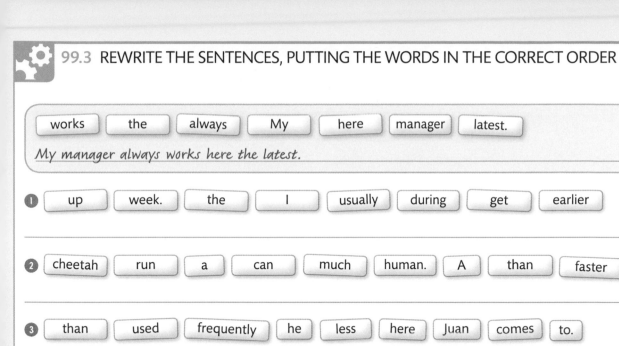

99.3 REWRITE THE SENTENCES, PUTTING THE WORDS IN THE CORRECT ORDER

| works | the | always | My | here | manager | latest. |

My manager always works here the latest.

❶ | up | week. | the | I | usually | during | get | earlier |

_____

❷ | cheetah | run | a | can | much | human. | A | than | faster |

_____

❸ | than | used | frequently | he | less | here | Juan | comes | to. |

_____

99.4 FILL IN THE GAPS USING THE PHRASES IN THE PANEL

Could you explain a bit _____ *more clearly* _____ how to do it?

❶ I should have looked _____ at my contract.

❷ My employees _____ when they're tired.

❸ Who _____ in the test, you or your sister?

❹ Joan gets up _____ in our family.

❺ My teacher said I should _____ in class.

❻ Lena has to _____ to get to our office.

❼ Our cat can _____ than our dog.

| work less efficiently | try harder | jump much higher | travel the farthest |
| more closely | ~~more clearly~~ | performed better | the earliest |

243

100 Adverbs of degree

Adverbs of degree can be placed in front of adjectives
and verbs to strengthen or weaken their original meaning.
Some adverbs can only be paired with certain adjectives.

100.1 MATCH THE PICTURES TO THE CORRECT SENTENCES

The two vases were only slightly different to each other.

My grandmother's house is extremely small.

1

Juan's cake was very popular. Everyone wanted more.

2

3

I don't think it's a particularly difficult mountain to climb.

4

Eric thought the test was fairly straightforward.

5

The house at the end of the road looks really unusual.

6

Phil's feeling remarkably fit despite how ill he was.

100.2 WRITE THE ADVERBS FROM THE PANEL IN THE CORRECT GROUPS

STRONGER	WEAKER
remarkably	

extremely   fairly   ~~remarkably~~   slightly

very   not particularly   barely   really

100.3 WRITE THE ADVERBS FROM THE PANEL IN THE CORRECT GROUPS

GRADING	NON-GRADING
slightly	

not particularly   totally   ~~slightly~~   fairly

utterly   completely   very   absolutely

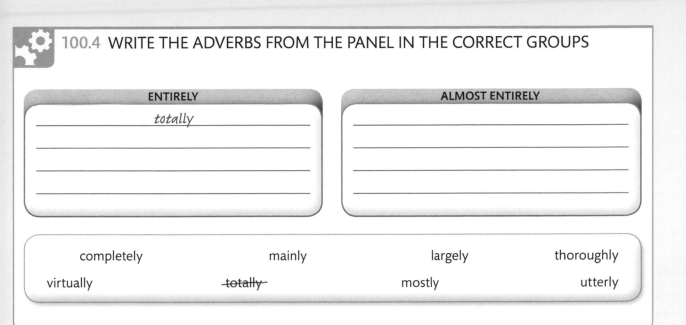

100.4 WRITE THE ADVERBS FROM THE PANEL IN THE CORRECT GROUPS

ENTIRELY

totally

ALMOST ENTIRELY

completely   mainly   largely   thoroughly

virtually   ~~totally~~   mostly   utterly

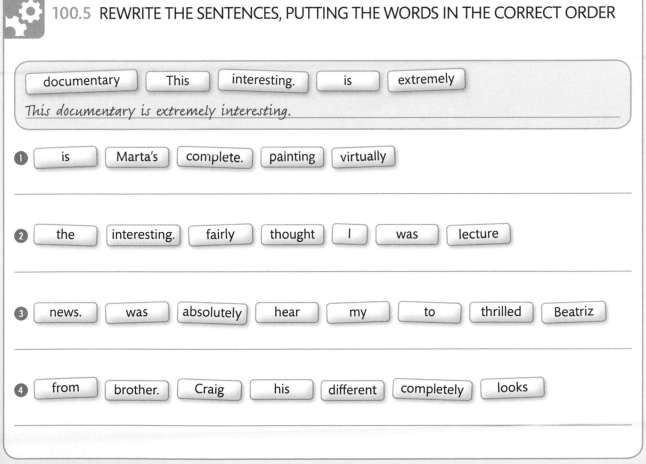

100.5 REWRITE THE SENTENCES, PUTTING THE WORDS IN THE CORRECT ORDER

documentary   This   interesting.   is   extremely

This documentary is extremely interesting.

1. is   Marta's   complete.   painting   virtually

2. the   interesting.   fairly   thought   I   was   lecture

3. news.   was   absolutely   hear   my   to   thrilled   Beatriz

4. from   brother.   Craig   his   different   completely   looks

100.6 MARK THE SENTENCES THAT ARE CORRECT

The rides at the fair were totally awesome. ✓
The rides at the fair were entirely awesome. ☐

1 Unfortunately, the hotel we stayed in was utterly awful. ☐
Unfortunately, the hotel we stayed in was remarkably awful. ☐

2 We found the music festival very brilliant this year. ☐
We found the music festival completely brilliant this year. ☐

3 The students' handwriting was barely legible. ☐
The students' handwriting was nearly legible. ☐

4 The food in the canteen is absolutely good. ☐
The food in the canteen is remarkably good. ☐

5 It was nearly impossible, but we reached the summit in the end. ☐
It was slightly impossible, but we reached the summit in the end. ☐

100.7 MATCH THE BEGINNINGS OF THE SENTENCES TO THE CORRECT ENDINGS

Saori's style of singing → is really quite unique.

wear jeans to work on Fridays.

1 The play had almost started — useless without its charger.

2 It's perfectly acceptable to — is really quite unique.

3 This old phone is absolutely — by the time we found the theater.

4 We were completely exhausted — writing his PhD thesis.

5 Jon is extremely talented — when we reached the summit.

6 Timothy has essentially finished — and should study art at college.

101 Adverbs of time

Adverbs of time are used to give more precise information about exactly when something happens. They can also refer to a continuing event or action.

101.1 MATCH THE PICTURES TO THE CORRECT SENTENCES

I've just knocked over that vase. I'm so sorry.

I haven't finished loading the dishwasher yet.

We've already packed everything for the move.

It looks like Sanchez is about to score!

Sarah looked like she was about to fall asleep.

The bus hasn't arrived yet. I'm going to be home late.

The chicken's not ready. It's still cooking in the oven.

101.2 MARK WHETHER EACH SENTENCE REFERS TO A PAST, ONGOING, OR FUTURE ACTION

It's still raining. Will it ever stop?
Past ☐
Ongoing ☑
Future ☐

❶ I'm about to leave work. Is it important?
Past ☐
Ongoing ☐
Future ☐

❷ Mona just called. She's at the café.
Past ☐
Ongoing ☐
Future ☐

❸ Jim has already seen that film.
Past ☐
Ongoing ☐
Future ☐

❹ George hasn't cleaned his bedroom yet.
Past ☐
Ongoing ☐
Future ☐

❺ Margaret still works in the HR department.
Past ☐
Ongoing ☐
Future ☐

Has Daniel finished painting the bedroom yet / ~~just~~?

① I have yet / just received a letter from an old friend.

② Mizuho has already / just been to Paris three times before.

③ Have you been introduced to Tonia's parents yet / just?

④ The judges are about to / just reveal the winner of the competition.

⑤ I've yet / just finished my final exam. It's such a relief.

⑥ I haven't finished the book you lent me already / yet.

⑦ Maria has yet / just told me she is quitting her job.

⑧ The concert had already / just begun by the time we arrived.

⑨ Lisa has yet / just returned from her trip around South America.

⑩ I was about to / just leave, when I remembered the oven was still on.

⑪ The new block on Park Street isn't finished just / yet.

⑫ Hurry up, everyone! The train is just / about to leave.

⑬ I've already / yet told Anna that the meeting has started.

101.4 MATCH THE BEGINNINGS OF THE SENTENCES TO THE CORRECT ENDINGS

We've just seen a bear — and its cubs in the forest.

all the money we saved.

about to give a speech.

1. Vanessa is still working

2. We have already spent

3. Has Zahra visited

4. Giuseppe's restaurant

5. Clive looks like he's

6. We still haven't heard

for the bank, isn't she?

the National Gallery yet?

back from the plumber.

is still the best in town.

101.5 MARK THE SENTENCES THAT ARE CORRECT

It looks like the band is about to go on stage. ✓
It looks like the band is about go on stage. ☐

1. Mesut still hasn't given back the $30 I lent him. ☐
   Mesut hasn't still given back the $30 I lent him. ☐

2. Leroy is still the best player on the team. ☐
   Leroy is yet the best player on the team. ☐

3. Has Timo still shown you around the new office? ☐
   Has Timo shown you around the new office yet? ☐

4. The guests have already eaten all of the birthday cake. ☐
   The guests have eaten already all of the birthday cake. ☐

5. I just have seen your brother walking out of the police station. ☐
   I've just seen your brother walking out of the police station. ☐

6. Jess is yet living in Aberdeen, isn't she? ☐
   Jess is still living in Aberdeen, isn't she? ☐

102 Adverbs of frequency

Adverbs of frequency show how often something is done, from something done very frequently ("always") to something not done at all ("never").

102.1 CROSS OUT THE INCORRECT WORDS IN EACH SENTENCE

Lou has to work late about once a month.   =   Lou ~~often~~ / **occasionally** works late.

1 Ola goes to the gym six days a week.   =   Ola goes to the gym **very often** / **sometimes**.

2 It rains in the desert once or twice a year.   =   It **hardly ever** / **regularly** rains in the desert.

3 I visit my gran on Tuesday and Thursday.   =   I **regularly** / **always** visit my gran.

4 Most Saturdays I go shopping with friends.   =   I **always** / **usually** go shopping on Saturday.

5 She goes running about three times a week.   =   She **occasionally** / **frequently** goes running.

6 We spend all our vacations in France.   =   We **always** / **sometimes** go to France on vacation.

102.2 WRITE THE ADVERBS FROM THE PANEL IN THE CORRECT GROUPS

ALL OR MOST OF THE TIME	SOME OF THE TIME	NOT OFTEN OR NOT AT ALL
always		

regularly   very often   almost never   ~~always~~   usually   occasionally

never   hardly ever   rarely   sometimes   nearly always

102.3 REWRITE THE SENTENCES, PUTTING THE WORDS IN THE CORRECT ORDER

| to | occasionally | work | Yasmin | cycles | summer. | in | the |

Yasmin occasionally cycles to work in the summer.

1 | ever | in | the | is | Karen | on | Fridays. | hardly | office |

_____

2 | I | about | my | once | a | parents | year. | visit |

_____

3 | photocopier | work | nearly | always | at | The | is | broken. |

_____

4 | three | the | week. | Mira | to | gym | times | a | goes |

_____

102.4 MATCH THE BEGINNINGS OF THE SENTENCES TO THE CORRECT ENDINGS

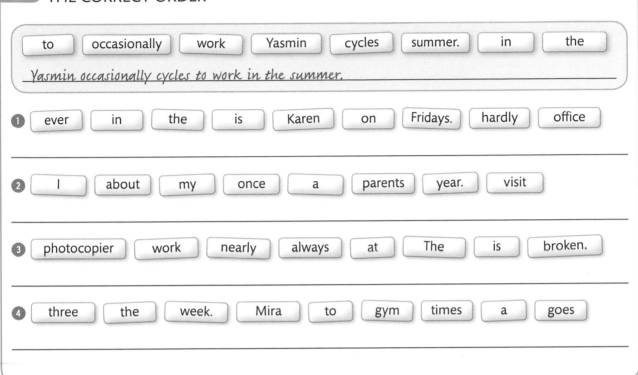

How often do you visit → your sister in Spain?

1 Benny's very reliable and — least five times a week.

2 Carlita goes swimming at — until after 10pm.

3 Ella often stays at work — is almost never late for work.

4 I come from central Australia, — every Sunday morning.

5 When do you usually — where it hardly ever rains.

6 Ania plays badminton with her cousin — finish work in the evening?

103 "So" and "such"

"So" and "such" are adverbs which can be used with certain words to add emphasis. They are similar in meaning, but they are used in different structures.

103.1 MATCH THE BEGINNINGS OF THE SENTENCES TO THE CORRECT ENDINGS

Beginnings	Endings
Your apartment is so much	that we couldn't fly a kite.
1 It was so windy	much better behaved than mine.
2 Your children are so	more spacious than mine.
3 The bride wore such	all decided to go swimming.
4 It was so hot that we	beautifully decorated cake before.
5 I've never seen such a	a stylish dress for the wedding.

Your apartment is so much → more spacious than mine.

103.2 MARK THE SENTENCES THAT ARE CORRECT

The photocopier's making such an awful noise. ☑
The photocopier's making a so awful noise. ☐

1 The cake that Carlos made for the party was such tasty. ☐
The cake that Carlos made for the party was so tasty. ☐

2 Your exam results are so better this year. ☐
Your exam results are so much better this year. ☐

3 This store sells such lovely clothes. ☐
This store sells such a lovely clothes. ☐

4 Your brother owns such a beautiful villa. ☐
Your brother owns a so beautiful villa. ☐

103.3 CROSS OUT THE INCORRECT WORDS IN EACH SENTENCE

> The children behaved ~~such~~ / so / ~~so much~~ badly that we sent them to bed.

1. Colm's job looks **such** / so / so much interesting, but it's very badly paid.

2. My new phone's **such** / so / so much better than my old one.

3. Everyone had **such** / so / so much a great time at the school reunion.

4. Hank is **such** / so / so much generous. He gave me a watch for my birthday.

5. The new intern works **such** / so / so much harder than the old one.

6. It was **such** / so / so much a shock when our boss said he was leaving.

7. Lorna's **such** / so / so much a talented musician.

8. The weather was **such** / so / so much bad that we decided to cancel the barbecue.

 103.4 REWRITE THE SENTENCES, CORRECTING THE ERRORS

> This book is so better than the author's last one.
> *This book is so much better than the author's last one.*

1. My little sister is a so good dancer. She should take classes.

   _____

2. The match was such a disappointing. No one scored.

   _____

3. The weather is so warmer in Florida. You should move here.

   _____

4. Kirsty's such a funny. She always makes me laugh.

   _____

5. Sandra is so much a good cook. Everything she makes is delicious.

   _____

104 "Enough" and "too"

"Enough" is used when there is the correct degree or amount of something. "Too" is used when something is more than necessary or wanted.

104.1 MATCH THE PICTURES TO THE CORRECT SENTENCES

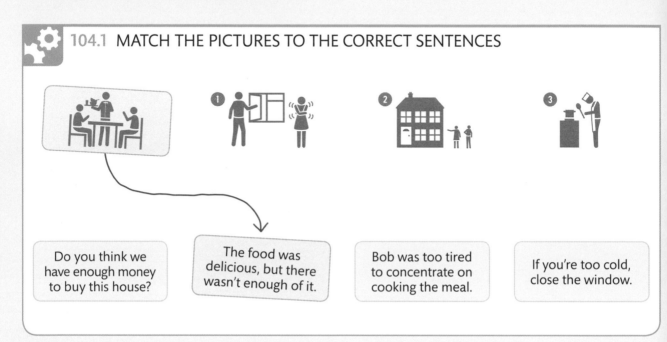

Do you think we have enough money to buy this house?

The food was delicious, but there wasn't enough of it.

Bob was too tired to concentrate on cooking the meal.

If you're too cold, close the window.

104.2 FILL IN THE GAPS USING THE PHRASES IN THE PANEL

Dan's _____old enough_____ to remember the 1960s.

1 I'm not _____ to afford those shoes.

2 Michael is _____ to watch that movie.

3 The water is _____ to go for a swim.

4 My neighbor always plays his music _____ .

5 This bookcase is _____ for me to move.

6 My French isn't _____ to understand Pierre.

7 The exercise was _____ for a total beginner.

too hard
rich enough
too loudly
old enough
too young
too heavy
good enough
warm enough

104.3 REWRITE THE SENTENCES, PUTTING THE WORDS IN THE CORRECT ORDER

was   spicy   The   for   food   India   Christopher.   too   in

The food in India was too spicy for Christopher.

① catch   last   bus.   We   enough   the   to   have   time

② should   sweater.   enough,   warm   If   put   you're   a   on   you   not

③ guests   food   tonight?   enough   Do   the   have   for   we   all

④ were   tickets   concert   expensive.   too   for   The   rock   the

⑤ enough   bottle.   Norbert   the   tall   isn't   reach   to

⑥ walked   we   there.   wasn't   The   so   far,   café   too

⑦ spoke   professor   The   hear.   us   too   for   to   quietly

⑧ enough   rent.   earn   I'm   but   not   the   rich,   pay   I   to

⑨ fast   but   I   enough.   best   wasn't   tried   my   race,   in   I   the

105 Prepositions

Prepositions are words that are used to show relationships between different parts of a clause, for example relationships of time, place, or reason.

105.1 MATCH THE PICTURES TO THE CORRECT SENTENCES

The meeting is on Monday morning.

He was so scared that he jumped up onto a chair.

There's a café by the church.

Peter works at the local airport.

Julie gave her teacher her homework after the lesson.

Mia was nervous before going in to speak to her boss.

Dan put the flowers on the table.

105.2 MARK THE SENTENCES THAT ARE CORRECT

Since quit her job, she's been happier. ☐
Since quitting her job, she's been happier. ☑

1. Before leaving for work, I wash the dishes. ☐
   Before to leave for work, I wash the dishes. ☐

2. I have an English class on Tuesdays. ☐
   I have an English class at Tuesdays. ☐

3. I don't know what to listen. ☐
   I don't know what to listen to. ☐

4. Al passed without study for the exam. ☐
   Al passed without studying for the exam. ☐

5. Kumi's listening the radio. ☐
   Kumi's listening to the radio. ☐

6. Emma's house is by the park. ☐
   Emma's house is for the park. ☐

7. Their office is next the library. ☐
   Their office is next to the library. ☐

8. After finishing work, I go swimming. ☐
   After to finish work, I go swimming. ☐

9. Jon wants to studying Spanish. ☐
   Jon wants to study Spanish. ☐

10. I live with Pete, with Dan, and with Ed. ☐
    I live with Pete, Dan, and Ed. ☐

105.3 FILL IN THE GAPS USING THE PREPOSITIONS IN THE PANEL

There are lots of great restaurants _____ *by* _____ our hotel.

1 My aunt is really good _____ making her own clothes.

2 My new house is _____ the National Museum.

3 In spite _____ the bad pay, Eleni loves her job.

4 You've been looking _____ that phone all morning.

5 Instead _____ going to college, I became a carpenter.

of   at

~~by~~   at

near   of

105.4 REWRITE THE SENTENCES, CORRECTING THE ERRORS

Michael and Amanda are looking forward **to go out** for dinner tonight.
Michael and Amanda are looking forward to going out for dinner tonight.

1 I'm not used **to wake up** so early each morning.

_____

2 My son is planning **to going** to college in New York.

_____

3 I'm sorry I haven't got around **to reply** to your email yet.

_____

4 Jean-Pierre used **to driving** a red sports car.

_____

5 Martin decided **to quitting** his job at the library.

_____

6 Virginie confessed **to steal** the bottle of wine.

_____

106 Prepositions of place

Prepositions of place are used to relate the position or location of one thing to another. Using a different preposition usually changes the meaning of a sentence.

 106.1 CROSS OUT THE INCORRECT WORDS IN EACH SENTENCE

Katie is ~~in~~ / ~~at~~ / on a bus to London.

① The dinner is **in** / **at** / **on** the table.

② Julian lives **in** / **at** / **on** the United States.

③ Mesut wasn't **in** / **at** / **on** the party.

④ I went to meet Ula **in** / **at** / **on** the airport.

⑤ Carmen works **in** / **at** / **on** France.

⑥ I bought it **in** / **at** / **on** the supermarket.

⑦ Mary stayed **in** / **at** / **on** bed all morning.

⑧ There are 20 rooms **in** / **at** / **on** the building.

⑨ Put the toys back **in** / **at** / **on** their box.

⑩ We went to London **in** / **at** / **on** the train.

⑪ Marta's left her keys **in** / **at** / **on** home.

⑫ Ben is sitting **in** / **at** / **on** the sofa.

⑬ The students are all **in** / **at** / **on** their desks.

 106.2 MATCH THE BEGINNINGS OF THE SENTENCES TO THE CORRECT ENDINGS

There's a great selection of movies | posters on your kitchen wall.

① Marina works at Z-Tech, the | number 16, Nelson Avenue.

② You have some lovely | playing at the theater downtown.

③ My uncle Tony lives at | software company on Park Street.

④ We keep the lawnmower | on the ninth and tenth floors.

⑤ The college library can be found | the bakery across the road.

⑥ I usually buy my bread at | in the shed behind the house.

106.3 LOOK AT THE PICTURES AND COMPLETE THE SENTENCES
USING THE PREPOSITIONS IN THE PANEL

We have a lovely photograph hanging
_____*above*_____ the couch.

4 Ian put his bag on the seat
_____ .

1 The castle sits _____
some ugly modern buildings.

5 There's a lovely park _____
my house.

2 I placed the final box of books
_____ the others.

6 The library is _____
the bank and the café.

3 Alan is working in the garage
_____ a car.

7 I found Craig and Robin hiding
_____ a tree.

on top of	behind	under	near
between	~~above~~	in front of	opposite

Prepositions of time are often used to talk about schedules and routines. They give information about when something happens, and how long it lasts.

107.1 MATCH THE PICTURES TO THE CORRECT SENTENCES

During the week I wake up at 7am.

Canada gets very cold in winter.

We'd better hurry. Our flight leaves in two hours.

I'm free on Wednesday and Thursday this week.

Jan has a bath in the evening before she goes to bed.

I usually make coffee when I get up in the morning.

It often gets far too hot in the summer in the city.

107.2 MARK THE SENTENCES THAT ARE CORRECT

Ted has plans on the afternoon. ☐
Ted has plans in the afternoon. ☑

1 I'm meeting Eliana at 6pm. ☐
I'm meeting Eliana on 6pm. ☐

2 Joe has his final exam at Friday. ☐
Joe has his final exam on Friday. ☐

3 She started working here on August. ☐
She started working here in August. ☐

4 I go to Angelo's café at lunchtime. ☐
I go to Angelo's café in lunchtime. ☐

5 Pat works from home at Thursdays. ☐
Pat works from home on Thursdays. ☐

6 I always have a nap in the afternoon. ☐
I always have a nap on the afternoon. ☐

7 Their wedding is on August the 15th. ☐
Their wedding is in August the 15th. ☐

8 The performance starts in 4 o'clock. ☐
The performance starts at 4 o'clock. ☐

9 Maria usually goes skiing in winter. ☐
Maria usually goes skiing on winter. ☐

10 My daughter was born at 1996. ☐
My daughter was born in 1996. ☐

107.3 MATCH THE BEGINNINGS OF THE SENTENCES TO THE CORRECT ENDINGS

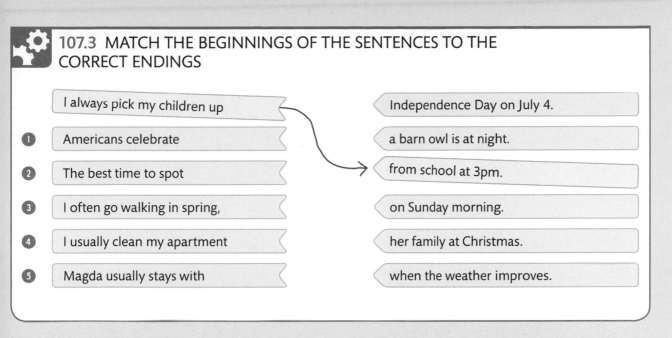

I always pick my children up	Independence Day on July 4.
① Americans celebrate	a barn owl is at night.
② The best time to spot	from school at 3pm.
③ I often go walking in spring,	on Sunday morning.
④ I usually clean my apartment	her family at Christmas.
⑤ Magda usually stays with	when the weather improves.

107.4 REWRITE THE SENTENCES, PUTTING THE WORDS IN THE CORRECT ORDER

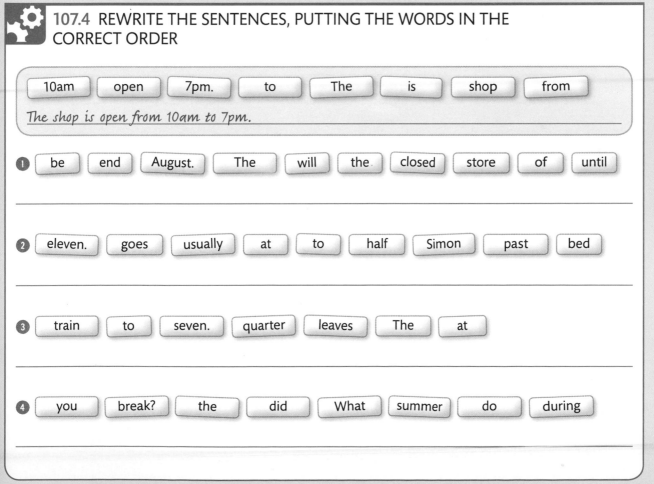

10am   open   7pm.   to   The   is   shop   from

The shop is open from 10am to 7pm.

① be   end   August.   The   will   the   closed   store   of   until

_____

② eleven.   goes   usually   at   to   half   Simon   past   bed

_____

③ train   to   seven.   quarter   leaves   The   at

_____

④ you   break?   the   did   What   summer   do   during

_____

107.5 FILL IN THE GAPS USING THE PHRASES IN THE PANEL

Wendy has been on vacation _____*for*_____ three days.

1 I usually go for lunch _____ 1 and 2pm.

2 I'm planning to work here _____ I retire.

3 Martin has worked here _____ October.

4 I lived in Spain for a couple of years _____ the 1970s.

5 Guests should leave their rooms _____ 11:30am.

until	during
~~for~~	since
between	by

107.6 REWRITE THE SENTENCES, CORRECTING THE ERRORS

Yasmin **is** a student here since last year.
Yasmin has been a student here since last year.

1 The café is open **for** 8am and 6pm.

_____

2 I'll be writing this essay **to** 10pm.

_____

3 I've been working here **since** about five months.

_____

4 We're traveling around Mexico from July **and** September.

_____

5 Mabel's lived in Madrid **from** she was a child.

_____

6 Camilla **is** my manager here since July.

_____

108 Other prepositions

Prepositions can be used to express relationships other than place and time, such as origin, ownership, and absence.

 108.1 MATCH THE PICTURES TO THE CORRECT SENTENCES

We went for a walk with our children this afternoon.	Elsa shouldn't have left the house without an umbrella.	My aunt's written a book about the town where she grew up.	I get a lot of work done when I travel by train.

 108.2 CROSS OUT THE INCORRECT WORDS IN EACH SENTENCE

I've just written a book ~~by~~ / ~~with~~ / about the history of European royalty.

1. *Macbeth* was written **by** / **without** / **about** William Shakespeare in the early 1600s.

2. Takumi went to the theater **by** / **with** / **about** his wife last night.

3. We found our way to the castle **by** / **without** / **about** too much difficulty.

4. I ordered boiled potatoes **by** / **with** / **about** my steak.

5. Most tourists travel around Tokyo **by** / **with** / **without** metro.

6. We need to talk **by** / **without** / **about** employing some more staff.

7. Sarah managed to finish the project **by** / **without** / **about** any help.

108.3 MATCH THE BEGINNINGS OF THE SENTENCES TO THE CORRECT ENDINGS

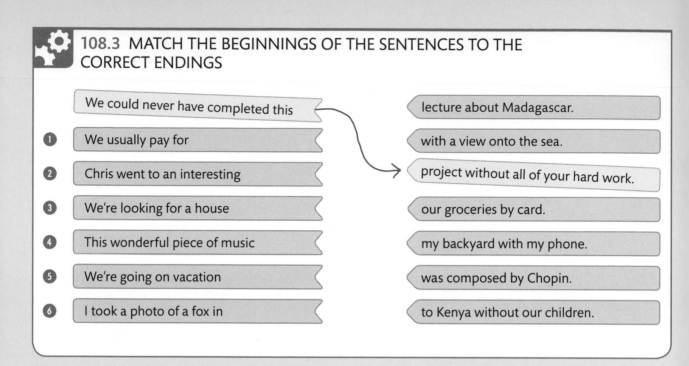

We could never have completed this — project without all of your hard work.

① We usually pay for

② Chris went to an interesting

③ We're looking for a house

④ This wonderful piece of music

⑤ We're going on vacation

⑥ I took a photo of a fox in

lecture about Madagascar.

with a view onto the sea.

our groceries by card.

my backyard with my phone.

was composed by Chopin.

to Kenya without our children.

108.4 REWRITE THE SENTENCES, PUTTING THE WORDS IN THE CORRECT ORDER

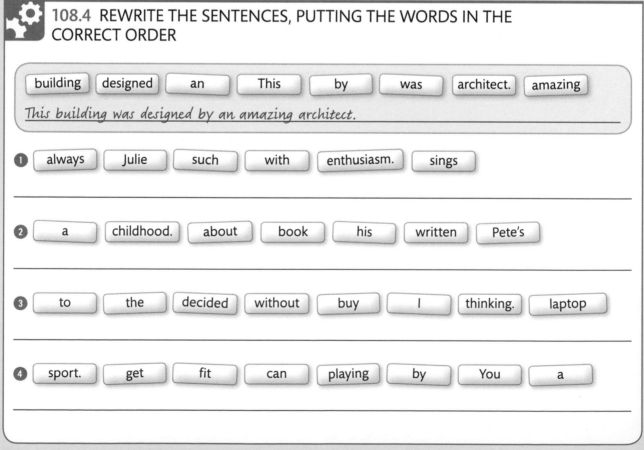

building | designed | an | This | by | was | architect. | amazing

This building was designed by an amazing architect.

① always | Julie | such | with | enthusiasm. | sings

_____

② a | childhood. | about | book | his | written | Pete's

_____

③ to | the | decided | without | buy | I | thinking. | laptop

_____

④ sport. | get | fit | can | playing | by | You | a

_____

109 Dependent prepositions

Some words must be followed by a specific preposition, called a dependent preposition. These words can be adjectives, verbs, or nouns.

109.1 MATCH THE PICTURES TO THE CORRECT SENTENCES

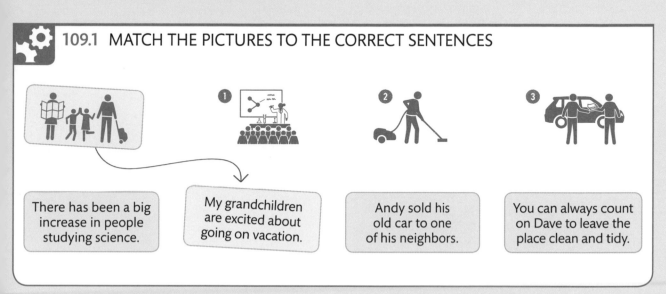

There has been a big increase in people studying science.

My grandchildren are excited about going on vacation.

Andy sold his old car to one of his neighbors.

You can always count on Dave to leave the place clean and tidy.

109.2 REWRITE THE SENTENCES, PUTTING THE WORDS IN THE CORRECT ORDER

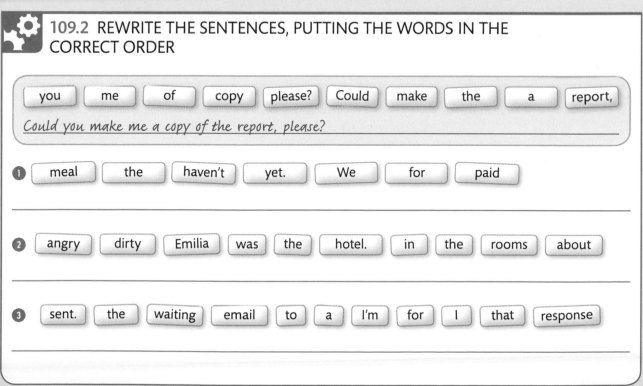

| you | me | of | copy | please? | Could | make | the | a | report, |

Could you make me a copy of the report, please?

1. | meal | the | haven't | yet. | We | for | paid |

_____

2. | angry | dirty | Emilia | was | the | hotel. | in | the | rooms | about |

_____

3. | sent. | the | waiting | email | to | a | I'm | for | I | that | response |

_____

109.3 CROSS OUT THE INCORRECT WORD IN EACH SENTENCE

 What do you think **about** / ~~on~~ my new haircut?

1  I was so proud **of** / **with** Katie when she passed the test.

2 There are lots of advantages **by** / **to** working from home.

3 This company is advertising **of** / **for** a new secretary.

4 Is everyone ready **for** / **of** the big exam tomorrow?

5 Stephanie has a very positive attitude **at** / **toward** her work.

6 The roadwork caused problems **for** / **with** many drivers.

7 I was so impressed **of** / **by** the room service.

8 My boss told us **to** / **about** be more punctual in future.

9 I don't agree **to** / **with** my husband about many things.

10 My son is afraid **of** / **with** spiders.

11 They've found another problem **for** / **with** my car.

12 Esther has talked **to** / **about** moving abroad for years.

109.4 FILL IN THE GAPS USING THE PHRASES IN THE PANEL

My daughter's asked _____*for*_____ a new laptop for her birthday.

1 I saw Leonard talking _____ a police officer yesterday.

2 There's been an increase _____ the number of thefts.

3 These animal toys should appeal _____ children.

4 Sangita is annoyed _____ her housemates.

5 My grandfather loves to talk _____ his childhood.

~~for~~   in

to   about

with   to

109.5 REWRITE THE SENTENCES, CORRECTING THE ERRORS

Will you have time to reply **at** my email today?
Will you have time to reply to my email today?

1 Ella is really upset **with** losing her mother's necklace.

_____

2 Bill is anxious **for** giving a speech at the conference.

_____

3 I have an excellent relationship **between** my manager.

_____

4 My teacher asked me what I know **for** Roman history.

_____

5 Erik has sold his bicycle **for** one of his cousins.

_____

6 I've been having a lot of problems **for** my internet router.

_____

110 Coordinating conjunctions

Coordinating conjunctions are words that link words, phrases, or clauses of equal importance. There are special rules for using commas with coordinating conjunctions.

110.1 MATCH THE PICTURES TO THE CORRECT SENTENCES

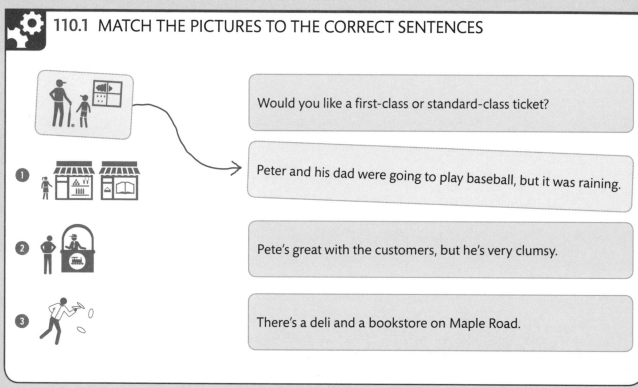

Would you like a first-class or standard-class ticket?

Peter and his dad were going to play baseball, but it was raining.

Pete's great with the customers, but he's very clumsy.

There's a deli and a bookstore on Maple Road.

110.2 MATCH THE BEGINNINGS OF THE SENTENCES TO THE CORRECT ENDINGS

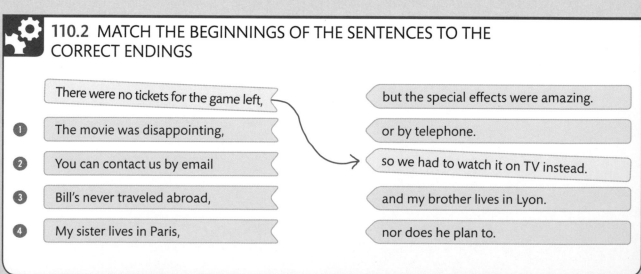

There were no tickets for the game left,

① The movie was disappointing,

② You can contact us by email

③ Bill's never traveled abroad,

④ My sister lives in Paris,

but the special effects were amazing.

or by telephone.

so we had to watch it on TV instead.

and my brother lives in Lyon.

nor does he plan to.

110.3 FILL IN THE GAPS USING THE COORDINATING CONJUNCTIONS IN THE PANEL

It's only 10am and _____ *yet* _____ I've already got all my errands done.

1 I've been to Ottawa, _____ I've never been to Vancouver.

2 It was raining, _____ we decided to go to the art gallery.

3 While walking, we saw an eagle, a puma, _____ a bear.

4 Ben has to choose between studying math, art, _____ psychology.

5 I did not like the food at the restaurant, _____ did I like the decor.

| and | ~~yet~~ | but | nor | or | so |

110.4 REWRITE THE SENTENCES, PUTTING THE WORDS IN THE CORRECT ORDER

can | or | to | We | the | center. | go | leisure | shopping

We can go shopping or to the leisure center.

1 bed. | to | so | tired, | Kim | went | feeling | was | she

_____

2 nor | live | at | doesn't | son | My | my | daughter. | home, | does

_____

3 planning | I | was | go | I | my | forgot | but | to | swimsuit. | swimming,

_____

4 grandchildren. | still | 76, | yet | his | with | he | soccer | Len's | plays

_____

111 Subordinating conjunctions

Subordinating conjunctions are used to connect words, phrases, and clauses of unequal importance. They're used to say why, where, or when something happens.

 111.1 MATCH THE BEGINNINGS OF THE SENTENCES TO THE CORRECT ENDINGS

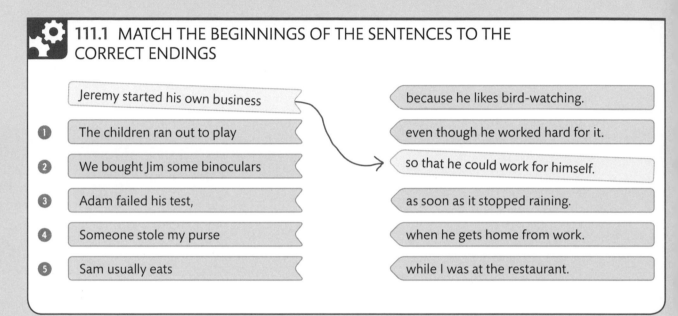

Jeremy started his own business

1 The children ran out to play

2 We bought Jim some binoculars

3 Adam failed his test,

4 Someone stole my purse

5 Sam usually eats

because he likes bird-watching.

even though he worked hard for it.

so that he could work for himself.

as soon as it stopped raining.

when he gets home from work.

while I was at the restaurant.

111.2 CROSS OUT THE INCORRECT WORDS IN EACH SENTENCE

You need to enter your password **in order to** / ~~so that~~ access your account.

1 Eli decided to go jogging, **so that** / **even though** it was raining.

2 Ella put on some sunscreen **because** / **so that** she didn't get sunburned.

3 **When** / **While** I finish this report, I'll give you a hand.

4 You need a passport **in order to** / **so that** enter most countries.

5 **Even though** / **Because** I prefer coffee, I decided to have a cup of tea.

6 Paolo decided to have a nap **although** / **because** he was feeling tired.

7 I made the dinner **when** / **while** my wife cleaned our apartment.

111.3 FILL IN THE GAPS USING THE SUBORDINATING CONJUNCTIONS IN THE PANEL

Regina called her parents _____ *as soon as* _____ her boyfriend proposed.

1 I read a newspaper _____ I was waiting for the train.

2 My dad bought some paint _____ he can decorate the kitchen.

3 I'm not going out _____ I've finished my homework.

4 Sally's moving to Spain, _____ she can't speak Spanish.

5 _____ you've written the report, can you send me a copy?

~~as soon as~~

When

even though

while

so that

until

111.4 REWRITE THE SENTENCES, CORRECTING THE ERRORS

Yuri got burned **so** he stayed in the sun too long.
Yuri got burned because he stayed in the sun too long.

1 The concert **begins** as soon as the singer **will arrive**.

_____

2 **Even although** I arrived early, there were no tickets left.

_____

3 Miguela is learning to juggle **in order for** impress her friends.

_____

4 Can you give me a call when **you will arrive**?

_____

5 I usually eat **while** my roommate gets home.

_____

6 I went to the supermarket **for** buy some groceries.

_____

112 More linking words

Some words can be used to show a relationship between two sentences or parts of a sentence. This can be cause, effect, emphasis, contrast, or comparison.

112.1 MATCH THE PICTURES TO THE CORRECT SENTENCES

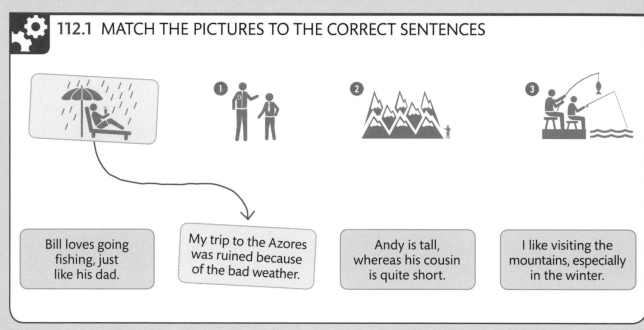

Bill loves going fishing, just like his dad.

My trip to the Azores was ruined because of the bad weather.

Andy is tall, whereas his cousin is quite short.

I like visiting the mountains, especially in the winter.

112.2 MATCH THE BEGINNINGS OF THE SENTENCES TO THE CORRECT ENDINGS

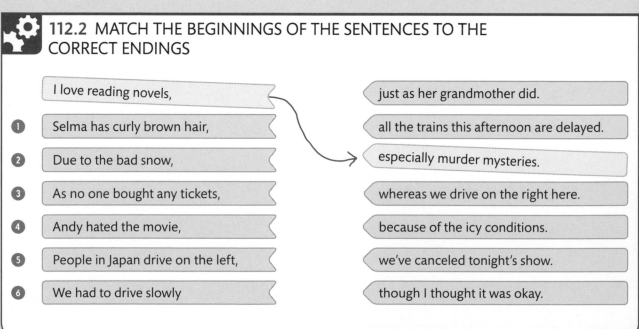

I love reading novels,

just as her grandmother did.

1 Selma has curly brown hair,

all the trains this afternoon are delayed.

2 Due to the bad snow,

especially murder mysteries.

3 As no one bought any tickets,

whereas we drive on the right here.

4 Andy hated the movie,

because of the icy conditions.

5 People in Japan drive on the left,

we've canceled tonight's show.

6 We had to drive slowly

though I thought it was okay.

112.3 CROSS OUT THE INCORRECT WORDS IN EACH SENTENCE

I love to travel, **especially** / ~~notably~~ to hot countries.

1 Lianne loves football, **whereas** / hence her brother hates it.

2 I was late for the interview **because** / because of the traffic.

3 The professor was sick. **As a result** / Especially, the lecture was postponed.

4 Frank is a zookeeper, **yet** / since he is terrified of mice.

5 I get on well with Saul, **so** / because we are going on vacation together.

112.4 LOOK AT THE PICTURES AND FILL IN THE GAPS USING THE LINKING WORDS IN THE PANEL

Ellie prefers to wear smart clothes, _____*whereas*_____ Dan likes to dress casual.

1 Magda loves gardening, _____ in the spring.

2 Omar visited Rome _____ he loves ancient history.

3 There are a lot of environmental problems _____ the bad pollution.

4 _____ her music teacher, Selma became a great pianist.

5 I wanted to come this morning, _____ the tickets had sold out.

| because | ~~whereas~~ | Thanks to | especially | because of | but |

Linking words overview

Conjunctions are linking words that describe the relationship between two parts of a sentence. They can be coordinating or subordinating.

113.1 WRITE THE LINKING WORDS FROM THE PANEL IN THE CORRECT GROUPS

COORDINATING CONJUNCTIONS

or
_____
_____
_____
_____

SUBORDINATING CONJUNCTIONS

_____
_____
_____
_____
_____

nor	in order that	after	so	and
even though	but	~~or~~	because	although

113.2 MARK THE USE OF THE CONJUNCTION IN EACH SENTENCE

Go home **as soon as** you're finished.
reason ☐   **condition** ☐   **time** ☑

① I was an actor **before** I worked here.
condition ☐   **time** ☐   **contrast** ☐

② Take a sweater **so** you don't get cold.
time ☐   **cause** ☐   **reason** ☐

③ I got a hot dog **because** I was hungry.
contrast ☐   **cause** ☐   **reason** ☐

④ Jo reads **while** she travels to work.
time ☐   **reason** ☐   **cause** ☐

⑤ I wore a hat **so that** I don't get burned.
contrast ☐   **time** ☐   **reason** ☐

⑥ Paula took a map **in case** she got lost.
cause ☐   **contrast** ☐   **condition** ☐

⑦ We will go running **unless** it rains.
reason ☐   **condition** ☐   **time** ☐

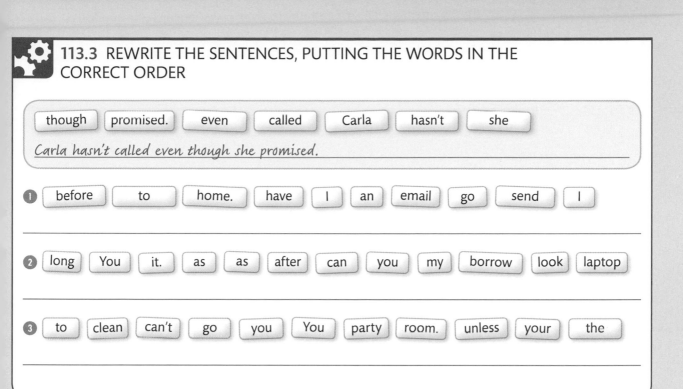

113.3 REWRITE THE SENTENCES, PUTTING THE WORDS IN THE CORRECT ORDER

| though | promised. | even | called | Carla | hasn't | she |

Carla hasn't called even though she promised.

1 | before | to | home. | have | I | an | email | go | send | I |

_____

2 | long | You | it. | as | as | after | can | you | my | borrow | look | laptop |

_____

3 | to | clean | can't | go | you | You | party | room. | unless | your | the |

_____

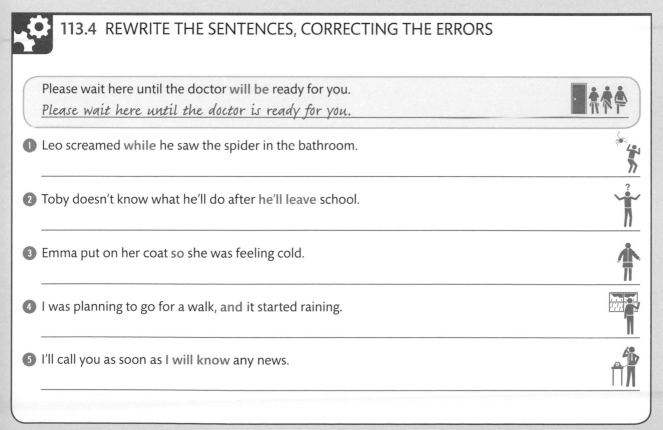

113.4 REWRITE THE SENTENCES, CORRECTING THE ERRORS

Please wait here until the doctor **will be** ready for you.
Please wait here until the doctor is ready for you.

1 Leo screamed **while** he saw the spider in the bathroom.

_____

2 Toby doesn't know what he'll do after **he'll leave** school.

_____

3 Emma put on her coat **so** she was feeling cold.

_____

4 I was planning to go for a walk, **and** it started raining.

_____

5 I'll call you as soon as **I will know** any news.

_____

275

114 Prefixes

Prefixes are small groups of letters which can be added to the start of many words to give them different meanings.

114.1 MATCH THE PICTURES TO THE CORRECT SENTENCES

I much prefer nonfiction, such as biographies, to fiction.

I'm worried about John. He's really overdoing it at work.

My girlfriend disapproves of me eating fast food.

I had a lot of fun with my coworkers at the office party.

114.2 CROSS OUT THE INCORRECT WORDS IN EACH SENTENCE

It's **impossible** / ~~unpossible~~ to start your own business without making sacrifices.

1 The police are looking for a man in his **mid-twenties** / **post-twenties**.

2 I've **misplaced** / **displaced** my glasses. Have you seen them?

3 The actor's performance was **prestandard** / **substandard**.

4 It was **inresponsible** / **irresponsible** to drive so quickly.

5 Clara is trying to **disprove** / **misprove** the allegations against her.

6 The teacher said their behavior was **unacceptable** / **inacceptable**.

7 The student's handwriting was quite **inlegible** / **illegible**.

114.3 FILL IN THE GAPS USING THE PREFIXES IN THE PANEL

> The book is coming out next week, but you can _____ pre _____ order it now.

| im |
| dis |
| ~~pre~~ |
| under |
| ir |
| un |
| il |
| re |
| mis |

1 We found Alexandra's cakes totally _____ resistible.

2 I _____ read your name. I thought it said Davies, not Davis.

3 Les failed the exam, but he can _____ sit next semester.

4 Andy was _____ honest about being fluent in Portuguese.

5 Emily was struggling to _____ tie her shoelaces.

6 It's _____ legal to drive without wearing a seat belt.

7 This cake is really _____ cooked. It's almost raw inside.

8 Don't be so _____ patient. The train will come soon.

114.4 REWRITE THE SENTENCES, CORRECTING THE ERRORS

> Katia is so **unpolite**. She never says "please."
> _Katia is so impolite. She never says "please."_

1 I realized I had the wrong key when I couldn't **dislock** the door.

_____

2 Ed's so **inreliable**. He's always late.

_____

3 You can **preapply** for the course next year.

_____

4 Ola was **incertain** what to think about Jim's haircut.

_____

5 I think she **overcharged** us. It should have cost more.

_____

115 Suffixes

Suffixes are small groups of letters which can be added to the end of many words to give them different meanings.

115.1 MATCH THE BEGINNINGS OF THE SENTENCES TO THE CORRECT ENDINGS

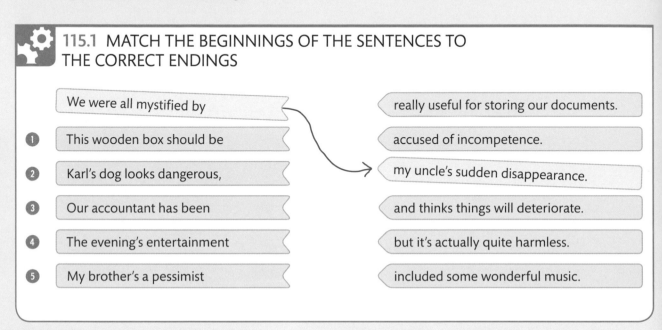

We were all mystified by → my uncle's sudden disappearance.

1 This wooden box should be · really useful for storing our documents.

2 Karl's dog looks dangerous, · accused of incompetence.

3 Our accountant has been · and thinks things will deteriorate.

4 The evening's entertainment · but it's actually quite harmless.

5 My brother's a pessimist · included some wonderful music.

115.2 WRITE THE SUFFIXES FROM THE PANEL IN THE CORRECT GROUPS

ADJECTIVES	VERBS	NOUNS
-able/-ible		

-al/-ial   -en   -ate   ~~-able/-ible~~   -ist/-ian   -less   -ism   -ance/-ence

-ity/-ty   -ful   -ify   -ic/-tic/-ical   -dom   -ize   -ous   -er/-or

115.3 CROSS OUT THE INCORRECT WORDS IN EACH SENTENCE

 Winning the lottery is a rare occurrence / ~~occurence~~.

① Alan works for a managment / **management** recruitment company.

② The café serves a selection of seasonnal / **seasonal** vegetables.

③ The fish are **plentiful** / plentyful in local rivers.

④ Kids love taking **inflatable** / inflateable toys to the beach.

⑤ I found the music festival very enjoiable / **enjoyable**.

⑥ She always shows great committment / **commitment** to her students.

115.4 REWRITE THE SENTENCES, PUTTING THE WORDS IN THE CORRECT ORDER

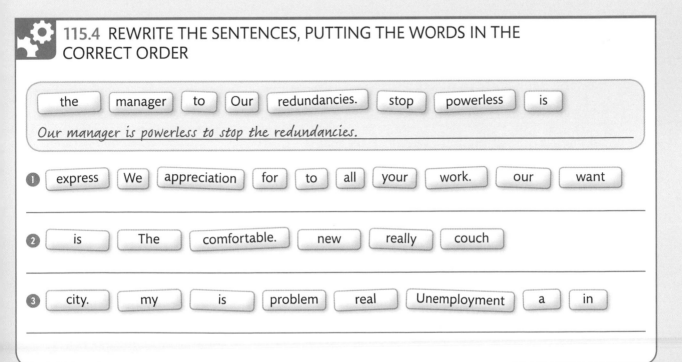

the · manager · to · Our · redundancies. · stop · powerless · is

Our manager is powerless to stop the redundancies.

① express · We · appreciation · for · to · all · your · work. · our · want

② is · The · comfortable. · new · really · couch

③ city. · my · is · problem · real · Unemployment · a · in

In English, there are several phrases which sound or look similar, but have different meanings. It is important not to get these confused.

116.1 MATCH THE BEGINNINGS OF THE SENTENCES TO THE CORRECT ENDINGS

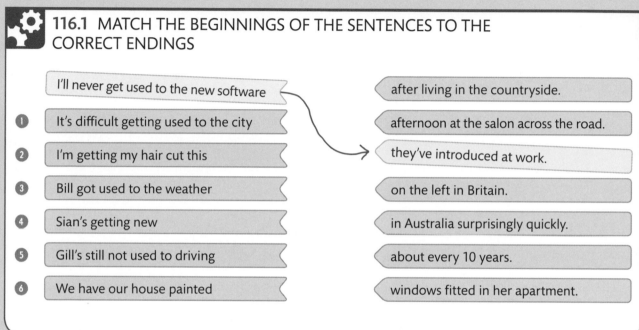

I'll never get used to the new software — they've introduced at work.

1. It's difficult getting used to the city — after living in the countryside.
2. I'm getting my hair cut this — afternoon at the salon across the road.
3. Bill got used to the weather — on the left in Britain.
4. Sian's getting new — in Australia surprisingly quickly.
5. Gill's still not used to driving — about every 10 years.
6. We have our house painted — windows fitted in her apartment.

116.2 MATCH THE PICTURES TO THE CORRECT SENTENCES

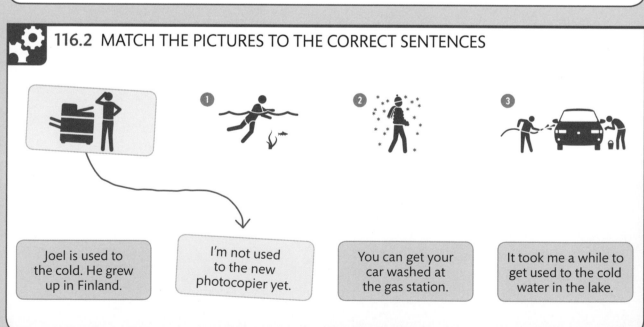

Joel is used to the cold. He grew up in Finland.

I'm not used to the new photocopier yet.

You can get your car washed at the gas station.

It took me a while to get used to the cold water in the lake.

116.3 MARK THE SENTENCES THAT ARE CORRECT

Will you get your car fixed before the trip? ☑
Will you get your car fix before the trip? ☐

1 I hated working nights at first, but then I got used to it. ☐
I hated working nights at first, but then I am used to it. ☐

2 Olga grew up in Moscow, so she used to cold winters. ☐
Olga grew up in Moscow, so she's used to cold winters. ☐

3 I am used to work as a lab technician before I became a teacher. ☐
I used to work as a lab technician before I became a teacher. ☐

4 Nico has his hair cut at the barbershop on Main Street. ☐
Nico has cut his hair at the barbershop on Main Street. ☐

5 I got my locks changed after our place was broken into. ☐
I got changed my locks after our place was broken into. ☐

116.4 REWRITE THE SENTENCES, PUTTING THE WORDS IN THE CORRECT ORDER

living | isn't | on | own. | his | used | Alfie | to

Alfie isn't used to living on his own.

1 a | on | delivered | gets | Sheila | Fridays. | pizza | always

_____

2 living | in | country. | not | I'm | to | a | used | rainy

_____

3 cleaned | a | I | once | teeth | month. | have | hygienist | my | the | by

_____

117 Sequencing and organizing

There are a number of words and phrases in English which help to explain the order of events. They can also be used to organize text and make it easier to understand.

117.1 FILL IN THE GAPS USING THE WORDS IN THE PANEL

overall	=	*in conclusion*
❶ for example	=	_____
❷ furthermore	=	_____
❸ next	=	_____
❹ first of all	=	_____

then   to begin with   for instance   ~~in conclusion~~   moreover

117.2 MATCH THE BEGINNINGS OF THE SENTENCES TO THE CORRECT ENDINGS

First of all, I find my recipe ⟶ book and kitchen utensils.

❶ Then I switch on the — in a bowl and mix them together.

❷ Next, I put all the ingredients — into a baking pan.

❸ After that, I pour the mixture — oven and find my ingredients.

❹ You can add extra ingredients, — the oven for about 25 minutes.

❺ Finally, put the cake into — such as nuts or dried fruit.

117.3 REWRITE THE SENTENCES, PUTTING THE WORDS IN THE CORRECT ORDER

to | all, | you | decide | you | live. | First | of | where | should | want

First of all, you should decide where you want to live.

1 type | should | the | you | of | choose | Furthermore, | want. | house | you

_____

2 an | house? | to | you | a | For | example, | live | do | want | in | apartment | or

_____

3 balcony? | the | instance, | a | property | Does | have, | for

_____

4 buying | should | house. | conclusion, | a | before | think | carefully | In | you

_____

117.4 CROSS OUT THE INCORRECT WORDS IN EACH SENTENCE

~~Firstly of all~~/ **First of all**, forests are home to so many local species.

1 **Additional / Additionally**, they provide employment to many people in the region.

2 **Farthermore / Furthermore**, many species are in danger of extinction.

3 **Meantime / Meanwhile**, the logging companies continue to destroy vast areas.

4 **In conclusion / By conclusion**, forests are in need of urgent protection.

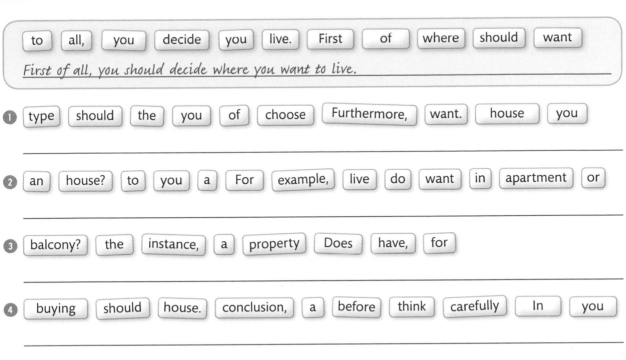

Correcting and changing the subject

Set words and phrases can be used to correct someone, disagree, change the subject, or concede a point.
They often come at the beginning of the sentence.

118.1 MATCH THE STATEMENTS TO THE CORRECT RESPONSES

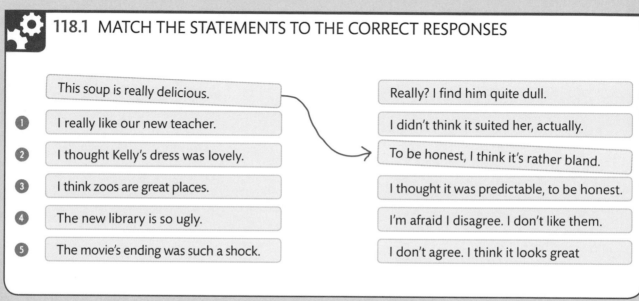

This soup is really delicious.

① I really like our new teacher.

② I thought Kelly's dress was lovely.

③ I think zoos are great places.

④ The new library is so ugly.

⑤ The movie's ending was such a shock.

Really? I find him quite dull.

I didn't think it suited her, actually.

To be honest, I think it's rather bland.

I thought it was predictable, to be honest.

I'm afraid I disagree. I don't like them.

I don't agree. I think it looks great

118.2 MARK THE BEST REPLY TO EACH STATEMENT

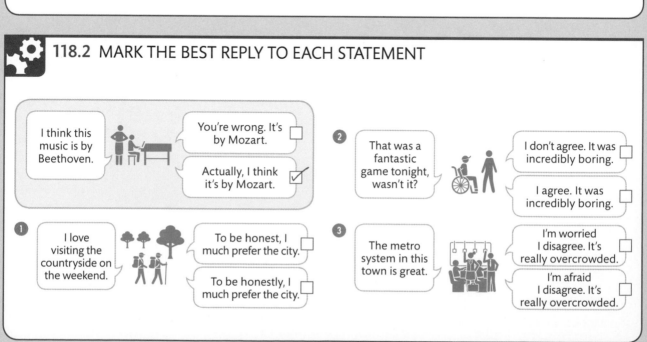

I think this music is by Beethoven.

You're wrong. It's by Mozart.

Actually, I think it's by Mozart. ☑

② That was a fantastic game tonight, wasn't it?

I don't agree. It was incredibly boring.

I agree. It was incredibly boring.

① I love visiting the countryside on the weekend.

To be honest, I much prefer the city.

To be honestly, I much prefer the city.

③ The metro system in this town is great.

I'm worried I disagree. It's really overcrowded.

I'm afraid I disagree. It's really overcrowded.

118.3 REWRITE THE SENTENCES, PUTTING THE WORDS IN THE CORRECT ORDER

| was | long, | be | thought | I | novel | to | latest | honest. | too | Claudia's |

I thought Claudia's latest novel was too long, to be honest.

① | a | really | she's | still | Anyway, | writer. | good |

_____

② | don't | I | I'm | she | think | is. | afraid |

_____

③ | was | very | is | As | saying, | I | she | talented. | I | think |

_____

④ | think | agree | you, | with | actually. | don't | I | I |

_____

⑤ | have | read | way, | her | By | novel? | the | first | you | ever |

_____

⑥ | much. | point | a | You | costing | about | have | too | books | her |

_____

⑦ | was | thought | Actually, | awful. | character | main | the | I |

_____

⑧ | about | see | character. | your | main | point | the | I |

_____

⑨ | Claudia's | you | told | new | novel! | like | I | wouldn't | I |

_____

Deciding and hedging

English uses a number of words and phrases to discuss the different sides of an argument or to make sentences sound less definite.

119.1 MATCH THE PICTURES TO THE CORRECT SENTENCES

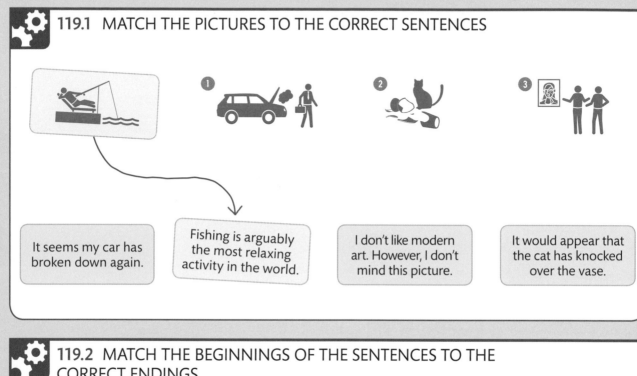

It seems my car has broken down again.

Fishing is arguably the most relaxing activity in the world.

I don't like modern art. However, I don't mind this picture.

It would appear that the cat has knocked over the vase.

119.2 MATCH THE BEGINNINGS OF THE SENTENCES TO THE CORRECT ENDINGS

In spite of the terrible weather,

nearby, I rarely eat there.

1 Although the restaurant is

are made using the finest ingredients.

2 However, whenever I go there,

I will go to the restaurant.

3 Of course, all the dishes

but on the other hand, it's good quality.

4 On the one hand, it's very expensive,

I always have a good time.

5 I might go out tonight.

I decided to go out with my friends.

6 Despite feeling tired,

Alternatively, I could relax in front of the TV.

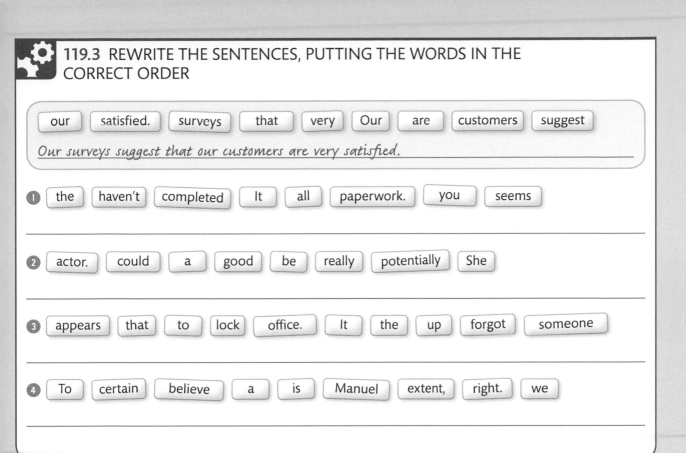

119.3 REWRITE THE SENTENCES, PUTTING THE WORDS IN THE CORRECT ORDER

| our | satisfied. | surveys | that | very | Our | are | customers | suggest |

Our surveys suggest that our customers are very satisfied.

1 | the | haven't | completed | It | all | paperwork. | you | seems |

_____

2 | actor. | could | a | good | be | really | potentially | She |

_____

3 | appears | that | to | lock | office. | It | the | up | forgot | someone |

_____

4 | To | certain | believe | a | is | Manuel | extent, | right. | we |

_____

119.4 MARK THE SENTENCES THAT ARE CORRECT

It looks that the thief entered through that window. ☐
It seems that the thief entered through that window. ☑

1 The figures suggest that we are losing a lot of customers. ☐
The figures recommend that we are losing a lot of customers. ☐

2 Despite of the delays, I enjoyed myself thoroughly. ☐
Despite the delays, I enjoyed myself thoroughly. ☐

3 In the one hand, I'm rich. In the other hand, I'm not very happy. ☐
On the one hand, I'm rich. On the other hand, I'm not very happy. ☐

4 To some extend, crime has increased in the past year. ☐
To some extent, crime has increased in the past year. ☐

120 Making conversation

Many words and phrases are used in English to ease the flow of conversation. These techniques are often called organizing, backchanneling, or stalling.

120.1 MARK THE BEST REPLY TO EACH STATEMENT

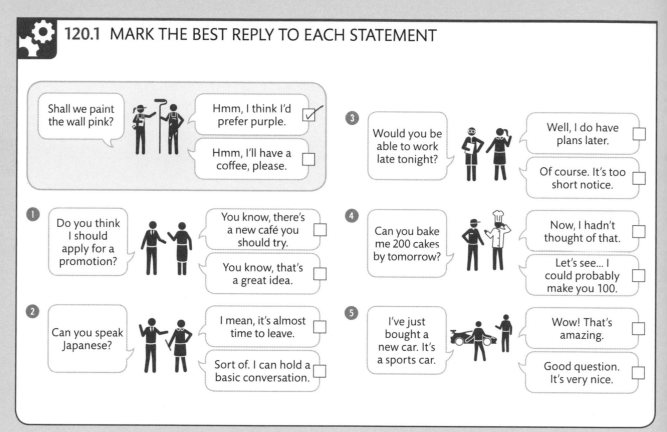

Shall we paint the wall pink?
- Hmm, I think I'd prefer purple. ✓
- Hmm, I'll have a coffee, please. ☐

① Do you think I should apply for a promotion?
- You know, there's a new café you should try. ☐
- You know, that's a great idea. ☐

② Can you speak Japanese?
- I mean, it's almost time to leave. ☐
- Sort of. I can hold a basic conversation. ☐

③ Would you be able to work late tonight?
- Well, I do have plans later. ☐
- Of course. It's too short notice. ☐

④ Can you bake me 200 cakes by tomorrow?
- Now, I hadn't thought of that. ☐
- Let's see... I could probably make you 100. ☐

⑤ I've just bought a new car. It's a sports car.
- Wow! That's amazing. ☐
- Good question. It's very nice. ☐

120.2 MATCH THE BEGINNINGS OF THE SENTENCES TO THE CORRECT ENDINGS

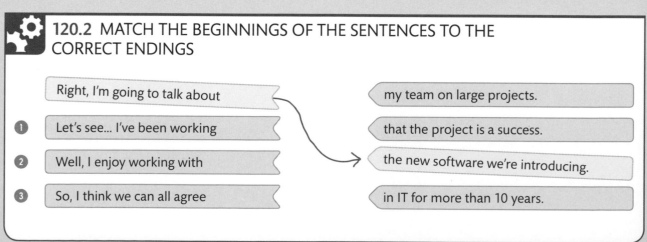

Right, I'm going to talk about — the new software we're introducing.

① Let's see... I've been working — in IT for more than 10 years.

② Well, I enjoy working with — my team on large projects.

③ So, I think we can all agree — that the project is a success.

120.3 REWRITE THE SENTENCES, PUTTING THE WORDS IN THE CORRECT ORDER

thinking | I'm | of | Paris. | to | moving | So,

So, I'm thinking of moving to Paris.

1 to | What | going | Really? | there? | you | are | do

_____

2 I'd | work | a | as | waiter. | like | to | Well,

_____

3 work. | know, | be | that | might | You | hard

_____

4 will | French. | I | practice | suppose | I | my | but | so,

_____

5 French? | Of | speak | But | course. | do | you | any

_____

6 like | Good | question. | I'd | but | yet, | Not | to.

_____

7 to | right. | do? | else | do | What | want | you | Oh

_____

8 travel | like | to | France. | I'd | see. | Let's | around

_____

9 sounds | Wow! | great | idea. | That | a | like

_____

Answers

NOTE: Some of the following answers can be written in different forms, for example with or without contractions.

01

1.1
1. Tony **makes** a huge breakfast for his family on Sundays.
2. I usually **eat** my lunch at 1pm at an Italian restaurant.
3. Fiona **meets** her friends at a café on Thursday evenings.
4. We sometimes **play** tennis with our friends on Saturday mornings.
5. My cousin **starts** work at 6am every morning.
6. The shop assistant **leaves** work at 6pm in the evening.
7. You **drink** a lot of coffee every morning.
8. Paolo usually **reads** a book in the evenings.

1.2
1. Greg works in a factory.
2. My dad watches TV every evening.
3. Michel plays the piano beautifully.
4. Jane brushes her hair in the morning.
5. Selma goes shopping after work.
6. Imran washes his clothes on Sunday.
7. Mary teaches French at a college.

1.3
1. I **am** a doctor at the local hospital.
2. Vicky **is** my eldest child.
3. We **are** from a town in Scotland.
4. Both my parents **are** lawyers.
5. You **are** a very good friend.
6. I **am** an American.
7. That policeman **is** so tall.
8. She **is** twenty-three years old.
9. It **is** cold outside.
10. I **am** fifteen today.
11. Our cat **is** black and white.
12. We **are** very excited.
13. They **are** students from France.
14. Jim **is** an architect.
15. My sister-in-law **is** from Japan.
16. I **am** so hungry!
17. You **are** very lazy.
18. My children **are** so tired.
19. I **am** forty-three years old.
20. They **are** late for work.
21. Claudia and Paolo **are** Italian.
22. My grandfather **is** retired.
23. We **are** from Pakistan.
24. Paul **is** disappointed.

1.4
1. Jack **has** a new car.
2. Jennifer **has** Abbie's bag.
3. We **have** a beautiful farm.
4. I **have** three sisters.
5. Bob **has** toothache.
6. My house **has** a large garage.
7. They **have** a new laptop.
8. We **have** so many books.
9. My dad **has** red hair.
10. You **have** an old phone.
11. My neighbors **have** a daughter.
12. Juan's house **has** three floors.
13. That bird **has** big eyes.
14. I **have** a new baby.
15. We both **have** headaches.
16. They **have** the same dress.
17. My grandparents **have** chickens.
18. You **have** a friendly cat.
19. My town **has** two museums.
20. Yuko **has** a painful back.
21. Our dogs **have** lots of toys.
22. We **have** an English class tonight.
23. Vineetha **has** a new haircut.
24. I **have** dinner at 6pm every day.

1.5
1. Brad goes camping in the forest every summer.
2. Hannah takes beautiful photos of the places she visits.
3. Emil leaves the office at 6pm each day.

1.6
1. I **start** work at 9am during the week.
2. You **are** an engineer.
3. Maria **has** coffee with Jules in the morning.
4. They **go** to work by train.
5. My dad **is** 67 years old.
6. Robert **finishes** work at 7pm.
7. We **have** an English lesson later.
8. Paul often **watches** a film in the evening.
9. Emma **goes** to bed early on Sundays.

02

2.1
1. She is not a doctor.
2. We are not from New Zealand.
3. My dad is not American.
4. They are not my dogs.
5. You are not Egyptian.
6. This is not my computer.
7. I am not an engineer.

2.2
1. You **do not** work in the library.
2. He **does not** eat meat.
3. Val **does not** watch TV in the evening.
4. I **do not** play football very often.
5. We **do not** get up early on Saturdays.
6. My grandparents **do not** have a car.
7. Nico **does not** work in the factory.
8. She **does not** go to work on Fridays.
9. I **do not** go to restaurants very often.
10. You **do not** have a cat.
11. They **do not** work outside.

2.3
1. He's not a teacher.
   He isn't a teacher.
2. Carla's not very tall.
   Carla isn't very tall.
3. You're not from Australia.
   You aren't from Australia.
4. They're not farmers.
   They aren't farmers.
5. We're not happy.
   We aren't happy.
6. You're not lawyers.
   You aren't lawyers.
7. She's not a doctor.
   She isn't a doctor.
8. It's not very cold outside.
   It isn't very cold outside.

2.4
1. I don't like Sam's cooking.
2. You don't look very happy.
3. Antonio does not live in Madrid.
4. Phil doesn't drive a car.
5. I'm not a doctor.
6. Diana doesn't have a computer.
7. I don't like cats.
8. Paolo does not get up at 6am.
9. My dad doesn't feel well.
10. They aren't from China.
11. My friends don't like chess.

2.5
1. Amy **doesn't work** as a receptionist in our office.
2. I **don't like** going to the health center.
3. Your company **isn't** very successful.
4. You **don't play** the violin very well.
5. Jean **doesn't cook** the dinner in the evening.
6. This TV show **isn't** very interesting.
7. Sonia and Rick **don't live** in Paris.
8. My son **isn't** a firefighter.
9. Our house **isn't** very big.
10. Sandra **doesn't work** late on Fridays.
11. My husband and I **don't relax** on weekends.
12. Edith and Sam **don't like** dancing in their free time.

03

3.1
1. **Are** you the new teacher?
2. **Is** she your sister?
3. **Are** we nearly home?
4. **Am** I on the list?
5. **Are** your dogs friendly?
6. Where **is** the front door?
7. **Is** Carlo still a teacher?
8. **Are** we late for the party?
9. Where **are** my shoes?
10. **Is** that Shelly's new car?
11. Who **is** the manager here?
12. **Am** I too late for the concert?
13. When **is** your birthday?
14. **Is** he here for the presentation?
15. Where **is** the bathroom?
16. **Am** I supposed to be at work?

⑰ Why **are** they angry?
⑱ **Is** it time to eat yet?
⑲ **Are** they coming to the seminar?

3.2
① **Does** Laura have a brother?
② **Do** they know your address?
③ **Does** Craig still live in Dublin?
④ Where **does** your mother work?
⑤ **Do** they know your father?
⑥ **Does** the restaurant serve fish?
⑦ **Do** you still have my book?
⑧ **Does** your house have a garage?
⑨ **Do** we have enough time?
⑩ How **does** Ben travel to work?
⑪ **Do** your parents have a car?
⑫ When **does** the lesson end?
⑬ **Do** you work on Saturdays?
⑭ **Does** she play any instruments?
⑮ What **do** you want for dinner?
⑯ **Do** I need to wear a dress?
⑰ What **does** he want this time?
⑱ **Do** they know what time it is?
⑲ Where **does** she buy her clothes?

3.3
① Does Danielle play baseball very often?
② Do you know how to play the electric guitar?
③ Does your daughter know how to drive a car?
④ What time do you get up in the morning?

3.4
① Does she like going to the theater?
② Does Carlo like Chinese food?
③ Do you like gardening?
④ Does he know how to play chess?
⑤ Does Cleo have breakfast every morning?
⑥ Does Jim have a lot of homework this weekend?
⑦ Do they live in London?
⑧ Does it rain often here?
⑨ Does Peter enjoy taking photos?
⑩ Does Sally know how to swim?
⑪ Do they play golf on Saturdays?

04

4.1
① Michelle is visiting a gallery.
② Pedro is hiking in the mountains.
③ Martin is cooking dinner for his family.

4.2
① You **are wearing** a beautiful red dress.
② Matilda **is reading** a travel book about Brazil.
③ My cat **is climbing** the apple tree.
④ I **am reading** such an interesting book.
⑤ Hetty and Paula **are drinking** some orange juice.
⑥ Phil **is practicing** for his piano lesson.

4.3
① Clara **is trying** on some new shoes.
② I **am writing** a letter to my girlfriend.
③ Sanjay **is learning** to drive.
④ Mel and Tim **are getting married** today.

⑤ Robin **isn't studying** for the French exam this afternoon.
⑥ Sam and Ashwin **are playing** baseball at the park.
⑦ My sister's friend **is performing** on stage now.

4.4
① Sam and Pete aren't playing cards in the living room.
② The children eat pizza once a week.
③ Julian is wearing a suit for the meeting.

4.5
① Are they going **to the festival?**
② What are we **eating for dinner?**
③ Is it **snowing outside?**
④ Why is Lisa **wearing such fancy clothes?**

4.6
① Chris isn't playing football today.
② Are your kids watching a football game?
③ My wife is visiting her friend this afternoon.
④ Where is Selma living at the moment?
⑤ Joe isn't wearing a tie today.

4.7
① Are they driving to the beach?
② Are you going swimming?
③ Is she watching a movie?
④ Is Nelson going shopping?
⑤ Is Ben listening to classical music?
⑥ Is Chrissie climbing the tree?
⑦ Are Sven and Olly singing?
⑧ Are you drinking apple juice?
⑨ Are they playing tennis?
⑩ Is my son reading a book?
⑪ Is Pavel speaking Russian?
⑫ Are you wearing a dress?

4.8
① I'm not going to the zoo.
② The dog isn't chasing a cat.
③ They aren't walking their dog.
④ Angela isn't wearing a dress.
⑤ We aren't playing chess.
⑥ I'm not eating Chinese food.
⑦ James isn't wearing your shirt.
⑧ You aren't reading a book.
⑨ She isn't cleaning her room.
⑩ Ed and Gus aren't watching a movie.
⑪ I'm not speaking French.
⑫ It isn't raining outside.

05

5.1
① Annabelle **explores** caves in her free time.
② João **doesn't like** dogs. He's really scared of them.
③ Is Dimitri still **building** the garage wall?
④ Brendan **loves** watching comedies on TV in the evenings.
⑤ Sid and Les **work** at the beauty salon.

5.2
① Kit **goes** scuba-diving with her friends on Fridays.
② Ben and Kelly **are dancing** at the club tonight.
③ Sai **puts** the dishes in the dishwasher each evening.
④ Bruce **is waiting** to go for a walk.

5.3
① Mary **doesn't send** letters often, but she **is writing** one to her mother now.
② I **am working** from home today, but usually I **work** in an office.
③ We usually **go** to Spain on vacation, but this year we **are going** to Mexico.
④ Helen **works** in a primary school. **She's teaching** math right now.
⑤ I **don't eat meat** very often, but tonight **I'm having** a steak.
⑥ It **doesn't rain** often in California, but today **it's pouring.**
⑦ My cousin **is performing** on stage now. I **love** her voice.
⑧ Rajiv **is wearing** a T-shirt now, but he always **wears** a shirt at work.
⑨ My dad **is sleeping** now. He **is** tired after the journey.
⑩ Juan normally **starts** work at 8am, but today **he's going** to the dentist.
⑪ Bob **is taking** a taxi to work today, but he usually **takes** the bus.

5.4
① My brother doesn't **work on Friday afternoons.**
② My mom usually bakes **a cake on the weekends.**
③ Where is your sister **living at the moment?**
④ Tom's new girlfriend **lives in a resort in Spain.**
⑤ What's dad cooking **in the kitchen?**
⑥ How often do you **play golf with your colleagues?**

5.5
① Do you play soccer on the weekend?
② Is Paula studying French at college?
③ Why is your dad wearing a suit today?
④ Clarissa usually works at home on Fridays.

5.6
① Lou wakes up at 7am each morning.
② Henry is performing at a country and western club tonight.
③ Tanya doesn't feel well, so she's not coming to the party.

5.7
① Steve **reads** in bed before he **goes** to sleep.
② Lisa and Tim **go** to the gym after work.
③ My mom **is playing** golf with her friend this afternoon.
④ Vernon **doesn't like** snakes. He really **hates** them.
⑤ We often **go** to the café by the park.
⑥ Craig **is walking** in the mountains with Rob this week.

06

6.1
write, draw, run, help, take, give, start, begin, work, send, listen, turn, come, read, smile

6.2
1 Be careful on the wet floor!
2 Take the second road on the right.
3 Don't sit there! It's Andrew's chair.
4 Let me help you with your bags, Vera.

6.3
1 Turn right **at the crossroads.**
2 Eat your **breakfast, Greg!**
3 Give the cake **to Layla.**
4 Please close **the window.**
5 Let's go to **the theater.**
6 Don't walk on **the grass.**
7 Take the first **road on the left.**
8 Don't touch **that vase!**

6.4
1 Turn left after the library.
2 Just give me a minute, please.
3 Let's go to the swimming pool.
4 Go straight ahead at the crossroads.
5 Please close the door.
6 Give the book to your brother.
7 Don't sing so loudly!

07

7.1
1 I **cleaned** my bedroom this morning.
2 We **played** football in the afternoon.
3 After his dinner, Alex **watched** a movie on TV.
4 My wife **visited** her parents yesterday.
5 Lucia **danced** with her friends at the party.

7.2
1 Terry usually takes the metro to work, **but yesterday he walked instead.**
2 I arrived at work early **so I checked my email.**
3 In the morning we walked to **the old town and visited the museum.**
4 Angela cried when she **heard the sad news.**
5 We usually go to France **but last year we traveled around Russia.**
6 Jemma washed the dishes **after she finished her dinner.**
7 Roger listened to some music **then started reading his new book.**

7.3
1 Amy felt sick, so she went to the doctor.
2 I usually walk to the café, but yesterday I drove.
3 Mia laughed when she heard Martin's joke.

7.4
1 Simone **tried** to open the door, but it was completely stuck.
2 Elena **decided** to wear a nice dress to the dinner party that evening.
3 Chan **washed** the dishes after she and Dan had eaten.
4 Stephan and Klara **hurried** to catch the last train home.
5 The waiter **dropped** the dishes onto the floor.
6 Megan **carried** the files into the office.

7.5
1 Marilyn **went** with Clive to the exhibition at the gallery.
2 I **saw** Phil and Dan at the party last night.
3 Sheila **swam** across the lake to the island.
4 I **drank** a large bottle of water after the race.
5 We **drove** to a beautiful resort in the mountains.
6 Carol **put** her cup down on the table.
7 Seb **did** his homework on the bus to school.
8 Omar **bought** a scarf for his wife at the market.
9 She **drew** a beautiful picture of a cherry tree.

7.6
1 You **were** at Paulina's party on Saturday.
2 Joanna **was** very tired after the flight to Australia.
3 My parents **were** delighted when I passed all my exams.
4 There **were** so many people waiting to buy a ticket.
5 I **was** upset when I lost my purse.
6 Liam **was** a pilot for more than 40 years.
7 There **was** a loud bang in the kitchen.
8 My cousins **were** famous dancers in the 1990s.
9 We **were** at the convention last year.

7.7
1 Robin **wanted** to go skiing in the winter.
2 Julie and Scott **drank** a lot of coffee at the café.
3 Eli **went** camping in the woods last summer.
4 Jon **played** rugby on Saturday afternoon.
5 I **watched** TV dramas until late last night.
6 We **went** to a jazz club to listen to live music.
7 Sadiq's dog **barked** in the yard all evening.
8 The pollution in my city **was** very bad.
9 Angelo **ate** an apple for his lunch.
10 Kyle **made** his bed after getting up in the morning.
11 Tina **played** the piano with her little brother.

08

8.1
1 Emily didn't go to the party **because she felt tired.**
2 The sports car cost a huge amount, **so we didn't buy it.**
3 Ben was upset because **Jenny didn't call him on his birthday.**
4 My uncle didn't enjoy the film **because he hates science fiction.**
5 The teacher shouted at me **because I didn't do my homework.**
6 Katie is very shy, so **she didn't talk to anyone at the party.**

8.2
1 Zehra didn't play football yesterday. She went fishing.
2 Michael did not like the burger he ordered, so he sent it back.
3 I didn't go out last night; I stayed in and watched TV instead.

8.3
1 There **weren't** enough sandwiches for everyone.
2 I **did not finish** mowing the lawn because I was tired.
3 The book **wasn't** interesting, so I watched TV instead.
4 Joe **didn't make** enough potatoes for everyone.
5 The students **didn't understand** the teacher.
6 There **weren't** many people at the concert last night.
7 It **wasn't** very warm outside, so we stayed at home.
8 My brother **didn't enjoy** the movie very much.

8.4
1 We **didn't speak** to Ellen.
2 They **were** happy.
3 They **weren't** late.
4 I **waited** for Carl.
5 Lola **didn't understand.**
6 Brendan **was** there.
7 They **didn't pay** the bill.
8 Hugh **talked** to me.
9 Claire **didn't eat** the cake.
10 She **went** swimming.

09

9.1
1 Did Salvador win the lottery?
2 Did Peter take a shower earlier?
3 Did they drink all the juice?
4 Did Nick wash the dishes?
5 Did Sam buy a sports car?
6 Did they build a new house?

9.2
1 Was it very windy on the island?
2 How was your band practice yesterday?
3 Why was Xander late for the meeting?

9.3
1 Did you take the dog for a walk?
2 How did you get home last night?
3 What was the food like in Greece?

9.4
1. **Why were you** both so late for work this morning?
2. **Was Katie** pleased with the present you got her?
3. **Did you take** any good photos while you were on vacation?
4. **What was the weather like** while you were in Greece?
5. **Where did you buy** that lovely suit, Vincent?

10

10.1
1. This time last year, Craig was on vacation in Hawaii.
2. I was decorating the kitchen on Wednesday evening.
3. I was mowing the lawn when you tried to call.

10.2
1. We **were sunbathing** when it **began** to rain.
2. When I **met** Tracy yesterday, she **was wearing** a lovely dress.
3. It **was** a beautiful day and the birds **were singing** in the trees.
4. I **heard** a loud bang when I **was watching** TV last night.
5. It **started** to rain while I **was talking** on the telephone.

10.3
1. We **were hiking in the Alps** this time last year.
2. Colm **was driving to work when he saw** a deer.
3. Who **were you talking to when I saw you** yesterday?
4. It was cloudy yesterday, but at least **it wasn't raining again**.

10.4
1. Mia **visited** Sydney while she **was traveling** around Australia.
2. The children **were reading** when I **entered** the classroom.
3. Ravi **saw** an old castle when he **was walking** through the forest.
4. The sun **was shining** when we **set off** on the journey home.

11

11.1
1. Daria **has** baked a delicious cake for everyone at the office.
2. My parents **have** decided to buy a little cottage in the country.
3. Ola **has** taken the day off and **has** gone to the new gallery in town.
4. We **have** decided when we're going to get married.

11.2
1. Hank **hasn't opened** the letter from his college yet.
2. My children **have washed** the car at last.
3. Kelly still **hasn't cleaned** her bedroom. It's so messy!
4. Danny **has painted** the bedroom and the living room.
5. Jess **has visited** Peru and Ecuador so far this year.

11.3
1. Fran and Leo **have gone** to the fair together.
2. Angelo **has not cooked** dinner for his family yet.
3. Jenny **has cleaned** all the windows in her apartment.
4. I **have not met** Nick's new girlfriend yet.
5. Morgan **has watched** this movie at least six times already.
6. Mr. Fernandez and his son **have left** the building.

11.4
REGULAR:
wanted, watched, helped, walked, asked
IRREGULAR:
given, done, seen, swum, put

11.5
1. I studied French in college a long time ago.
2. I haven't lived in Venezuela since 2009.
3. Kevin first visited Munich in 1997.
4. Enzo finished the report on Friday.
5. Sebastian has worked as a chef for 10 years.

11.6
1. Owen **started** work here in 2017.
2. I **have spoken** to Tina about this twice today already.
3. How many countries **have you visited** so far?
4. Gloria **has never tried** windsurfing before.
5. Fabio **has lived** in England for more than 15 years.

11.7
1. I've just been to the dentist for a filling.
2. They've gone to the library.
3. Yes, she's been shopping with her friends.
4. Yes, I've just been for a run.
5. No, she's gone for a walk with the dog.

11.8
1. Of course, I've visited it many times.
2. Yes, I tried it when I went to Athens last year.
3. Yes, I moved here in 1997.
4. Yes, I saw *Macbeth* when I went to London.
5. Yes, I've tried it twice since I've been in Malaysia.

12

12.1
1. Val has been learning to dance tango **for more than six months.**
2. Jess has been running today **and looks very tired.**
3. Have you been living at this **address for a long time?**
4. I've been eating too much cake lately, **so I want to go on a diet.**
5. I haven't been running for ages, **so I don't feel very fit.**

12.2
1. Colin has been looking for a new house all year.
2. My brother's been painting the kitchen since Sunday.
3. It's been raining for more than a week.

12.3
1. I **have been cleaning** the house because my parents are coming tomorrow.
2. You **have been building** that wall all day. Are you nearly finished?
3. Joe **has been fishing** all afternoon, but he hasn't caught anything yet.
4. We **haven't been playing** tennis together for very long.
5. How long **have** you **been training** for the marathon, Jon?
6. Josh **has been painting** a lovely landscape this afternoon.
7. Matt and Heather **have been studying** for their exam all evening.
8. I **haven't been reading** this book for very long.
9. Jane **has been traveling** all summer.
10. **Has** Robin **been walking** all day? He looks exhausted.
11. I **have been trying** to cook a new recipe today.
12. Ed **hasn't been feeling** well, so I told him to go to the doctor.
13. My friend **has been touring** Europe with his band.
14. My manager **has been sleeping** at his desk all afternoon.

13

13.1
1. The play **had started** by the time we arrived at the theater.
2. Ben liked Sal, even though he **had met** her only a few times.
3. I **hadn't eaten** Indian food before, so I didn't know what to expect.
4. Justin called his sister, but she **had gone** to bed.
5. Edith **hadn't seen** her niece for years so was delighted when she visited.
6. Amber felt so happy that she **had passed** her exam.

7 My uncle was upset because I **hadn't called** him recently.

8 Christine worked late, because she **hadn't finished** her project yet.

9 There were a lot of delays because a bus **had broken down**.

10 When we arrived at the station, we discovered the train **had left**.

11 Amy couldn't take her flight because she **had forgotten** her passport.

12 My son looked bored because he **had been** inside the house all day.

13 The house looked shabby because we **hadn't painted** it in years.

14 Jane was excited about going to Rome. She **hadn't been** to Italy before.

13.2

1 Pete had almost finished tiling the wall by the time I got home.

2 I had just sat down with my drink when it started to rain.

3 Janine felt really cold because she'd been outside too long.

4 Tony had called for a taxi an hour earlier, but it still hadn't arrived.

13.3

1 Craig **arrived** late to work because he **had missed** the train.

2 Marie **hadn't ridden** a bike for years, so she **found** it difficult.

3 Dana **was** delighted that she **had passed** her driving test at last.

4 James **had prepared** breakfast when Caitlin **got up**.

5 She **had visited** San Francisco once before, when she **was** seven.

6 I **hadn't met** Karl before, but we **had** lots in common.

7 We **had seen** the play once before, but we **enjoyed** it anyway.

14

14.1

1 Maya had been working here for five years when I started.

2 It had been raining for a week before the sun came out.

3 I got sunburned because I'd been lying in the sun all day.

4 We went to see that movie everyone had been talking about at work.

5 Vlad had been studying English for a year when he moved to Toronto.

6 My computer hadn't been working properly for ages, so I bought a new one.

7 We only found the hotel after we'd been driving for more than an hour.

8 I'd been training for years before I won my first marathon.

9 Carol had been cooking all morning, so she was exhausted.

10 I went to the doctor because I hadn't been feeling well all week.

14.2

1 Marion had been learning Spanish **for six months before she went to Spain.**

2 The forest looked beautiful because **it had been snowing all night.**

3 Kelly had been practicing all week, **so her performance was perfect.**

4 Clive had been complaining **about the bad smell all week.**

14.3

1 Nina **had been shopping** all morning and **needed** a coffee.

2 Carla **had been living** in Paris for 10 years when she **met** Liam.

3 Chris **felt** exhausted because he **had been playing** football all day.

4 Phil **had been watching** TV when the telephone **rang**.

5 Jill **had been feeling** ill all day, so she **went** to bed early.

6 The kids **had been watching** TV all afternoon because it **was** so cold outside.

7 Jo **had been studying** for years before she **passed** the exam.

8 Ahmed **had been working** for hours before he finally **left** the office.

15

15.1

1 I **used to live** in London, but I moved to Paris 10 years ago.

2 When I was a teenager, I **would go** fishing on Saturdays. Now I prefer photography.

3 There **didn't use to be** any factories here. There were beautiful woods.

4 When I worked, I **would get up** at 5am. Now I relax in the morning.

5 Did you **use to ride** a bike when you were a child?

15.2

1 Dana used to play soccer with her friends when she was a child.

2 Chris didn't use to have such long hair.

3 I visited Prague three times when I was a child.

4 Maria used to believe in ghosts when she was little.

5 I used to know Andre well when I was a student.

15.3

1 I would **try** to save money when I was at college.

2 My brother **used** to read comics when he was a kid.

3 Did **you use to** play computer games when you were young?

4 I **didn't use** to read novels, but I really enjoy them now.

16

16.1

1 When I saw Sam earlier this morning, he **was mopping** the floor.

2 Ron and Tim **have worked** at the salon for more than 10 years.

3 Danny **didn't understand** what the man was saying.

4 When I was a kid, I **used to be scared** of spiders.

5 I love travel, but I **haven't been** to New York before.

6 I discovered the loggers **had cut down** almost all the trees.

7 Pavel went outside and **built** a snowman in the park.

8 We were delayed, and the concert **had started** by the time we arrived.

9 Ash **had been studying** Spanish for years before he moved to Madrid.

10 We **have been hiking** all morning. Let's have a break, shall we?

11 It was a beautiful day, and the sun **was shining** through the window.

16.2

1 How long have you **been studying English?**

2 Pedro has been living in his apartment **for more than six months.**

3 It had been raining all night, **and the garden was flooded.**

4 Chrissie loves trying new dishes, **but she's never tried Vietnamese food.**

5 Peter was walking home **when he bumped into an old school friend.**

6 Did you go to the new exhibition **at the museum last weekend?**

16.3

1 Aditya wasn't feeling well, so he went home.

2 You used to go to my school, didn't you?

3 How long have you been working in this office?

4 Ed had been working here for ages when I met him.

16.4

1 When I arrived at the venue, I realized I **hadn't brought** the tickets.

2 By the time we arrived at the theater, the play **had begun**.

3 I **haven't seen** that movie yet. Jon told me it's great.

4 Sophie **has been cooking** all morning. She's exhausted.

5 Harry looked great. He **was wearing** his new suit.

6 Natalia **was sunbathing** when she noticed a monkey in a tree.

7 I **didn't go** to the party on Friday. I was at a concert.

8 Len **has been decorating**. He has paint on his clothes.

9 Jamie **had been practicing** for months before yesterday's show.

10 I **called** my dad this morning to wish him a happy birthday.
11 Bill **was taking** a bath when he heard a knock at the door.

16.5
1 I was sleeping soundly when my alarm clock rang.
2 After we'd eaten, Marco helped me to clear the table.
3 I've been dreaming of going abroad all year.

16.6
1 It **was** my gran's birthday yesterday.
2 I **used to** like mathematics, but now I prefer chemistry.
3 When I walked into the room, Juan **was talking** on the phone.
4 We were sailing to Crete when I **saw** a dolphin.
5 You look hot, Karen. **Have** you **been running?**
6 When Dan **had finished** the cleaning, he went to the park.
7 We **were** lost for three weeks before the helicopter spotted us.
8 **Have** you **lived** in this house for a long time?
9 I **cycled** all the way to London yesterday.
10 We **were walking** through the woods when we saw a bear.
11 When Ben was a child, he **wanted** to be an astronaut.
12 **Did** you **enjoy** your vacation last week?

17

17.1
1 Prediction
2 Future plan
3 Prediction
4 Future plan
5 Future plan
6 Prediction
7 Future plan

17.2
1 Ted told me he's going to travel around Egypt next year.
2 Ben's brought his guitar. I think he's going to sing.
3 Cal has the ball. Is he going to score?
4 I think Angela is going to fall off the ladder!
5 Oh dear! The waiter's going to drop all the plates.
6 Sam's writing on the wall. His dad's going to be furious.
7 Look at those clouds. I think it's going to rain.

17.3
1 Is Gerald going to win the race?
2 Is Aziz going to sail to Ireland?
3 Is Fiona going to teach us about statistics?
4 Are we going to run out of milk soon?

17.4
1 My son **is going to cook** for us tonight.
2 **Is** Jess **going to study** French at college?
3 Katie **isn't going to** teach us next year.
4 It looks like it **is going to** rain again.
5 **Are** they **going to** sing another song for us?

6 I'**m going to** sell my bike. I never use it.
7 Emily **is going to** fix the shower for us.
8 Pete **isn't going to play** rugby with us today.
9 Dad'**s going to get** perfume for Mom's birthday again.

18

18.1
1 Ronaldo **won't go** to bed before midnight.
2 The kids **will have** a great time in Florida next summer.
3 You **will love** the new coat I just bought for the winter.
4 Mia **won't eat** anything with meat in it.
5 My car broke down, so I **will take** the train to work today.
6 Eric **will want** to eat steak and fries for his dinner.
7 Noah **will win** the 400m race at the track competition.
8 My children **won't like** that flavor of ice cream.
9 Charlotte **will marry** her boyfriend this year.
10 I **will stay** at home and watch TV tonight.
11 Arnie **will go** swimming with Bob and Sue.

18.2
1 Decision
2 Prediction
3 Decision
4 Offer

18.3
1 I know he will win the competition.
2 I will definitely wear a warm coat if it's cold.
3 The new office will certainly be an improvement.

19

19.1
1 Present
2 Future
3 Present
4 Present
5 Future
6 Future
7 Present
8 Future
9 Future
10 Present

19.2
1 The exam **is** next week. I'm nervous!
2 The bus to London usually **departs** at 5pm.
3 Phil **is taking** his children to the library tomorrow.
4 Lech won't be at work tomorrow. He **is traveling** to Berlin.
5 I can't come to the meeting tomorrow; I **have** a doctor's appointment.
6 Mel and Phil **are getting** married this weekend.

19.3
1 We **are going** to a party later if you want to join us.
2 The train from Glasgow **arrives** at 10:15pm.
3 I **am going** fishing with my father this afternoon.
4 Terry **is working** all next weekend to earn a bit of extra money.

20

20.1
1 Will you be coming into college later? **I need some help with my project.**
2 In the year 3000, I think **people will be living on the moon.**
3 I can give you a lift. I'll be **driving past the library anyway.**
4 Will we be having a meeting **about the new company logo?**
5 I'm sure people won't be driving **flying cars in 20 years' time.**
6 Mia is going to be bringing her **new boyfriend to the party tonight.**
7 I'm working as a waiter now, but I hope **I'll be running my own restaurant in 10 years.**
8 Will you be playing soccer **with us this weekend?**
9 Enzo's studying French. He hopes **he'll be working as a translator in a few years.**
10 I can post your letter. I'll be going **to the post office this afternoon anyway.**
11 In 10 years' time, I hope **I'll be living in a nice house in the country.**
12 Tomorrow evening, Femi's band **are going to be performing at Funky Joe's.**
13 I guess Liz won't be coming to work **today. She looked terrible yesterday.**
14 Marco hopes that he'll be working **as an actor in a few years' time.**
15 Sophie will be traveling to Paris next **Thursday to see her mother.**

20.2
1 Request
2 Neutral question
3 Neutral question
4 Neutral question
5 Request

20.3
1 I'**ll be living** in a villa by the time I'm 40.
2 Marie is **going to be talking** about the sales figures.
3 We'**ll** all **be relaxing** on the beach next week!
4 Cas **will** probably **be earning** lots of money before too long.
5 Is Martin **going to be playing** any of his new songs?
6 I think humans **will be exploring** other planets by 2050.

21

21.1
1 Amelia **will have moved** to Cairo by the end of September.
2 By the end of this year, we **will have been living** here for 25 years.
3 **Will** Pedro **have finished** the painting by the time we return?
4 The paint **will have dried** by tomorrow morning.
5 By four o'clock, we **will have been waiting** here for two hours.
6 I'm sure he **will have won** more than 10 medals by the end of the year.
7 I think by the end of the year Rio **will have asked** Yukio to marry him.
8 By the time she's 22, Suzy **will have finished** college.
9 We **will have completed** the project by the end of May.
10 Sam **will have graduated** by this time next year.
11 **Will** you **have finished** the assignment by early October?
12 How many countries **will you have visited** by the time you're 40?
13 By the time I'm 25, I **will have been studying** for six years.
14 I **will have left the country** by the time you get here.
15 Dan **will have retired** by the time he's 60.
16 By this time next week, we**'ll have been** married for a year!
17 Sam **will have been cooking** all day by the time the dinner's ready.
18 By the end of tonight, I**'ll have written** this essay.

21.2
1 Don't worry. I'm sure we'll have put up the tent by sunset.
2 Will Dan have made that chair by the time we come back?
3 It looks like they won't have finished the building by next month.

21.3
1 Anika **will have been acting** for 10 years by the end of the year.
2 I'm afraid I **won't have painted** the kitchen by the time you return.
3 By December, I **will have been** learning the piano for six months.
4 The guests **will have eaten** all the food by the time Tom arrives.
5 Leroy **will have turned** 18 by the end of next month.
6 In a year's time, Katie **will have been living** in Rome for 20 years.

22

22.1
1 I thought Hugo would have been promoted by the end of the year.
2 Pari was going to buy a kitten for her daughter.
3 Did you think you'd still be working here in 2021?
4 I thought Sam would pass the final English exam.
5 Penny was going to clean her house if she had time.
6 I knew Michelle would become a successful singer one day.
7 Beccy wasn't going to do the English course, was she?

22.2
1 Christopher **thought he would go** traveling when **he finished** college.
2 Farouk **was going to start** cycling to work in the new year.
3 I **was going to cook** dinner when I **got** home from work.
4 Pablo **had** the ball. I **thought he was going to** score.
5 I **was** sure Danny **would finish** the wall soon.
6 I **thought** Ania **would win** the athletics competition.
7 My sister **was going** to get a cat when she **moved** house.
8 The radio **said it was going to snow** tonight.
9 Craig **thought** he **would visit** Japan in the summer.
10 **We were going to see** a new band playing at Club 9000.
11 I **was** sure **he was going to talk** about the company's problems.
12 Kelly **was** sure she **was going to see** some dolphins on vacation.

23

23.1
1 Are you meeting my sister for dinner this evening?
2 They will have finished the stadium by the end of the year.
3 By August, I will have been working here for one year.
4 It's clear that Petra isn't going to win.
5 Derek thought he would study engineering at college.
6 Does the lesson begin at half past three?
7 In 10 years' time I'll be living in Spain.

23.2
1 I thought I was going to be late, **but I made it to work just on time.**
2 Tomorrow's lecture about **volcanoes will be very interesting.**
3 Tim thought the meeting **would have started by now.**
4 Sorry, I'm busy at the moment, but **I will have finished in 10 minutes.**

23.3
1 Sue tells me she **is going** to start learning Spanish next year.
2 You look tired. **I'll** get you some coffee.
3 Look at those clouds. **It's going to** rain soon.
4 **I'll** help you with those bags, Edith.
5 Look! He **is going to** ask his girlfriend to marry him.
6 I **am going to** see a play at the theater. I've already got the tickets.
7 In the future, I think people **will** travel to other planets.
8 **I'll** have the chocolate cake on the right, please.

23.4
1 The forecast said it was going to rain later.
2 If you're not careful, you'll smash a window.
3 I hope Silvia's going to sing all her hits tonight.

23.5
1 Our company **is not going to** make a profit this year.
2 I don't think my son **will be** an artist when he grows up.
3 I can't meet you tomorrow. **I'm playing** tennis with Antoine.
4 **We're going to miss** the beginning of the play. Let's hurry!
5 Sal **will have been working** at the diner for 10 years in August.
6 I **was going to eat** another piece of cake, but I remembered I was on a diet.

23.6
1 My son thinks we will be driving flying cars in the future.
2 Seb won't have finished the decorating by the time you get back.
3 Look! That child's going to fall off that wall.
4 It's Angie's party tonight. I'll bring some snacks and cakes.
5 The train had broken down, so I knew I was going to be late.
6 I'm going to buy that house I saw a couple of times last week.
7 Suki is joining us for dinner at the Hotel Bristol.
8 When I turn 40, I will have been living in Lisbon for 20 years.
9 I am traveling to Paris by train this afternoon.
10 I know! I'll buy my grandmother a new scarf.
11 John knew there were going to be bad delays on the trains.
12 Do you think you'll have finished the essay by the time I arrive?
13 This time next year, I hope I'll be studying medicine at college.

24

24.1
① The alarm **is tested** once a month at my workplace.
② The sculpture **is displayed** in the main hall.
③ The Eiffel Tower **is visited** by millions of tourists each year.
④ Lunch **is eaten** in the college cafeteria.
⑤ The band **is expected** to perform its greatest hits.

24.2
① This program is used by many students.
② Her new dress is being made by a famous designer.
③ Our apartment is cleaned every Thursday.
④ The train is usually driven by Martin.

24.3
① The game is usually played in Central Park each September.
② The play is being performed on stage later tonight.
③ Solar panels are being used by an increasing number of people.

24.4
① English **is not understood** by many people here.
② A new shopping mall **is being built** near the park.
③ Some shows **are watched** by millions of people each day.
④ The food **is being prepared** at home today.
⑤ The castle **is surrounded** by dense forests.
⑥ Our products **are** usually **dispatched** within two days.
⑦ Latin **is not studied** by many young people.
⑧ Guests **are** always **provided** with a complimentary lunch.
⑨ My computer **is being repaired** at the moment.
⑩ Kelvin **is being taught** how to juggle today.
⑪ The children **are** always **supervised** by two adults.
⑫ A lot of old factories **are being knocked down**.
⑬ The crime **is being investigated** by the police.
⑭ Students **are expected** to be punctual at all times.
⑮ I'm staying with Claire while my house is **being decorated**.
⑯ The play **is being performed** in French tonight.
⑰ That course **is** usually **taught** by Eduardo.
⑱ All our plastic and glass **is recycled** by the council.
⑲ Ron **is being investigated** for fraud.
⑳ My hair **is cut** by a stylist from Ecuador.
㉑ The car **is being washed** right now.
㉒ Karim's performance **is being recorded** tonight.

25

25.1
① The temple in my town was built in 1482.
② We couldn't use the kitchen because it was being painted.

③ Patrick was surrounded by all the books he had to read.
④ The roof was repaired by my father.
⑤ I was taught how to drive by my aunt.
⑥ John's birthday cake was made by his grandmother.
⑦ Our cat was being looked after by a friend.

25.2
① When we got home, **we discovered the house had been broken into.**
② Karen was so upset **because she hadn't been invited to the party.**
③ I hadn't been told it was Rajiv's birthday, **so I didn't have a present for him.**
④ Many houses have been damaged **by the recent hurricane.**
⑤ Have all the staff been informed **about tomorrow's meeting?**
⑥ Has your car been fixed yet? **It's been in the auto repair shop for ages!**

25.3
① The play **was interrupted** by the smoke alarm. We had to evacuate the theater.
② Dan's room was filthy. It **hadn't been cleaned** in weeks.
③ That old factory near my house **has been demolished**.
④ All of the plants on the balcony **have been watered**.
⑤ The mail **hasn't been delivered** yet. I'm still waiting.
⑥ Most of the forest **was cut down** last year.
⑦ The spy **was being followed** by two men in hats.
⑧ Malcolm **has been fired**. He was so lazy!

25.4
MODEL ANSWERS
① All of the cake that Jemima had made was eaten.
② All the money from the bank's safe was stolen.
③ My brother was injured in a car accident yesterday.
④ All the tables in the restaurant have been booked.
⑤ Lots of tower blocks were being built in the suburbs.
⑥ That part of the country hadn't been explored before.
⑦ They were so happy that their cat had been found.
⑧ I wasn't informed that the office was closed on Friday.
⑨ All the tickets for tonight's movie have been sold.
⑩ That mountain has never been climbed before.
⑪ A lot of buildings have been destroyed by the earthquake.
⑫ It's cold. The window has been left open.

26

26.1
① The new stadium **will be opened** by the president.
② All the food **will be cooked** by our new chef, Luigi.
③ Our house **won't be finished** by the end of the year.
④ The prisoner **will be released** after 30 years.
⑤ **Will** the show **be presented** by a new DJ?
⑥ My latest novel **will be published** in January.
⑦ The water **will be turned off** on Thursday morning.
⑧ The lecture **will be given** by Professor O'Brien.
⑨ Dinner **will be served** in the dining room between 7 and 9pm.
⑩ All the laundry **will be done** by the time you get back.
⑪ **Will** the students **be given** a test at the end of the course?

26.2
① Will the dress have been altered before her wedding day?
② I hope my house will have been sold by next month.
③ I'm sure we'll have been visited by aliens by 2100.

26.3
① By 2030, intelligent robots **will have been developed**.
② I'm sure our car **will have been repaired** by the beginning of next week.
③ The computer **will have been replaced** before you start work.
④ I think Jane **will have been fired** by this time next year.
⑤ By 2050, many more galaxies **will have been discovered**.
⑥ Do you think the criminals **will have been caught** by then?
⑦ All our staff **will have been trained** by the end of the week.
⑧ **Will** the project **have been completed** by the time we return?
⑨ All the issues **will have been resolved** before we release the product.
⑩ I hope the kitchen **will have been painted** by the time we move in.
⑪ Our new bed **will have been delivered** by the end of the month.
⑫ The decision **will have been made** by Friday evening.

27

27.1
① All computers should be turned off before leaving the office.
② Protective glasses must be worn at all times.
③ We should have been told about the exam.
④ Can the meeting be postponed until later in the week?
⑤ All the tourists should be given a guidebook.
⑥ You could have been killed running across that street!
⑦ Our car should have been repaired weeks ago.

27.2
① All the floors must be mopped at the end of the day.
② That ugly building should have been demolished years ago.
③ The mountain can be climbed with the help of ropes.
④ Our forests must be protected from destruction.
⑤ You wouldn't have been stung if you'd remained calm.

27.3
① Bicycles should only be ridden **if you are wearing a helmet.**
② The dentist told me that **one of my teeth must be removed.**
③ Clara should have been given **more time to finish her assignment.**
④ Everyone should be warned that **a tiger has escaped from the zoo.**
⑤ The dish could have been improved **if we'd used better ingredients.**
⑥ The steak should be fried **for one minute on each side.**
⑦ The accident might have been avoided **if the car hadn't been going so fast.**

28

28.1
① It has been revealed that the company is losing a lot of money.
② That old house across the road is said to be haunted.
③ The movie star is rumored to be in a relationship with her co-star.
④ The new gallery is reported to contain a lot of modern art.
⑤ The mountain is known to be dangerous to climb.
⑥ It has been reported that many houses have been destroyed.
⑦ There are said to be many beautiful temples in Japan.

28.2
① I'm hoping that I will **get promoted** to senior manager soon.
② My colleague often **gets criticized** for the quality of her work.
③ The bedroom's **getting redecorated** next week.
④ My aunt's car **got stolen** from the parking lot at work.
⑤ Samantha **got bitten** by a dog in the local park.

28.3
① This store **is known** to sell high-quality shoes.
② It **has been reported** that Ella is going to start performing again.
③ The grass **gets cut** once a month by our gardener.
④ It **is rumored** that we are going to have an exam today.
⑤ All the dishes **got washed** by Danny.

29

29.1
① Food tastes awful when you add too much salt.
② If my dog gets hungry, he barks loudly.
③ If you misbehave, you get sent to detention.

29.2
① When it gets too cold, **we light the fire.**
② If you squeeze a balloon hard enough, **it explodes.**
③ Water boils if you **heat it long enough.**
④ Eggs usually break when **you drop them.**
⑤ If you keep cooling water, **it eventually freezes.**
⑥ If you don't pay your bills on time, **you get fined.**

29.3
① If the phone rings, please **answer** it.
② **Let me know** if you have any problems at all.
③ **Don't eat** it if you don't like it.
④ When you buy something expensive, always **keep** the receipt.
⑤ If it's sunny tomorrow, **make sure** to use sunscreen.

29.4
① If it **stops** raining, I'll finish painting the fence.
② If Janine works very hard, she **will pass** her exams.
③ If I **don't get** the job, I'll be very upset.
④ Sally **will lose** her job if she keeps missing deadlines.
⑤ If it doesn't rain tomorrow, we **will have** a picnic.
⑥ If I **get** a raise, I'll definitely go on an expensive vacation.
⑦ Sarah will go fishing on Saturday if she **has** time.
⑧ If we take this path, we **will get** there more quickly.

29.5
① Phil would buy a new television if he had more money.
② If I didn't have a headache, I'd definitely come to the party.
③ I'd visit you more often if I had more time.
④ If I was young again, I would go traveling around the world.

29.6
① Tony would buy a villa if he won the lottery.
② If we had more money, we would start our own business.
③ I'm sure David would help you if you asked him.
④ If Ania went traveling, she'd go to Vietnam.

29.7
① If Fleur **had gone** to bed earlier, she **wouldn't have felt** tired all day.
② Simon **would have gone** to jail if the police **had caught** him.
③ If Marco **had known** there was a test, he **would have studied** for it.
④ I **would have brought** an umbrella if I **had known** it was going to rain.
⑤ If Chris **hadn't scored**, we **wouldn't have won** the championship.
⑥ If I **had known** you were coming, I **would have cleaned** the apartment.
⑦ I **would have bought** you a present if I **had known** it was your birthday.
⑧ Dom **wouldn't have been** alone on his birthday if he **had invited** his friends.
⑨ If I **hadn't slept** through my alarm, I **wouldn't have** arrived late for work.
⑩ Abbie **would have studied** art if she **had gone** to college.
⑪ If we **had arrived** early, we **wouldn't have missed** the train.
⑫ Libby **would have won** the race if she **had been** faster than Nina.
⑬ We **would have gone** camping if **we'd known** it was going to be so hot.
⑭ If Lou **hadn't worked** so hard, the project **wouldn't have been** such a success.

29.8
① If I hadn't brought the umbrella **I'd be very wet now.**
② If Ed had scored higher on his tests, **he'd be going to a good college now.**
③ I'd be at work now **if I hadn't missed the 7am train.**
④ Chloe wouldn't be sitting outside now **if she'd remembered her key this morning.**
⑤ Gordon wouldn't be in prison **if he hadn't stolen the painting from the gallery.**

29.9
① Jemma **wouldn't be** so tired now if she'd gone to bed earlier.
② If they **had finished** the decorating, we wouldn't be sleeping in a camper.
③ If Emma **had listened** to our advice, she would be more successful now.
④ I wouldn't be such a good athlete if I **hadn't trained** so hard.
⑤ If Len had fixed my car, I **wouldn't be walking** to work today.
⑥ Tim **would love** it here if he had decided to join us.
⑦ Karen wouldn't have to stand if she **had reserved** a seat.
⑧ If I hadn't lost my job, I **wouldn't be living** with my sister.
⑨ If you **had kept** practicing, I'm sure you'd be a famous singer today.

29.10

1 If I **had to** make a choice, I would say I prefer dogs.

2 **I would have graduated** by now if I'd continued with my studies.

3 If you **don't hurry up**, you're going to be late for school.

4 You would have had a great time at the party if you **had come**.

5 We'd be on vacation now if we **hadn't missed** the flight.

6 When water **gets** hot enough, it boils.

7 **I will go** to the doctor if my leg still hurts tomorrow.

8 The soup **would taste** better if I had added more salt.

9 I always drink plenty of water if I **get** too hot.

10 It **would have been** a perfect party if the dog hadn't eaten the cake.

11 **I will repair** the roof this afternoon if the weather's good.

12 **I would be** very scared if I ever saw a UFO.

30

30.1

1 You **can have** an ice cream if you're really good.

2 If you'd asked her to marry you, she **might have said** yes.

3 We **could go** camping if I take a few days off work.

4 If she had practiced more, Helena **could have been** a great singer.

5 If I have some free time later, I **might do** some gardening.

30.2

1 Unless you get up now, **you're going to be late.**

2 She'll leave the firm **unless we start paying her more.**

3 Unless you turn the music down, **the neighbors will complain.**

4 You'll get sunburned **unless you wear sun protection.**

5 Unless you start working harder, **you're not going to graduate on time.**

6 Angelica will get annoyed **unless you reply to her email.**

7 Unless there's bad weather, **we'll reach the summit before noon.**

30.3

1 Had business been better, the company wouldn't have gone bankrupt.

2 Had Pamela been richer, she would have bought a larger house.

3 Had you studied harder, the exam wouldn't have been so difficult.

4 Had Paul attended the meeting, he would have known about the new project.

5 Had the weather been better, their trip would have been more enjoyable.

31

31.1

1 Second
2 First
3 Zero
4 Third
5 First
6 First
7 Zero
8 Second
9 Third
10 Second

31.2

1 If I had more money, I'd go on vacation to Rome.

2 We would have packed warmer clothes if we'd known it was so cold here.

3 They could play baseball if it stopped raining.

4 If you keep practicing, you will win the championship.

31.3

1 I would have passed the test if I'd studied.

2 If Mia had more time, she'd start a hobby.

3 If it's sunny tomorrow, I'll go swimming.

4 If you heat ice, it turns into water.

5 I'd have caught the bus if I hadn't overslept.

6 If my team doesn't win, I'll be disappointed.

7 If Mel won the lottery, she'd buy a villa.

8 If I had seen Rob, I would have said hello.

9 If I'm late again, my boss will be so angry.

10 If she had asked me, I would have helped her.

11 If you went to bed earlier, you'd feel less tired.

32

32.1

1 Likely
2 Didn't happen
3 Didn't happen
4 Unlikely
5 Didn't happen
6 Unlikely
7 Unlikely
8 Likely
9 Likely
10 Unlikely

32.2

1 What if Vicky became a famous actress? **She really enjoys drama, after all.**

2 Suppose you lost your job at the café. **Where do you think you'd work?**

3 Suppose we get lost in the forest. **We may not be able to find the path.**

4 Let's prepare some more food **in case more people arrive.**

5 Take some water with you **in case you get hot while you're jogging.**

6 I'm nervous about going on stage tonight. **What if the audience don't like me?**

32.3

1 Check the gallery's website in case it is closed on Mondays.

2 Suppose the factory closed. What would the town do?

3 What if we come across a bear? There are lots of them in the mountains.

4 It's your interview tomorrow. Set an alarm in case you don't wake up.

5 What if we won the lottery? What would we do with the money?

6 Take a good book in case you get bored waiting.

33

33.1

1 I wish I had a job where I could work outside.

2 Simone wishes she'd remembered to bring her camera.

3 Martin wishes he knew how to ski.

4 Pete wishes he had a better car.

5 Ronaldo wishes he hadn't broken his guitar.

6 Joan wishes she had a lawn mower.

7 We wish it was sunny, so we could go to the beach.

33.2

1 Can no longer happen
2 Can no longer happen
3 Could still happen
4 Can no longer happen
5 Could still happen

33.3

1 I wish I **didn't work** so late all the time. I'm so tired in the evenings.

2 We're lost! We **should have planned** our route a little better.

3 Ed, I wish **you would** stop singing out of tune all the time.

4 If only **I could** cook! Everything I make is a disaster.

34

34.1

1 Are the children waiting?
2 Is there a good restaurant on Park Street?
3 Can Fu speak fluent French?
4 Is Jean going to win the game?
5 Should Peter tell Amy about the party?
6 Has Kelly bought a gift for her dad?

34.2

1 Did Anthony start his new job at the bank?
2 Does Wayne want to come to the zoo with us?
3 Did Harleen work for us a few years ago?
4 Does Henry like classical music?
5 Do Lara and Michael go to the same school?
6 Do they own the bookstore by the park?

34.3

1. Does Tina still work at the boutique?
2. Do you prefer cats or dogs?
3. Did the children enjoy the fair?
4. Did you manage to move that box?
5. Does Selma go jogging often?
6. Did you help clean up after the party?
7. Do you often go abroad on vacation?
8. Doesn't Clara have two large dogs?
9. Have you ever read *Little Women*?
10. Don't you like fast food, Phillippe?
11. Have you ever had a driving lesson?
12. Did you enjoy the art exhibition?
13. Did you remember to feed the dog?

34.4

1. **Does** Dora work in a bank?
2. **Are** your colleagues coming to the party?
3. **Do** we start work at 10am on Fridays?
4. **Does** Marlon really live in a mansion?
5. Did Bill **work** for the government?
6. **Were** there many animals in the forest?
7. **Does** Marcel come from Argentina?
8. Did you **go** to the theater last night?
9. **Have** you seen Anika's new car?
10. **Is** Tom going to finish the report today?
11. Did Bruce **live** in Glasgow?
12. **Was** John at the airport to meet you?
13. **Do** you take a shower in the evening?
14. **Is** there any juice left?
15. **Have** we got enough time left?
16. **Is** your brother coming later?
17. **Do** Claire and Sam have any children?
18. **Does** Tim play soccer on the weekend?
19. **Are** those your tools on the table?
20. Did Elsa **have** a boyfriend named Gus?
21. **Does** Ash still work at the café?
22. **Is** your daughter still in college?
23. **Has** Sheila seen your new house yet?

34.5

1. Has she finished the painting yet?
2. Have you been to India?
3. Are you coming to the party later?
4. Is Jackie still a teacher?
5. Did you remember to lock the door?

34.6

1. Has Ed lived in New York for more than 10 years?
2. Are Katia and Pavel getting married in June?
3. Did Claudia take a flight to Rio de Janeiro?
4. Does Mia go swimming every evening after work?
5. Did you remember to buy some water?
6. Are Ron and Lily playing tennis this afternoon?

35

35.1

1. **What** did you buy at the market?
2. **Why** is Lena laughing so much?
3. **Which** of these bags is yours?
4. **How** does your dad feel today?
5. **Who** is going to teach the course?
6. **Whose** car is parked outside?
7. **How** quickly can you finish it?

8. **Where** does your cousin live?
9. **When** does the hardware store close?
10. **Whose** diary is on the desk?
11. **When** did you last see Maria?
12. **How** many times has he been to Kenya?
13. **Why** did she quit the course?
14. **Where** is the entrance?
15. **Who** did you invite to the party?
16. **How** long does it take to get there?
17. **Which** car should I buy?
18. **Where** did I put my glasses?

35.2

1. Where is the classroom?
2. Whose phone is this?
3. Why did you do that?
4. How long did you wait?
5. Who did you meet earlier?
6. Which house is yours?
7. When does the movie start?

35.3

1. When did you start playing the guitar, Tom?
2. How does the soup taste, Gustav?
3. Which way do you think we should go?

35.4

1. What is the date today?
2. What's the name of your business?
3. Which train are you taking, the 1pm or the 3pm?
4. Which do you prefer, skiing or snowboarding?
5. What time are they arriving?
6. If you had to choose between dogs and cats, which would you choose?

35.5

1. How often do you read?
2. When can we have our meeting?
3. When is the movie being released?
4. How often do you perform in public?
5. When do you finish work?

35.6

1. How many people work **in your department**?
2. Where are they going **to build the new airport**?
3. Whose coat has been left **on the back of that chair**?
4. Which way is it **to the bus station**?
5. What time does **the concert start**?
6. When does the train **to Glasgow leave**?

36

36.1

1. **What would you do** if you saw a ghost?
2. **When do you think** you will finish building the house?
3. **How do you feel** after the race?
4. **How often do you** water your plants?
5. **Why do you both** look so happy?

36.2

1. What time does the train leave?
2. What is your name?
3. How was the movie?

4. When did you get this dog?
5. Why did you phone me earlier?
6. Who can speak English here?
7. Who should I call to complain?
8. When do you start work?
9. What is this button for?
10. Which dress do you prefer?
11. Why aren't you at work today?
12. What do you eat for breakfast?
13. Where does David live?

36.3

1. What **is she going** to sing for us next?
2. Where **did you buy** that lovely dress?
3. What **happened** to your leg, Paul?
4. **Whose** bicycle is that in the yard?
5. Why **do you have to** watch so much TV?
6. How **do you feel** about losing your job?
7. Where **do you cycle** to on Sundays?
8. How many times **have you visited** New York?
9. Why **are you** so angry, Anthony?
10. How old **are the twins** today?
11. What time **do you eat** your lunch?
12. When **did you last go** camping, Sam?

37

37.1

1. I went with an old friend from school.
2. An artist from Australia painted it.
3. It was a present from my boyfriend.
4. We saw a play by William Shakespeare.
5. I'm going to have fish and chips.
6. Angelica. She has so much experience.
7. There was a terrible storm last week.

37.2

1. Subject question
2. Subject question
3. Object question
4. Subject question
5. Subject question
6. Object question
7. Object question

37.3

1. Who **played golf** with you yesterday?
2. What **did you see** at the movies last night?
3. Who **married** Sonia at the end of the movie?
4. What **did you catch** while fishing yesterday?

37.4

1. Who **did I see** you playing golf with on Sunday?
2. Who **stole** the money from the bank?
3. Who **left** this terrible mess?
4. What **are you going** to wear to the wedding?
5. Who **lives** in that huge castle?
6. What **did you give** the cat to eat?
7. Who **won** the race this afternoon?

38

38.1
1. Do you know **what time the lesson begins**?
2. Do you know **where the bus station is**?
3. Could you tell me **how to get to the national gallery**?
4. Do you know **how much a ticket to Oslo costs**?
5. Could you tell me **if breakfast is still being served**?
6. Could you tell me **why this is so expensive**?
7. Do you know **whether the train goes to Swansea**?

38.2
1. Could you tell me where Lizzy lives?
2. Do you know why the school is closed?
3. Do you know if the course has begun yet?
4. Could you tell me why you did that?

38.3
1. Do you know if Emma has brushed the yard?
2. Could you tell me whose that old car is?
3. Do you know if the car will be ready by 5pm?
4. Could you tell me where the station is?
5. Do you know when you will finish the report?

39

39.1
1. Brian was a Spanish teacher, **wasn't he?**
2. Mark is Mike's cousin, **isn't he?**
3. There aren't any tickets left, **are there?**
4. There's a nice café near the park, **isn't there?**
5. That was such an exciting movie, **wasn't it?**
6. It's not going to rain today, **is it?**

39.2
1. Your grandmother likes tea, **doesn't she?**
2. Gerald has finished the gardening, **hasn't he?**
3. Luca didn't pass the English exam, **did he?**
4. Carla worked in a bakery, **didn't she?**
5. We should buy a new fridge, **shouldn't we?**
6. You haven't seen my glasses, **have you?**
7. Mike can swim, **can't he?**

39.3
1. The hat on the left is gorgeous, **isn't it?**
2. That ride was really scary, **wasn't it?**
3. You're Daniel's cousin, **aren't you?**
4. I think our team's going to win, **isn't it?**
5. We aren't going to catch our plane, **are we?**
6. You've read that book before, **haven't you?**
7. The guests don't look very happy, **do they?**
8. Bill plays the guitar really well, **doesn't he?**
9. Chloe will do the shopping for you, **won't she?**
10. I should have brought an umbrella, **shouldn't I?**
11. Martin doesn't like cooking much, **does he?**
12. Paul looks absolutely exhausted, **doesn't he?**
13. We've been waiting here for 30 minutes, **haven't we?**
14. You're not listening to anything I say, **are you?**

40

40.1
1. Does he?
2. Did you?
3. Isn't it?
4. Have you?
5. Did she?
6. Is she?
7. Hasn't he?
8. Was it?
9. Is he?

41

41.1
1. Yes, there is.
2. No, I don't.
3. No, we won't.
4. Yes, I do.
5. Yes, we are.
6. Yes, there were.
7. Yes, he can.
8. No, I haven't.
9. No, I wouldn't.

42

42.1
1. Is Joe playing tennis on Thursday?
2. Have they knocked down the apartment block?
3. Is Jean-Paul learning to cook?
4. Is Rob going to win the race?
5. Does Chrissy do exercises each morning?
6. Will they play all their greatest hits?
7. Did Claire and Ben get married last week?
8. Does Aziz work late every evening?
9. Did Jessica take the dog for a walk?

42.2
SUBJECT QUESTIONS:
Who wrote this book?
What happened next?
Who called earlier?
Who drove you to work?
OBJECT QUESTIONS:
Who did you invite?
What did you buy?
Who do you live with?
What does John do for work?

42.3
1. Open question
2. Closed question
3. Closed question
4. Open question
5. Closed question
6. Closed question

43

43.1
1. Emilia said she wanted to come to the park with us.
2. She said her husband was from Alabama.
3. He said it was extremely hot in Adelaide.
4. She told me that she was a lawyer.
5. My son said he wanted to quit school.
6. Our boss told us we had to work harder.
7. They told me they owned a villa in Spain.

43.2
1. She told me she was a Canadian citizen.
2. Rob said he had won a huge amount of money.
3. Ella said that Phil's 18th birthday party was great fun.
4. Ted told me he went backpacking around Europe last year.

43.3
1. She **said** that she **traveled** around the world a lot for work.
2. She **told** me that her new boyfriend **was** from Ethiopia.
3. Silvio **told** Maria that he **lived** in Milan with his family.
4. Mike **said** that he **felt** sick, so he went home.
5. She **told** me that her brother **worked** in a travel agency.

44

44.1
1. Jan said she would give me a call later that evening.
2. Benedict said he was seeing his grandma later that day.
3. George told me he'd arrived at the hotel hours earlier.
4. Matt and Mable said they were going to the movies to see a thriller.
5. Danny said he couldn't afford to come on vacation with us this summer.
6. Gemma told me that my new dress looked great.
7. Katie said she'd give the camera back to me the next day.

44.2
1. Archie told me that his car had broken down.
2. Betty said she'd seen a wolf in the woods last year.
3. Malcolm told Mel that he works in a salon.

44.3
1. Cath told me she **had** posted the letter a few days ago.
2. The weather forecast said it **was** going to be sunny yesterday.
3. Angela told me she **had** already mowed the lawn.
4. Miles told us that the company **was** losing money before it went bankrupt.

⑤ In February, Lisa told me that she **had had** a great idea for a vacation.

⑥ Emil said he **would** visit me in Japan that summer.

44.4

① Harry told me they were going to the zoo on Thursday.

② The shop assistant told me they didn't have a shirt in my size.

③ Michelle said she didn't want to go to the party last night.

④ The manager said the hotel was fully booked in July.

⑤ Jenny told me that she'd worked on a farm when she was a student.

⑥ Billy's mom said he would pass all his exams.

⑦ Robert told me he was writing a novel set in Ancient Rome.

⑧ She said that she lives in a house near the bus station.

⑨ Carlo said he was going to buy a new car that afternoon.

45

45.1

① Don **reminded me to buy** some milk on the way home.

② My parents **encouraged me to study** medicine in college.

③ Tina's sister **explained that she would be** late to the recital.

45.2

① Wayne admitted that it was the first time he'd made pancakes.

② Archie's boss threatened to fire him if he didn't work harder.

③ Sergio asked me to marry him while we were on vacation.

46

46.1

① Pedro explained that he **didn't work on Fridays.**

② Paul's mom told him **not to draw on the walls.**

③ Monika reminded me **not to forget my passport.**

④ I said that I didn't want **to drive to the restaurant.**

⑤ I told my brother I couldn't **come because I was feeling ill.**

46.2

① My colleague mentioned that the printer wasn't working.

② Mark explained that he didn't like dogs.

③ Myra phoned to say that she wasn't coming to the meeting.

④ Jon tried to persuade me not to eat any more cake.

47

47.1

① The artist asked us what we thought of his painting.

② Georges asked me if I'd ever been to Paris.

③ Dave asked if I'd like to go fishing with him.

④ Jon asked me why I was dressed as a clown.

⑤ Mom asked if I'd done the dishes yet.

⑥ My stylist asked me what I wanted.

⑦ The waiter asked me what I wanted to drink.

47.2
MODEL ANSWERS

① He asked me **where you live.**

② Sue asked me **what I thought.**

③ Amy asked us **if she should bring something.**

④ Paul asked **why I left.**

⑤ They asked me **where I had been.**

⑥ The girl asked me **where the station is.**

⑦ She asked **where the exit was.**

⑧ Mia asked me **if I own a car.**

⑨ They asked me **who he is.**

47.3

① Peter asked **if you were coming to the** performance later.

② My teacher asked **me if I'd decided to** study math at college.

③ Lou asked **me where I wanted to go** on Saturday.

④ The waiter asked **if we wanted to order** more drinks.

⑤ Susan asked **me what time we usually have** our lunch break.

⑥ She asked **me if I wanted to go to the** movies with her.

⑦ Claire asked **her kids if they wanted mint or** strawberry ice cream.

⑧ Fran asked **how long we had lived in** San Francisco.

⑨ Pete asked **whether I could help him move house** this weekend.

47.4

① Paul asked if he **could** borrow my T-shirt.

② Danny wanted to know if it **is raining / was raining** here.

③ Hiroshi asked whether you **are coming** to the lecture later today.

④ Shona asked me if I **would post** this letter for her.

⑤ My granddaughter asked me how long **have been knitting / I had been knitting** for.

⑥ Antonia asked me where you **are living** at the moment.

⑦ Greg asked me who the singer **is / was** in the band we saw last night.

⑧ I asked the architect if he knew when they **are going to finish / were going to finish** the block.

⑨ Ella asked me who **won / had won** the marathon yesterday.

⑩ My children asked me today if I **believe / believed** in ghosts.

⑪ Patsy wanted to know who **directed / had directed** the new comedy.

48

48.1

① Steph told me that she really missed her friends and family.

② Les told me Christine had paid for lunch the previous week.

③ Rohan tells me he really doesn't want to work this Saturday.

④ Mia told Dan that her daughter dreamed of becoming an actor.

⑤ Jiya once told me she'd be a famous singer by 2015.

⑥ Lou told me they were going to the theater the following day.

⑦ Angela tells me she's never been to the Tower of London.

48.2

① Ruth explained why the results were so bad.

② Phil said he'd finish the garden last Wednesday.

③ Carla asked whether she could leave the office early.

④ Liam told me he had visited Paris the previous year.

⑤ Ken asked Katie if she wanted to dance with him.

48.3

① Karen told me she was going to Vietnam for her honeymoon.

② Mike said he wanted to be a police officer when he was a kid.

③ Sophia mentioned that she has a spare ticket.

49

49.1

① Main
② Auxiliary
③ Auxiliary
④ Auxiliary
⑤ Main
⑥ Main
⑦ Auxiliary
⑧ Main
⑨ Auxiliary
⑩ Main

49.2

① You **should** call your grandma. It's her birthday.

② The students **have** all handed in their papers.

③ Sandra **isn't** coming to the party tonight.

④ My son **could** already swim when he was three.

⑤ I **had** already left by the time Jim arrived.

⑥ I **didn't** like her boyfriend. He was rude.

⑦ You **mustn't** speak so loudly in the library.

49.3
TRANSITIVE:
want, **bring**, **throw**
INTRANSITIVE:
arrive, **come**, **smile**

50

50.1
1. Action
2. State
3. Action
4. Action
5. State
6. State
7. Action

50.2
1. We **know** Jenny very well.
2. This soup **tastes** awful.
3. Chris **wants** an ice cream.
4. Our vacation **cost** a lot of money.
5. Craig **understands** Spanish.
6. I **recognized** that man.
7. My son **hates** vegetables.
8. Dom's pie **smelled** great.
9. Your book **sounds** interesting.

50.3
ACTION VERBS:
try, **read**, **eat**, **kick**, **drive**
STATE VERBS:
be, **contain**, **know**, **hear**, **own**

50.4
1. Fatima **is writing** a book about her childhood.
2. It **is raining** outside. Let's watch something on TV.
3. Marco **is playing** guitar on stage now.
4. Rosita **has** two sisters, who live in the United States.
5. Claude **hates** all salad and vegetables.
6. I **am reading** a travel guide to Los Angeles.

51

51.1
1. **plan** planning **planned**
2. play **playing** **played**
3. **do** doing **done**
4. **like** liking **liked**
5. **find** **finding** found
6. **write** **writing** written
7. finish **finishing** **finished**
8. **buy** **buying** bought
9. read **reading** **read**
10. **tell** **telling** told
11. **hope** **hoping** hoped
12. swim **swimming** **swum**
13. **go** **going** gone
14. **cry** crying **cried**
15. **begin** beginning **begun**
16. **say** **saying** said
17. **love** loving **loved**

51.2
1. Carla has **finished** all of her assignments.
2. Marsha's **planning** a surprise party for Ed.
3. Marion is **going** to get married this fall.
4. We hadn't **planned** to stay in, but it started raining.
5. We want **to go** to the art exhibition tomorrow.

51.3
1. **Writing** new vocabulary in a notebook helps me to remember it.
2. Tim's English teacher asked if he'd **done** his homework.
3. My husband keeps **forgetting** his keys. It's so frustrating.
4. My children don't **want to go** to school this morning.
5. I go **swimming** most weekends with my friends.
6. Everyone had **sung** Happy Birthday by the time I arrived.

52

52.1
1. I finally **managed** to buy a house after saving for years.
2. Alberto has **finished** painting the landscape.
3. We **arranged** to meet for a drink after work.
4. My brother **considered** buying a sports car when he turned 40.
5. I really **enjoyed** meeting your friends at the party.

52.2
1. My dad has **decided** to start studying Spanish.
2. My colleague **offered** to help me finish the report.
3. I really **enjoy** running on the weekend.

52.3
1. Carlo enjoys **going** to the theater each Friday.
2. Rob and Phil intend **to buy** a house this year.
3. Ellie is planning **to visit** Sydney while she's in Australia.
4. I don't feel like **playing** football this evening.
5. Margo refused **to eat** the ice cream Jed offered her.
6. My boss agreed **to let** me go home early from work.

52.4
1. I wish I hadn't told Jon about my job.
2. I was driving home when I decided to stop for a cup of coffee.
3. I will remember to pick Angela up later from the airport later.
4. Do you remember the time you first met Paul at the conference?
5. I used to drink coffee, but I decided to stop a long time ago.

6. The professor thanked the organizers and then talked about the experiment.
7. You were supposed to meet Paul. Did you remember to do that?
8. I'll always remember when I saw Angela for the first time.
9. The professor was talking about the experiment and continued to do so.

53

53.1
1. Alfred spends a lot of time playing golf after work.
2. Janice watched the kids playing in the park.
3. Marco tried to sell his old car to me.
4. My boss wants me to work more quickly.
5. Helena heard people talking in the room next door.
6. My aunt borrowed a lot of money from my dad.
7. My mom wants me to clean my room immediately.
8. Hanif asked me to help him use the new software.
9. Yuri bought an ice cream for his girlfriend.
10. Tom reminded Peter to buy some tickets for the concert.

53.2
1. My parents expect me to keep my room clean.
2. Gus's boss allows him to finish early on Fridays.
3. Danny watched the children playing on the lawn.
4. Don reminded me to phone my grandmother.
5. The principal told us to walk more slowly.
6. I can imagine Katie becoming an actor one day.
7. Ravi spent his summer lying on the beach.
8. Eleanor wants her dog to be more friendly.
9. Mona asked me to buy some milk from the store.

54

54.1
1. Emma is talking **about** quitting her job.
2. Ania finally admitted **to** stealing the jewelry.
3. My dad tried to prevent me **from** studying art in college.
4. Our company believes **in** doing the best possible job.
5. Frank apologized **for** forgetting my birthday.
6. I want to ask my tutor **about** doing the exam again.
7. We congratulated Sandra **on** winning the competition.
8. Paul objected **to** Danny eating a burger in the office.
9. We decided **against** buying a house in the country.

10 We're all looking forward **to** visiting you soon.

11 I need to concentrate **on** passing all my exams this spring.

12 Peter is worrying **about** his interview tomorrow.

13 The council banned people **from** taking dogs onto the beach.

14 Chloe accused me **of** stealing her idea for the presentation.

15 Leo's parents tried to stop him **from** marrying the girl he loved.

55

55.1

1 It's taken me a long time to get over this cold.

2 Tony works out at the local gym each evening.

3 My mother takes care of my sons on Fridays.

4 We checked into the hotel and went to our room.

5 I've heard from Bill. He's got some shocking news.

6 I get along very well with my brother.

7 I meet up with my friends most weekends.

55.2

1 Jen and Hugo eat out very often.

2 You should try it on before buying it.

3 The music was loud so I turned it down.

4 I've always looked up to my brother.

5 We've run out of milk.

6 We checked into the hotel at noon.

7 Rob meets up with Nina on Fridays.

8 Does Pete always show up on time?

9 I was annoyed because he woke me up.

10 I'm staying in to watch the game tonight.

11 Sharon handed in her essay early.

12 The caterpillar turned into a butterfly.

13 It's heavy. Please help me pick it up.

55.3

1 Ramon is **getting over** the flu.

2 It was lovely **to hear from you**.

3 She told the children **to sit down**.

4 Here's your coat. **Put it on please**.

5 We need **to check into the hotel**.

6 I spotted a coin and **picked it up**.

7 Riku **gets up** at 9:30am on Saturdays.

8 The baby's crying. **You woke him up**.

9 I love cooking so I **don't eat out often**.

10 The café has **run out** of coffee.

11 Femi **grew up** in New York.

12 The airplane **takes off** in one hour.

55.4

1 I work out in the gym most evenings.

2 Camila really looks up to her English teacher.

3 Rachel takes after her father.

4 It's so hard to keep up with Libby.

5 We ran out of food so I made some more.

6 I didn't get on with my brother when we were young.

7 We got back from our trip to Wales on Thursday.

8 I usually get up later on the weekend.

9 My dad's car is always breaking down.

55.5

SEPARABLE:

turn on, throw away, fill up, wake up

INSEPARABLE:

do without, get through, go over, come across

55.6

1 A break on the coast sounds like the ideal **getaway**.

2 There has been another **outbreak** of the disease in the city.

3 The café was a **rip-off**! We paid $20 for a bowl of soup.

4 After the **downpour**, the sun came out again.

5 It's important to make a **backup** of any work you do.

6 There have been so many **dropouts** from the course this year.

7 All the students were given a **handout** with important information.

8 Following her **break-up** with Charlie, Ola was very unhappy.

9 We haven't had **snowfall** like this for years. There's snow and ice everywhere.

56

56.1

1 You should learn how to use a computer.

2 Could I have another piece of cake?

3 You must not run in the corridor.

4 My sister can speak four languages fluently.

5 Can I give you a hand with your shopping?

6 Could you lend me your pen for a moment?

7 That letter must be from Ken's college.

56.2

1 You mustn't be late for work again.

2 Can I get you a drink?

3 Can I help you with your bag?

56.3

1 Can I help you clean up?

2 Should Phil study math in college?

3 Can Graham play the violin?

4 Does Peter have to go to the meeting?

5 Can she have another chocolate?

6 Could Angela drive us to the party?

56.4

1 Leroy can't repair your oven.

2 My grandma couldn't speak Welsh.

3 You shouldn't eat more red meat.

4 Louisa can't swim well.

5 Students don't have to wear uniforms.

6 You can't have another piece of cake.

57

57.1

1 Jamie can't lift that box. I'll help him.

2 Emma can make beautiful dresses.

3 I can't solve this. It's too difficult.

4 Chris can repair your car.

5 I can't climb that mountain.

6 Rita can cook the most amazing dishes.

7 Chloe can speak three languages.

57.2

1 Jonathan can play the guitar.

2 We can't open the door.

3 Amy can sing really well.

4 Lizzie cannot drive a car.

5 Femi can climb trees.

6 Marion can speak five languages.

7 Derek can't move that piano.

57.3

1 My grandmother could **make wonderful cakes.**

2 I couldn't fix your phone. **You need a new one.**

3 When I was a child, **I could run much faster.**

4 Martha could play the piano **when she was four years old.**

5 I couldn't come to the party **because I felt ill.**

6 When she was six, **Jen could already speak six languages.**

57.4

1 I'll be able to speak it fluently by the summer.

2 I won't be able to take my flight without it.

3 In the future we'll be able to travel to other planets.

4 I'm hoping I will be able to fix it soon.

58

58.1

1 Formal

2 Informal

3 Formal

4 Informal

5 Formal

6 Formal

7 Informal

58.2

1 Request

2 Offer

3 Request

4 Offer

5 Request

6 Request

7 Offer

58.3

1 Can I take your coat?

2 May I take your order?

3 Shall I carry it for you?

58.4

1. **Could I sit** here, please?
2. **May I make** an appointment, please?
3. **Could I have** a piece of your pizza?
4. **Can I get** you something to drink?
5. **Can I have** the chicken and a salad, please?
6. **Could you tell** me the way to the museum?

59

59.1

1. You should take it out for a walk.
2. You should put on some sunscreen.
3. You should try talking to a native speaker.
4. He should join a club or take up a hobby.
5. She should try to relax before bed.
6. You could make a little card for her as a gift.
7. He should eat less cake and exercise more.
8. You should go home and get some sleep.
9. You should try to save money regularly.

59.2

1. It's going to rain. You **had better** take an umbrella.
2. The train's been cancelled. We **had better** take a taxi.
3. It's icy outside. You **had better not** drive tonight.
4. I'm late for the meeting. I **had better** call my boss.

59.3

1. If I were you I'd try jogging.
2. You really must visit the castle.
3. You ought to go to the barbershop.
4. He should get a cat. They're quite independent.
5. You could wear jeans and a shirt.

60

60.1

1. You have to go. It's about the new IT system.
2. You must call her right away!
3. You won't have to do any when the summer break comes!
4. In that case, you don't have to take your medication any longer.
5. The council must do something to stop people from littering.
6. I have to keep to the speed limit.
7. Yes, all our workers must wear a helmet at all times.
8. He had to go home because his daughter's unwell.
9. You must not lift anything heavy for two weeks.

60.2

1. I **don't have to** wear a suit for work, but I wear one anyway.
2. I'm staying in bed because I **don't have to** go to work today.
3. You **must not** stay in the sun too long. You'll get burned.
4. You **must not** touch that pan. It's hot.
5. You **don't have to** be great at tennis to enjoy it.
6. I have a secret, but you **must not** tell anyone else.

60.3

1. Everyone will have to leave before 5pm.
2. You will have to inform your manager.
3. Brenda will have to go home early today.
4. She will have to pay for the damage.

60.4

1. The managers had to apologize.
2. Greg had to eat all the broccoli.
3. Joe had to work very hard today.
4. I had to rest all this week.

61

61.1

1. It looks like Sam could win this race.
2. Look! Janet must have passed her driving test.
3. He can't be the plumber. He's wearing a suit.

61.2

1. Alina drank all the water. She **must** have been really thirsty.
2. I can't read this. I **might** need new glasses.
3. Ben **can't** have stolen the vase. He was with me all evening.
4. The journey home takes ages. The children **must** be so bored.
5. I can't find my wallet. I **must** have dropped it somewhere.

61.3

1. I can't find my purse. I **might have left it on** the bus.
2. I keep sneezing. I think I **might have a** cold.
3. Veronika is crying. She **must have failed** her test.
4. What's that animal with brown fur? It **could be a bear**.

61.4

1. That must be so interesting.
2. There might be a burglar downstairs.
3. It must have cost a lot of money.
4. She can't be feeling very happy.
5. You can't have followed the recipe properly.

62

62.1

1. It looks like my team **might win** tonight's game!
2. I **might take** some driving lessons if I can afford them.
3. I think the train **might have been** canceled.
4. I can't find my keys. I **might have left** them at work.
5. If you don't hurry you **might miss** the deadline!
6. I think we **might be** lost. We had better ask someone.
7. I **might not finish** the building by the end of the year.

62.2

1. I might have forgotten to turn off the iron.
2. The forecast said it might snow later.
3. Karl might not come to the party this evening.
4. Jon may have gone away for the weekend.

62.3

1. I might not be able to come to the movies.
2. I might go to the zoo next weekend.
3. Sue might be delayed because of the traffic.
4. It looks like it might rain later.

63

63.1

1. Russia is **a** huge country. It took me seven days to cross it by train.
2. While hiking in Scotland, I spotted **an** eagle soaring above us.
3. Bill took me on **a** date to **the** most expensive bar in town.
4. Where can you get **a** good cup of coffee in **the** evening?
5. **The** food in Italy was absolutely delicious.
6. When I was **a** child, I wanted to be **an** actor.
7. **The** first train to Madrid leaves at 4:30 from platform 4.
8. It's going to rain this evening. Don't forget to take **an** umbrella.
9. Do you live in **a** house or **an** apartment?
10. I saw **a** wolf and **a** bear in Canada. **The** bear was catching fish.
11. Neil Armstrong was **the** first man to set foot on **the** moon.
12. Last week, I went to see **a** show with my cousin.
13. My brother used to be **a** chef. He's **an** optician now.
14. While I was in Rome, I visited **the** Colosseum.
15. **The** cakes in that bakery are the best in town.
16. I had **a** cup of coffee and **a** croissant. **The** coffee was cold, though.
17. Is there **a** good hotel where I can stay in your town?
18. **The** book that I just finished was really interesting.

63.2

1. **There are some mugs** in the dishwasher.
2. I have **some pencils** here.
3. **There are some sandwiches** for you.
4. Mary has **some beautiful dresses**.
5. Hassan caught **some big fish**.
6. **There are some cafés** in town.
7. There **are some watches** on the counter.
8. Marco climbed **some high mountains**.
9. **There are some bags** in the kitchen.
10. **There are some people** running outside.
11. There **are some big hotels** by the shore.
12. Ola sang **some beautiful songs**.

63.3

1. Clara works in **an** office.
2. Do you have **any** brothers or sisters?
3. There are **some** banks on my street.
4. There aren't **any** cookies in the cupboard.
5. Is there **a** hospital near here?
6. We visited **an** interesting exhibition today.
7. Are there **any** good restaurants nearby?
8. London is **a** very big city.
9. Is there **a** swimming pool in your town?
10. There aren't **any** students in the classroom.
11. There are **some** nice cafés near my house.
12. I tasted **the** best pasta while I was on vacation.

63.4

1. The president is visiting the **north of the country next week.**
2. The rich always complain **that they don't earn enough.**
3. The buildings in the **capital are really beautiful.**
4. The coffee in this café **is the best in town.**
5. I had a great trip, but **the weather was disappointing.**
6. The press were waiting **outside the star's apartment.**

63.5

1. Children start school when they are seven in my country.
2. The children wanted to know the way to the school.
3. Bears often visit people's yards to look for food.
4. Residents were warned that there could be a flood soon.

63.6

1. My sister-in-law is a doctor at the local hospital.
2. The perfume you bought for your wife is in my bag.
3. Try not to get water all over the bathroom floor.
4. I'm going to climb the highest mountain in my country.
5. You really should go to bed. You're exhausted.
6. The food was excellent during our trip to Morocco.
7. The phone has been ringing all morning.
8. Is there a museum I can visit in your town?
9. I rode an elephant when I visited India last year.
10. You might see lions while you're on safari.
11. Christopher has a hot dog for lunch every day.
12. I ride my bike to the office each morning.
13. Only rich people can afford to go to that restaurant.

64

64.1

1. It's so warm outside. I'm going to invite **some** friends over for a barbecue.
2. **The** new secretary seems good but doesn't have much experience.
3. I read **some** really good books during my last vacation.
4. What happened in **the** kitchen? It's such a mess.
5. **The** shirt Liam bought for **the** party cost more than $80.
6. My cousin has **a** really friendly dog.
7. While walking in the park, I spotted **a** rare bird.
8. I have **a** lot of friends who still live with their parents.
9. Paula has left **some** money on **the** kitchen table for you.
10. I think Brazil would be **a** fascinating country to visit.
11. I've just baked **some** cupcakes. Would you like to try one?
12. **The** cake you made for the fair was absolutely delicious.
13. My family's big. I have three brothers and **a** sister.
14. The blue whale is **the** biggest animal that has ever existed.
15. I asked **the** waiter for **a** large cup of coffee.
16. **The** saxophone is **a** difficult instrument to play.
17. India is **the** country I'd most like to visit.
18. We saw **a** bear on our trip through **the** mountains.

64.2

1. I don't go to work on Fridays. I look after my young son.
2. My son rides **a** bike to school each day.
3. In my country, people usually retire when they're about 60.
4. Colm works as **a** scientist at a large research centre.
5. You should make sure you get plenty of sleep before **the** exam tomorrow.
6. Irma buys her paint from the store by **the** café.
7. Bill got married to **a** woman he met at work.
8. **The** band I went to see last night was awful.
9. I'm still in touch with the friends I made while on vacation.
10. My aunt thought she saw **a** wolf in the woods today.
11. **The** shoes I bought yesterday are far too big.
12. My mom says that cats are much cleaner than dogs.
13. While I was traveling in Australia, I saw **a** kangaroo.
14. **The** president gave **a** long speech at the conference.

65

65.1

1. **This** is my new boyfriend, Dan.
2. **That** book is so interesting.
3. **That** was such a tasty pizza!
4. I'd like **those** grapes, please.
5. Do you like **this** shirt?
6. I want to see **that** movie tonight.
7. **These** are your glasses, right here.
8. Where did you buy **those** jeans?
9. Is **this** my cup of coffee?
10. **Those** shoes look great on you!
11. **This** is the perfect car for a family.
12. Is **that** your new motorcycle, Andy?
13. Who made **these** cakes?
14. **These** are my parents, Anna and Charles.
15. **This** wardrobe's so heavy!

65.2

1. That is my new house. It's just by the ocean.
2. This is your desk and computer.
3. That was an amazing goal. You should have seen it!

65.3

1. Those boots really suit you.
2. This is one of the best books I've read.
3. I'm sure I've seen this movie before.
4. I don't think this meat is cooked properly.

65.4

1. That is one of the most beautiful **castles that I've ever seen.**
2. I'll have a half kilo of those potatoes **and a bag of these apricots, please.**
3. Your most important role is **that of spokesperson for our company.**
4. The cars we drive today are safer **than those our parents used to drive.**
5. I like these jeans here, but I prefer **those with the stripe on them over there.**
6. This is the best coffee I've **ever had. It's absolutely delicious.**

66

66.1

1. We had no time to make lunch, so we went out for burgers instead.
2. I've missed the train again. I'm having no luck this week!
3. None of the clothes I tried on suited me.
4. We wanted a room with a view, but the receptionist said that there were none available.
5. I couldn't call you because there was no reception where I was.
6. I wanted to order apple pie, but there was none left.
7. None of my friends believed I saw a ghost.

66.2

1. There **aren't any** free seats.
2. I **have no** money left.
3. There **weren't any** more tickets.
4. Kinga **doesn't have any** friends at work.
5. It **takes no** time to get there.
6. There **was no** doubt that he did it.

66.3

1. **No** vegetarian food had been ordered for the convention.
2. There are **no** places left on the English course.
3. **None** of the staff wanted to work on Saturdays.
4. Amelia wanted to buy salad, but there wasn't **any** in the shop.
5. There was **no** time to think about the exam questions.
6. I called five hotels, but **none** had a free room for tonight.

7 There wasn't **any** milk left, so I went to the shops.
8 I had **no** energy left after work, so I watched some TV.
9 **None** of my friends wanted to go see a movie with me.
10 There weren't **any** seats free on the train home.
11 I wanted to try one of Sarah's cakes, but there were **none** left.
12 **No** dentists were available to see me, so I went home.

67

67.1
1 David and his wife visit the Poconos every March.
2 I go to the Indian restaurant in town every Monday.
3 Each of us was given a sandwich and a drink.
4 Every morning, Luis buys a coffee before work.
5 This shampoo works for every type of hair.
6 Each member of the team was given a prize.
7 Maddy gave each of her children a thousand dollars.

67.2
1 I go hiking with my dog every summer.
2 Mona has a different type of earring in each ear.
3 Our boss spoke to each employee in turn about the redundancies.
4 Each player was given a medal by the president.

67.3
1 Our manager has spoken to **each employee about the factory closing.**
2 We gave every child at the party **a present and some cake.**
3 My sister loves jewelry and **wears a bracelet on each wrist.**
4 Every Thursday, I play golf **with one of my work colleagues.**
5 Oscar makes sure he does **some exercise every morning.**
6 The bakery near my house sells **every kind of bread you can think of.**
7 Each city we visited in Spain **had incredibly beautiful architecture.**
8 Every time I hear that song, I **remember the first time I heard it.**
9 I love that author. I've read **every one of her books.**

68

68.1
1 **Neither** Dan nor Belinda could remember the way to the theater.
2 **Both** of my brothers go hiking in the hills on the weekend.
3 **Neither** of us could resist another piece of cake.
4 Janet could afford to buy **either** the skirt or the dress.

5 I invited **both** Sheila and Bill to my apartment in Paris.
6 **Both** Steve and Louis work really hard in their English class.
7 Let's eat out **either** on Wednesday or Thursday.
8 **Neither** of the managers were at the meeting, unfortunately.
9 I had to take **both** the cat and the dog to the veterinarian.
10 Ramon can play **both** the electric and acoustic guitar.
11 Chetana didn't really like **either** of the paintings on sale.

68.2
1 Neither Gabriela nor Carlos came **to the party last night.**
2 My niece wants to be either an **actress or an accountant.**
3 Lisa wants both a puppy **and a laptop for her birthday.**
4 Neither the apple pie nor **the cheesecake appealed to my aunt.**
5 I want to see either an action film **or a comedy tonight.**
6 Both my brother and sister **still live with our parents.**
7 Neither the electricity nor the water **works properly in my new house.**

68.3
1 Either my cousin or my parents **are** going to pick you up from the airport.
2 Neither Paula's car nor her bike **is** working properly.
3 I hope either the steak or the fish **is** on the menu today.
4 Both the food and the drink **were** really overpriced.
5 Neither my brother nor my sister **is** coming tomorrow.
6 Either a cat or a dog **makes** a great pet for a family.
7 Neither of us **wants** to go to the conference.
8 I don't really like either of the **dresses** she bought.
9 Neither the boss nor the workers **were** pleased about the deal.
10 We're thinking about adopting both of the **puppies** we saw.

69

69.1
1 car
2 castle
3 chess
4 thought
5 waterfall

69.2
COMMON NOUNS:
town, flower, hope, scissors
PROPER NOUNS:
France, September, George, Jupiter

69.3
1 When I finished my dinner, I washed all the **dishes**.
2 I bought my new **watch** in Switzerland.
3 A lot of **people** were waiting on the platform.
4 We need to protect endangered **species**.

69.4
1 Tim asked to borrow the **dictionary**.
2 The **trains** always **leave** on time.
3 The **women were** talking about the past.
4 The mayor visited the **factory** in our city.
5 I think there **is a mouse** in the kitchen.
6 **Those stories were** wonderful.
7 The **sheep was** standing in the road.
8 The **boxes are** full. We need to buy more.
9 Carla rested her **foot** on a cushion.
10 Ellie asked the **man** for directions.
11 Maria put her **babies** into the **cots**.

70

70.1
COUNTABLE:
question, apple, city
UNCOUNTABLE:
sugar, knowledge, money

70.2
1 Is there a bag of rice in the pantry?
2 Can you get a carton of juice?
3 Would you like a piece of cheese?

70.3
1 **There's some** milk in the fridge.
2 I **didn't buy any** eggs at the store.
3 We **didn't see any** bears in the mountains.
4 **There's some** juice left.
5 I **got some** gifts for my birthday.
6 I **don't have any** fruit in my bag.
7 We **have some** important information.
8 There **isn't any** rice in the cupboard.
9 I **have some** money saved for the vacation.

70.4
1 How much meat is there?
2 How many cups of tea are there?
3 How much coffee have you made?
4 How many bars of chocolate do we have?
5 How many jars of jam are there?
6 How much juice will we need?
7 How much milk is there?
8 How many bowls of cereal are there?
9 How many bananas do you have?
10 How many bags of flour did you buy?
11 How many cartons of milk are there?

71

71.1
1. Athletics **consists of a number of sports**, such as running and the high jump.
2. I think the news **is really boring**, but my parents always watch it.
3. The United States **has a population** of more than 300 million people.
4. Measles **is an illness** that usually affects children rather than adults.
5. *The Adventures of Sherlock Holmes* **is my favorite book**. I read it every summer.

71.2
1. The Netherlands **is** one of the world's biggest exporters of fresh flowers.
2. Gymnastics **wasn't** my first choice of sport.
3. *The Three Musketeers* **has** remained a popular novel since its publication in 1844.
4. Mathematics **was** my favorite subject when I was at school.

71.3
1. My family usually gets together each Christmas.
2. The company have hired a couple of new managers.
3. The government is refusing to reveal any details.
4. All the staff are going out for a meal after work.

72

72.1
1. Pablo has so many qualifications, **but he has almost no experience.**
2. We had quite a bit of difficulty finding **our way to the right block.**
3. Chiara has great ideas, **but not enough money to develop them.**
4. Don's had plenty of success, **and he's won three awards this year.**

72.2
CONCRETE:
pencil, **car**, **tree**, **table**
ABSTRACT:
happiness, **love**, **time**, **belief**

72.3
1. I met people from many different **cultures** at college.
2. After a lot of **thought**, I've decided to quit my job.
3. Being able to play an instrument is a great **skill** to have.
4. I've visited the museum a few **times** this year.
5. Don't give up **hope**! Your team might win.
6. I have a terrible **memory** for people's names.
7. It takes a lot of **time** to learn a foreign language.
8. Venice is famous for its **culture** and history.
9. Trisha loves to share her **memories** of the past.

10. There's a lot of **space** in my new apartment.
11. My uncle is always driving everywhere at high **speed**.
12. I made some lasting **friendships** while traveling.
13. There isn't enough **time** to finish the project.

73

73.1
1. During the heat wave, we kept the air-conditioning switched on all day.
2. My mother-in-law had her birthday party in the town hall.
3. I went to pick up my theater tickets from the ticket office.
4. Sally had a terrible headache, so she asked her boyfriend to get her some painkillers.
5. Marc looked at the night sky as he relaxed on his camping trip.
6. Alberto stood at the front door with his suitcase, waiting for the taxi.
7. As Ellie felt the first raindrops fall, she regretted not bringing a raincoat.

73.2
1. We've been waiting at this **bus stop** for an hour.
2. Graham cleans his **bathroom** on Saturday morning.
3. I like your new **haircut**, Ed. It looks great.
4. My **sister-in-law** works in the main hospital.
5. You'll need a **bottle opener** for those drinks.

73.3
1. The police are investigating the break-in at the bookstore.
2. The teapot fell onto the kitchen floor.
3. I bought some toothpaste at the drugstore.
4. I got up at sunrise and had a bowl of breakfast cereal.
5. Darren bought a birthday card for his son.

74

74.1
1. cardinal
2. ordinal
3. cardinal
4. cardinal
5. ordinal
6. ordinal
7. cardinal

74.2
1. nine thousand
2. 848
3. 417
4. six thousand, five hundred
5. nine hundred and fifty-eight
6. 97
7. three thousand, five hundred and ninety
8. three hundred and fifty-nine

74.3
1. six million, eight hundred and forty thousand, two hundred and fifty
2. fourteen million, two hundred and twenty thousand, nine hundred and two
3. ninety million, three hundred and ten thousand

74.4
1. twelve point five
2. twenty-seven point five percent
3. two-thirds
4. thirty-two percent
5. six and three-quarters
6. fourteen point nine five
7. nineteen percent
8. two-fifths
9. six point three four
10. eight and a third
11. seventy-nine point four percent
12. eight and a half

75

75.1
1. **Lots of students** also have a part-time job.
2. Only **a few of my friends** came to my barbecue on Saturday.
3. There are **some good bands** performing tonight.
4. I sent **a few postcards** while I was traveling.
5. There is **lots of juice** in the fridge if you want some.

75.2
1. There **isn't** enough sugar to make a birthday cake.
2. The burger costs six euros? I'm afraid that's **too much**.
3. Do we have **enough** money to buy a car?
4. There are **too many** people on the bus this morning.
5. There **isn't enough** chicken to make dinner for everyone.
6. I bought **too much** fruit. Please take some!
7. **Is** there enough orange juice in the fridge for breakfast?
8. There are only two seats left. There are **too many** of us here.

75.3
1. **A lot of** people visit the mountains on the weekend.
2. I'm not rich, but I try to donate **a little** money to charity every month.
3. Sadly, there are **few** Sumatran tigers left in the world today.
4. I met **quite a few** new clients at the conference.
5. I have **little** patience for people who are always late. I'm always on time!
6. There's **quite a bit of** snow. Let's build a snowman!
7. **Lots of** people came to Craig's 40th birthday party.
8. Do you need some help with that report? I have **a little time** I can spare.
9. Be careful! That vase is worth quite **a bit of** money.

⑩ There are **a few** paintings in the museum I haven't seen. Can we stay a bit longer?
⑪ There are very **few** people I would lend money to, but my brother is one of them.
⑫ I don't have lots of friends, but I've got **a few** who I'm really close to.

75.4

① I spent **less** time on this essay than I did last time.
② The lecture was almost empty. There were **fewer** than 10 students there.
③ I'm earning **less** money with my new job, but the conditions are better.
④ **Fewer** people eat meat today in comparison with a decade ago.
⑤ The train leaves in **less** than half an hour. We should hurry!
⑥ There was much **less** traffic than usual on the way to work.
⑦ There are **fewer** than 5,000 black rhinos left in the wild.
⑧ **Fewer** young people are studying languages than in the past.
⑨ It's **less** than 10 minutes' walk to the historic part of the city.

75.5

① We didn't go shopping because we didn't have enough money.
② The weather was awful, but at least I made a few friends there.
③ There is much less traffic in the city than 15 years ago.
④ A male African elephant can weigh more than seven tons.
⑤ I received a lot of presents for my 30th birthday.

75.6

① Marco was making **far too much noise**, so Ellie went out to the café.
② I'm afraid it's bad news. Our company is making **less money than** it did last year.
③ Unfortunately **very little** can be done about the bad weather.
④ Do we have **enough pasta** to make lunch for all the family?
⑤ We have **lots of things** to pack. Do you think there's room in the box?
⑥ **Few people** come to the restaurant on a Monday evening. It's almost empty.
⑦ There are **quite a few sandwiches** left. Help yourself to one!
⑧ There was a **lot of people** waiting on the platform for the train.
⑨ There were **quite a few clothes** I liked, but I didn't buy any.
⑩ **Fewer than 10 people** work for our company. It's very cozy here.
⑪ The safari park costs **less than $5** to visit. It's a real bargain.
⑫ We have **quite a bit of time** before we need to leave.

76.1

① Almost all our customers are happy with the service they receive.
② About half of the students failed the exam this year.
③ Just under a third of all people own a cat in my country.

76.2

① There are as many as two exams **each month on my college course.**
② Well over half of the country **consists of mountains and forests.**
③ Almost none of the money is left **following the expensive carnival.**
④ Approximately 75% of Earth's **surface is covered in water.**
⑤ As many as 7 out of 10 people **can speak a second language.**

76.3

① You could be fluent in English in as little as two months.
② In most cases, people recover quickly from food poisoning.
③ The children have eaten almost all the cakes.
④ About half the students failed the final exam.
⑤ As few as one in ten applications are successful.
⑥ Well over three-quarters of students use social media.
⑦ In a minority of cases, people go to prison.
⑧ There are as many as 25 public parks in my city.
⑨ My house is just under a mile away from the station.

77.1

① us
② you
③ him
④ she
⑤ it
⑥ they

77.2

① Kelly's so angry with him.
② Paula asked me to marry her.
③ Do you know what happened to them?
④ Mike gave her the money.

77.3

① They went to the same music festival as last year.
② I play soccer with my friends every weekend.
③ We visited Venice for our 20th wedding anniversary.

77.4

① She saw him working in a shop in Edinburgh.
② He gave us a ride to the movie theater.
③ He offered her a flower.

77.5

① Jane cooked a new dish, but **it** tasted awful. **She** was so disappointed.
② Tom asked Roger to water the plants. **He** watered **them** and went home.
③ The commuters waited for the train. **They** were angry because **it** was delayed.
④ Mike told his parents he wanted to study drama. **They** replied that **it** was a great choice.
⑤ Shona bought a coffee for Brian. **He** thanked **her** for **it**.

78.1

① yourself
② yourselves
③ him
④ her
⑤ itself
⑥ ourselves
⑦ them

78.2

① I asked **myself** if I should leave my job.
② You should pride **yourself** on your work, Phil.
③ Did Daniel injure **himself** when he fell off the wall?
④ Ed and Flora are teaching **themselves** to cook.
⑤ Sarah is preparing **herself** for the interview.
⑥ Did you and Claire enjoy **yourselves** at the party?

78.3

① Tim **shaves** when he gets up in the morning.
② Angela **cut herself** while she was chopping the onions.
③ The door **opened**, and my uncle walked into the room.
④ Chan **hurt himself** when he slipped on the ice.
⑤ Janet **feels** better after her illness.

78.4

① I baked the cake myself. I hope you like it.
② Most stores close at 5pm in my town.
③ Did the children behave themselves during the class?
④ Annie asked Peter and me to move the boxes.
⑤ The child sat by himself reading a book.
⑥ How was the party? Did you enjoy yourselves?
⑦ We were talking to each other when the phone rang.

78.5

① My wife is going to paint the house herself.
② Carlos admired himself in the mirror before leaving.
③ The CEO herself offered to help clean the office.
④ I enjoyed the evening, but the movie itself was bad.

78.6

① My grandpa is a carpenter and **built this table himself.**
② My cats hate each other **and fight almost every day.**
③ Betty is very selfish and **only thinks about herself.**
④ My sister and I call each other **every day to share the latest gossip.**
⑤ The children played in the park, **throwing snowballs at one another.**
⑥ Lee and Ben are helping **each other with their homework.**

78.7

① Sharon is teaching **herself** how to knit.
② It's hard to tear **yourself** away from a really good book.
③ Martin shaves each morning when he gets up.
④ I made some tea while the cake baked in the oven.
⑤ We found **ourselves** in a strange part of town. We were lost.
⑥ My grandparents have convinced **themselves** to go swimming each day.
⑦ How was the fair? Did the children enjoy **themselves** there?
⑧ The truck started to reverse, so we moved out of the way.
⑨ I'm familiarizing **myself** with the new software.
⑩ Jim and Ula are decorating their new house **themselves.** It's so much cheaper.
⑪ My arm really hurts. I hope I haven't broken it.
⑫ Our café prides **itself** on its excellent service.
⑬ I find it so hard to concentrate with all that noise.
⑭ It looks like the weather is improving. Let's go out.

79

79.1

① What would you prefer? Tea or coffee?
② There's a meeting in room 10.
③ I'm not feeling very well at all.
④ It was nothing. Probably just the cat playing.
⑤ Yes, it's half past five
⑥ Of course. Pass it here.
⑦ No one's heard of him, sorry.

79.2

① Everyone's asking why you're not at the party!
② Did you buy anything when you were at the grocer's?
③ I was exhausted after checking everything.

79.3

① I know absolutley **nothing** about electronics.
② Libby doesn't want **anything** to eat at the moment.
③ I don't get on with my brother. We have **nothing** in common.
④ I didn't buy **anything** while I was at the store.
⑤ There's **nothing** to do here. I'm bored!
⑥ I think I just heard **something** downstairs.

80

80.1

① **you** your **yours**
② he **his his**
③ **she her** hers
④ **it** its **its**
⑤ we **our ours**
⑥ **they their** theirs

80.2

① I saw the children playing with their dog.
② You look very excited with your new present.
③ There's Silvia taking her dogs for a walk.

80.3

① Where is their house?
② This desk is yours.
③ Is that my charger there?
④ These books aren't theirs.
⑤ That is her coat.
⑥ Are these his glasses?
⑦ Which of these cups is mine?

80.4

① **Their** IT system is modern, but **ours** needs replacing soon.
② These earrings are **mine**, but that bracelet is **hers**.
③ **My** bag is the yellow one. Which one is **yours**?
④ The large boxes are **theirs**, but these small ones are **ours**.
⑤ **Her** parents live in the countryside, while **mine** live in the city.
⑥ If this is **yours**, then I don't know which laptop is **mine**.
⑦ Stacey put **her** lunch in the fridge. Are these sandwiches **yours**?
⑧ Katya parked **her** car by the park. Where did your parents park **theirs**?
⑨ We drive **our** cars on the right, whereas they drive **theirs** on the left.
⑩ **Your** father drives a sports car, but **mine** rides a bike.

80.5

① Mary and Don's uncle
② Ben's son
③ The students' grades
④ Sam and Ayshah's cat
⑤ Debbie's house
⑥ My parents' dog
⑦ Marco and Kate's car
⑧ My grandparents' house
⑨ Elsa's grandchild
⑩ Beth's parrot
⑪ The people's choice

80.6

① The women's clothes are downstairs.
② Pick the babies' toys up, please.
③ Your car's new, while mine is old.
④ That book is yours, and this one is mine!
⑤ Tom's computer is slow.
⑥ Hurry up! It's time you left for work.
⑦ My town is bigger than yours.
⑧ The children's food is here.
⑨ That bag over there is yours.
⑩ These are the ladies' coats.
⑪ My parents' house is small.
⑫ The men's changing room is there.
⑬ The dog can't find its home.

80.7

① I don't have any money **left to go on vacation this year.**
② The nearest town has a swimming pool **and a bowling alley.**
③ Have you got any free time **to help me with this project?**
④ My dad hasn't got a phone or **an email account.**
⑤ My wife's from a big family and has **two brothers and two sisters.**
⑥ Has your brother got **red hair and a long beard?**
⑦ I'm very worried that my son **doesn't have any friends at college.**

80.8

① Yes, I do. How can I help?
② No, she hasn't. Why do you ask?
③ Yes, I do. It's in my bag.
④ No, we don't. There's one tomorrow.
⑤ Yes, it has. There are two lines.

81

81.1

① I met a man who has sailed around the world.
② The book that you lent me was really exciting.
③ The dessert that Misha ordered looks delicious.
④ Laura invited some people who she knows from college.
⑤ The palace that I was hoping to visit was closed.
⑥ Sanjay is moving to a house that is close to the sea.
⑦ I loved the band which performed on stage.

81.2

① My son has a camera which takes wonderful photos.
② The milk that you bought yesterday has turned sour.
③ The woman who was just speaking to you is incredibly rich.
④ Where did you get the hat you're wearing?

81.3

1. Ben works for a company **which produces kitchen equipment.**
2. Do you like the shirt **that I bought at the market today?**
3. Fatima showed me the dog **that she wants to adopt.**
4. Betty is playing a woman **who dreams of becoming an astronaut.**
5. This is the villa **which we're planning to buy.**
6. There are only two stores **that sell that particular part.**
7. My dad studied with the woman **who lives over the road.**
8. Does Mira have an umbrella **that she could lend me?**

82

82.1

1. Den has a new sports car, which he spent all his savings on.
2. The Statue of Liberty, which is on a small island, is popular with tourists.
3. Sam has a lovely dog, which he takes for a walk each morning.

82.2

1. My new sweater, **which is** made of wool, cost $40.
2. I teach many international students, many of **whom** are Indian.
3. David's cat, **which is** usually very calm, just scratched me!
4. My wife, **who** is an optician, enjoys her job very much.
5. He has two daughters, both of **whom** are lawyers.

82.3

1. I've recently bought a house, which I'm now decorating.
2. My nephew, who is only seven years old, is learning to play the violin.
3. The singer thanked her fans, many of whom were at the event.
4. My car, which I only bought last week, has already broken down.
5. Jill, who has worked here for 15 years, is extremely reliable.

82.4

1. Defining
2. Non-defining
3. Non-defining
4. Defining

83

83.1

1. I'll never forget that afternoon **when** Paula told me she wanted to move to another country.
2. Jane, **whose** sister you work with, is giving the speech this afternoon.
3. A long break and some sunshine is exactly **what** Kelly needs right now.
4. Toni's café, **where** you worked as a student, has closed down.
5. I'm interviewing a woman **whose** brother used to work here.
6. I'm looking forward to a time **when** we don't have to work so late.
7. That sofa is just **what** we need for the living room.
8. The companies have an agreement **whereby** they share customer data.

83.2

1. I thought it was Monday **when** Manuela was supposed to come.
2. I have no idea **what** he's bought me for my birthday.
3. We visited the part of India **where** my parents grew up.
4. Liam, **whose** report you've just read, is an excellent lawyer.
5. Stratford-upon-Avon, **where** Shakespeare was born, is lovely.

83.3

1. In 2008, when I got my first job here, I worked in the warehouse.
2. This is Miguel, whose sister works in the HR department.
3. I'm not sure what this is, but I know I like it.
4. I've already broken the phone that I bought last week.

83.4

1. 2013 was the year **when I decided to study art.**
2. This is the store **where we buy our groceries.**
3. That singer, **whose songs Jane loves**, is performing tonight.
4. This dress is exactly **what I need for Abigail's party.**

84

84.1

1. I want to finish this puzzle, **however long it takes.**
2. Catrina said she'd support me, **whichever decision I make.**
3. You can wear whatever you like **for John's birthday dinner tonight.**
4. Tony tries to visit his parents **whenever he gets the chance.**
5. Whoever was in the kitchen last **has left a terrible mess.**

84.2

1. **Whatever** did Jon do to make you so angry with him?
2. We're going to be late, **whichever** route we take.
3. Elsie told me that she'd be there to help **whenever** I needed her.
4. The engagement's not a secret. You can tell **whoever** you want.
5. **Whoever** won first prize must be a really good artist.
6. **Whenever** I hear that music, I always think of Paris.
7. My new kitten follows me **wherever** I go in the house.

84.3

1. I'm going to study drama, **whatever** my parents say.
2. John's in front of the TV **whenever** I go to see him.
3. **Wherever** Andy's gone, he's forgotten his wallet.
4. **Whoever** painted this clearly has a vivid imagination.
5. I do some gardening **whenever** I have a spare moment.
6. **Whichever** student answers this question will win a prize.
7. I'm going to finish this novel, **however** long it takes!
8. **Whatever** it is John's cooked, it tastes absolutely terrible.
9. **However** much Anthony earns, he always wants more.

85

85.1

1. There was such a mess after the party.
2. There's been an explosion at the laboratory.
3. There's going to be a jazz band at the concert hall tonight.
4. There are some lovely hats for sale in that store.
5. There was some awful pollution on the beach.
6. I'm afraid there isn't any chocolate cake left.

85.2

1. There **is** still some milk in the fridge.
2. There **were** huge crowds yesterday.
3. There **hasn't been** an inspection so far.
4. There **aren't** any cakes left, sorry.
5. There **was** a storm last night.
6. There **will be** a presentation tomorrow.
7. There **is** a heatwave at the moment.
8. There **have been** no thefts since June.
9. There **will be** rain later today.

85.3

1. There have been a lot of complaints **about the poor service at the restaurant.**
2. There will be a meeting to **discuss the forthcoming redundancies.**
3. There's going to be a party **to celebrate our silver wedding anniversary.**

④ There weren't many **cars in my village when I was a child.**

⑤ There are not enough **seats for all the people here.**

85.4

① There **were** a lot of visitors at yesterday's exhibition.

② There **aren't** any tickets for the show this evening.

③ There **is** a lot of sugar in the recipe for Cathy's cake.

④ **Is there** a party to celebrate Olive's 90th birthday tomorrow?

⑤ There **is** going to be a soccer match this afternoon.

⑥ **Was** there enough room for all the guests?

⑦ Do you know if there **is** another train tonight?

⑧ There **has been** some terrible weather recently.

⑨ There **weren't** many students at the lecture.

⑩ Bill's so busy at work. There **is** a deadline soon.

⑪ There **is** water all over the floor. What happened?

⑫ I'm sure there **won't be** another unexpected election this year.

85.5

① There's plenty of food in the fridge.

② There is a large dog in the street.

③ Are there any good cafés in your town?

④ There are a lot of people selling fruit and vegetables.

⑤ There won't be another bus today.

⑥ Do you know if there is any rice left?

⑦ There are lots of people waiting outside.

⑧ Will there be an exam at the end of the course?

⑨ Is there going to be a meeting this afternoon?

86

86.1

① Awful! It's pouring.

② It was in 1564, I think.

③ It's quarter to three.

④ No, it's just a five-minute walk.

86.2

① Distance

② Day / Date / Month / Year

③ Weather

④ Time

86.3

① It is essential that all candidates **arrive 15 minutes before the interview.**

② It's often said that **absence makes the heart grow fonder.**

③ If you don't start working harder, **it's unlikely you'll pass the exam.**

④ It was so nice to meet **you and your husband at the party.**

⑤ It is difficult for foreigners to **pronounce some words in my language.**

⑥ It is dangerous to drive **too fast on the highway.**

⑦ It would be great if **we could meet for coffee next weekend.**

⑧ It's been impossible for me **to find a free moment to call you.**

⑨ It's such a shame that it **rained every day on our vacation.**

⑩ It was a surprise to discover **that we share the same birthday.**

⑪ It is wonderful to lie in a field **and look up at the stars.**

⑫ It's been 40 minutes. It looks **like the bus isn't coming.**

86.4

① It is true **that** being a doctor involves a lot of hard work.

② It is important **to** lock all the doors when you go out.

③ It is useful **to** write down important information in a notebook.

④ It is possible **that** Andre forgot that the party is tonight.

87

87.1

① It's honey, not sugar, that **you should add to the cake.**

② It was the manager, not the intern, **who broke the photocopier.**

③ It was Neil Armstrong, not Buzz Aldrin, **who first walked on the moon.**

④ It was Poland that I visited, **not Germany.**

⑤ It's on Tuesday that we're meeting, **not Thursday.**

⑥ It was James, not John, who **I saw at the theater.**

87.2

① What I really hate is people singing out of tune.

② What Karen needs is to get more sleep.

③ What I enjoyed most were the fascinating ruins.

87.3

① **The person** I admire most in the world is my grandfather.

② **The one thing** I'll never forget is when I won the national prize.

③ **The reason** they gave for firing me was ridiculous.

④ **The country** I loved visiting most was Montenegro.

⑤ **The subject** I enjoyed most at school was history.

87.4

① It's the location that I like most about my home.

② What I want to do is travel around the world.

③ The animal I'd like to see while on safari is the tiger.

④ What Dave disliked most was the bad acting.

⑤ It was my neighbor who told me about the flood.

88

88.1

① Hardly had it stopped raining when the children ran out to play.

② Only after my departure did I realize that I had forgotten to say goodbye.

③ No sooner had I arrived at the airport than I decided I wasn't going to leave the country.

④ Never before have we achieved such amazing results.

⑤ Little did we know that the boy would one day become president.

⑥ Rarely have I had such a positive response to a proposal.

⑦ Only when I opened the letter did I realize that I was going to college.

88.2

① **Not since the 1980s have I known such** a hot summer.

② **Only sometimes do you witness such** kindness from strangers.

③ **No sooner had we finished the project** than the next one began.

④ **Little did they suspect how expensive** the vacation would be.

88.3

① Neither do I!   ② So am I.   ③ So do I.

89

89.1

① Ella woke up before dawn and **made herself a strong cup of coffee.**

② I need to tell my parents I'm leaving college, **but I'm not sure how.**

③ We need to hire a new mechanic **but don't know where to find one.**

④ I'd like to cook something special **for dinner, but I can't decide what.**

⑤ I hope Jamie comes to the wedding, **but I don't think he will.**

⑥ Someone with real talent painted **this, but we don't know who.**

89.2

① Neither of them, to be honest.

② At the market on Church Road.

③ A bit tough, actually.

④ Monday morning, 9am.

89.3

① I asked Charlie to stop playing soccer, but he didn't.

② I'm trying to make an omelet, but I don't know how.

③ I want to move to a new area, but I don't know where.

④ I really enjoy skiing, but my brother doesn't.

⑤ Someone's left a present, but I'm not sure who.

6 I want to buy one of these laptops, but I'm not sure which.
7 Catalina said she'd come to the party, but I don't think she will.
8 There is a museum somewhere, but I'm not sure where.
9 I tried to lift the box, but I wasn't strong enough.
10 My wife can swim really well, but I can't.
11 I want to study something at college, but I'm not sure what.
12 Anne and Si passed the exam, but Matt didn't.

90

90.1
1 There are fewer factories here than there used to be.
2 I was going to buy some shoes but couldn't afford to.
3 I tried to fix the bathtub but wasn't able to.

90.2
1 There aren't as many cars on the streets **as there used to be.**
2 I meant to call my grandma on her birthday, **but I completely forgot to.**
3 Sean could have studied at Oxford University, **but he chose not to.**
4 Liz hasn't completed as much work **as she intended to.**
5 I've eaten much more cake **than I meant to.**

90.3
1 He didn't want to.
2 Yes, she's determined to.
3 Yes, she seemed to be.
4 That's right. He promised.
5 There's no need to be.

90.4
1 This software is more complicated than it needs to be.
2 Mia didn't come to the party even though she promised.
3 I'd love to try hang gliding, but I don't have the courage.

90.5
1 Maurice wasn't at the convention, even though he had hoped to be.
2 I was thinking of studying French at college but decided not to.
3 Shelly isn't at school today, but she ought to be.
4 I wasn't able to go on the trip, but I did want to.
5 The dish isn't vegetarian, even though it's supposed to be.

90.6
1 Lisa invited me to visit Spain, and I told her I'd love to.
2 We asked Mario to play golf with us, but he didn't want to.
3 I wanted to see you this summer, but I won't be able to.

4 We can alter the dress for you. Would you like us to?
5 I've never seen the Great Wall of China, but I'd love the chance to.
6 Gerard doesn't have a motorcycle now, but he used to.
7 Mary was going to buy a dog, but she decided not to.
8 I dream of buying that apartment, but I can't afford to.

91

91.1
1 There aren't any cafés here, but **there are some nice ones by the park.**
2 The computers at work are much **slower than the ones in my old office.**
3 If you need to borrow a raincoat, **you can take one of mine.**
4 I don't own a drill, I'm afraid, **but my brother-in-law does.**

91.2
1 Cathy refuses to get a phone, though her boyfriend **has got one.**
2 I really don't like this sofa, but I **like the red one** over there.
3 There isn't any juice left, but I think **there's some** in the fridge.
4 I love your boots. I saw **some similar ones** in the boutique by the park.
5 I liked the look of the cakes in the bakery, so I **bought some.**

91.3
1 My car is ruined. I need to buy a new one.
2 We don't like fishing, but our dad does.
3 We'd like a dessert. Could you recommend one?
4 I really like cooking, and so does my husband.
5 If that dress is too expensive, we have cheaper ones, too.
6 Zhao liked the artwork, but I didn't.
7 I own few books myself, but there are lots at the library.
8 That looks delicious. Can I try some?

91.4
1 We'd prefer it if you did.
2 I don't think so, sorry.
3 I'm afraid I don't.
4 I hope so.
5 I'm afraid not.
6 I did it this morning.

92

92.1
1 My boyfriend gave me a **beautiful gold** necklace for my birthday.
2 My grandma's knitting me a **dark-green woolen** sweater.

3 We went to see the **ancient Aztec** ruins while in Mexico.
4 We adopted a **cute friendly** kitten from the shelter.

92.2
SIZE:
little, tiny, massive
SHAPE:
diamond-shaped, round, square
AGE:
young, ancient, old
COLOR:
pink, light-blue, red
NATIONALITY:
Argentinian, Vietnamese, French
MATERIAL:
china, cotton, steel

92.3
GENERAL OPINION:
awful, good, nasty, wonderful,
SPECIFIC OPINION:
clever, friendly, delicious, beautiful

92.4
1 I read this exciting new French novel while on vacation.
2 That small old brown dog belongs to Harry.
3 Ebru made this lovely white silk dress.

92.5
1 Claude has a **beautiful old Indian** rug in his living room.
2 Nigel's bought himself a **big red American** sports car.
3 Catalina keeps her jewelry in a **small black wooden** box.
4 My granddaughter is engaged to a **charming tall young** man.

92.6
1 Everyone found the presentation extremely **boring**.
2 The instructions are so **confusing**. I don't know what to do.
3 Selma and Bob are **interested** in wildlife.
4 We were all **amazed** when Sharon won the race.

93

93.1
1 Ola is a very talented cook.
2 It was boiling hot outside.
3 They were ecstatic when they won the tournament.
4 My new shoes are not very comfortable at all.
5 Our plumber is not particularly reliable.
6 Marty was really hungry and ordered two hamburgers.

93.2
1 Extreme
2 Absolute
3 Classifying
4 Extreme

93.3
GRADABLE:
interesting, **cold**, **intelligent**, **large**
NON-GRADABLE:
awesome, **square**, **perfect**, **wooden**

93.4
1 The weather was extremely **bad. It rained every day.**
2 The cookies that Ellie made **were not very tasty.**
3 I found the exam almost **impossible to finish in time.**
4 Our business is reasonably **successful, but it could do better.**
5 This antique vase is quite **unique. There are no others like it.**
6 Martin was absolutely **terrified when he saw the bear.**

93.5
1 The food at the wedding wasn't particularly impressive.
2 Hikaru speaks fairly good English, but she makes mistakes.
3 The rooms in the hotel were really awful.
4 Our old car is still in reasonably good condition.

93.6
1 I can't criticize his cakes. They're absolutely **perfect.**
2 The clothes here are of good quality and **reasonably** priced.
3 The concert was absolutely **awful**. She simply can't sing!
4 There's a wonderful **medieval** castle in my town.
5 The software is **fairly** easy to use and won't cause too many problems.
6 It's **freezing** outside! Make sure you wear a hat.

94

94.1
1 Al's new car is faster than mine.
2 The weather was colder than we'd hoped for.
3 Mount Everest is higher than K2.
4 The festival was better than I had expected.
5 Our house is larger than our neighbor's.
6 The Eiffel Tower is taller than the Statue of Liberty.

94.2
1 faster 2 more beautiful 3 happier
4 hotter 5 younger 6 thinner 7 colder
8 more complicated 9 earlier 10 more tiring
11 worse 12 more popular 13 bigger 14 lazier
15 better 16 angrier 17 closer 18 more difficult

94.3
1 Danny's dog is much **larger than mine.**
2 The wedding was more **extravagant than I'd expected.**
3 Karen is only slightly **older than her husband.**

4 Going to work by bike is **less stressful than taking a train.**
5 Electric cars are much more **common than they were 10 years ago.**
6 I'm less sporty than my **elder brother. I prefer reading to football.**
7 My daughter is much more **sensible than she used to be.**

94.4
1 The countryside is far **more quiet** than the city.
2 The Caspian Sea is **more shallow** than the Black Sea.
3 The new software we have to use couldn't be **more simple.**
4 The road was **more narrow** than I thought, and I scratched the car.
5 Jane is really mad with you. I've never seen anyone **more angry.**

94.5
1 Lisbon is much farther than Seville.
2 The Sahara Desert is hotter than the Atacama.
3 I feel happier since I moved to Barcelona.
4 The weather in California is much better than in Montana.
5 A cheetah is faster than a lion.
6 Tom is only slightly taller than his brother, Joe.
7 These jeans are much tighter than my old ones.
8 The old buildings in my town are more beautiful than the modern ones.
9 My new apartment is slightly smaller than my old one.
10 My city has a worse transportation system than yours.
11 The staff in this hotel are much more friendly than in the other one.
12 This book is much more interesting than the last one I read.

94.6
1 The castle is **quite a bit older** than the skyscrapers.
2 She was **just a bit quicker** than me in the race.
3 The weather was **much better** than was forecast.
4 A salad is **a lot healthier** than a hamburger.
5 My colleagues are **much more experienced** than me.
6 A cruise liner is **a lot bigger** than a sail boat.
7 I go to bed **slightly earlier** on Sunday evenings.

95

95.1
1 The more responsibility I take on, **the more stressed I get.**
2 The faster he drove, **the more scared she became.**
3 The more I earn, **the more I seem to spend.**
4 The longer I live here, **the more I want to move away.**
5 The more you study, **the easier the exam will be.**

6 The farther Joe walked, **the more tired he became.**
7 The colder it gets, **the more clothes you should wear.**

95.2
1 The **bigger the cake**, the more there will be to eat.
2 Ola's getting **more and more skilled** at the guitar.
3 It's getting **colder and colder**. Don't forget your scarf!
4 The faster you work, the **earlier you'll finish** the project.
5 My nephew gets **taller and taller** every time I see him.

95.3
1 The more, the merrier.
2 The sooner, the better.
3 The stronger, the better.
4 The more glamorous, the better.

95.4
1 Everyone is getting more and more concerned about climate change.
2 Philip's sunflowers keep growing taller and taller.
3 The exam gets harder and harder each year.
4 Robots are becoming more and more sophisticated.

96

96.1
1 I'm sure your pasta will be as tasty as usual.
2 Dogs are not so easy to look after as cats.
3 I hope the movie is as good as the book.
4 This hat is twice as expensive as the other one.
5 The results are not as good as we had hoped.
6 I hope the new chef is as talented as Jean-Louis.

96.2
1 I'm not as confident as I was before.
2 The food wasn't half as good as we'd hoped.
3 Rome is nowhere near as big as Paris.
4 He told us to finish as quickly as possible.
5 It's not quite as cold as last winter.
6 Ula doesn't call as much as she used to.
7 The journey took twice as long as usual.
8 Ben was as quiet as a mouse.
9 Ed is almost as old as my aunt.
10 It cost just as much as it did last time.

96.3
1 The exam was just **as** hard as I had expected.
2 The skyscrapers here are nowhere near **as** big as in Shanghai.
3 This restaurant is **twice as** expensive as the others.
4 The café is **almost as** big as the church.
5 The house is **not quite** as easy to find as we thought.
6 The singer was nowhere **near** as good as I hoped.
7 The play lasted twice **as** long as I expected.

314

8 It's **not nearly** as cold as we'd imagined.

9 The supermarket was not **quite** as busy as I feared.

10 The dress is **twice as** big as I thought it would be.

11 The other buildings are nowhere near **as** tall as the clock tower.

12 The company results were not quite **so** good as last year's.

13 The new store will be as popular **as** the others.

14 This was **not nearly** as easy to make as I expected.

97

97.1
1 The pianist played the most beautiful music I've ever heard.

2 The Eiffel Tower is still the tallest structure in Paris.

3 Parrots are some of the most intelligent animals.

97.2
1 Pablo has the strangest **taste in music in our class.**

2 Glasgow is the biggest **city in Scotland.**

3 Ania has the curliest hair **in my family.**

4 China has the largest **population in the world.**

5 Our soccer team was the least **successful in the league.**

97.3
1 sweetest 2 most frightening 3 best
4 slowest 5 easiest 6 happiest
7 most careful 8 worst 9 thinnest 10 dirtiest
11 smartest 12 heaviest 13 biggest
14 most boring 15 most beautiful
16 most dangerous 17 tidiest 18 newest
19 most expensive

97.4
1 That café is one of the most expensive places to eat.

2 We bought this vase because it was the most attractive.

3 My grandma always says the sweetest things about me.

97.5
1 The Mississippi is the longest river in the United States.

2 The sailfish is the fastest fish in the ocean.

3 Death Valley is the hottest place on earth.

4 Bungee jumping is the most exciting thing I've ever done.

5 Mont Blanc is the highest mountain in France.

6 My sister is the most creative person I know.

7 I felt like the luckiest person alive when I won the lottery.

8 Some of the oldest paintings can be found in local caves.

97.6
1 This is the **worst** coffee I've ever drunk.

2 Daniel is the **fastest** boy in my class.

3 I think this has been the **hottest** day of the year so far.

4 This feels like the **slowest** train I've ever been on.

5 Ashalata is the **friendliest** manager at work.

6 This is the **least** expensive car we have on sale at the moment.

7 That's the **most exciting** news I've heard today.

8 Mr. Clarke is the **strictest** teacher in school.

9 Michael lives the **farthest** away from our office.

10 That was one of the **saddest** movies I've ever seen.

97.7
1 Elvira was **the fastest** cyclist in the race.

2 I chose **the least expensive** drink on the menu.

3 This is **by far the tastiest** hamburger I've ever eaten.

4 The Burj Khalifa is one of **the tallest** buildings in the world.

5 It's **the worst** summer I've ever known.

6 This is **the best book** I've read for ages.

7 Paul **is the happiest** person I know.

8 Anna is **the most worried** of us all about tomorrow's inspection.

9 London is **the biggest** city in England.

10 Don is **easily the tallest** person in our class.

11 Feng is **one of the most talented** musicians I know.

12 Claire's is **by far the cheapest** salon in town.

98

98.1
1 Tim **kindly** helped Jo with her bags.

2 The kids played **happily** with the dog.

3 This bus is moving so **slowly**!

4 Charles **greedily** ate all the chocolate.

5 It started to rain **heavily**.

6 Carla shouted **angrily** at her computer.

7 Ed's mom thinks he drives too **quickly**.

8 My doctor told me to eat **healthily**.

9 Magda waited **nervously** for her results.

98.2
1 noisily 2 reluctantly 3 well 4 shyly
5 happily 6 long 7 calmly 8 straight
9 easily 10 hard 11 softly 12 dangerously
13 repeatedly 14 clumsily 15 late 16 badly
17 fast 18 stylishly

98.3
1 That child has been waiting **patiently for more than an hour.**

2 Anne advised me to arrive **early for the interview tomorrow.**

3 George left the room quietly, **so as not to wake up the baby.**

4 The number of people studying **English has increased rapidly.**

5 Alina is doing fine after **her operation last week.**

6 I think I answered all **the questions in the test correctly.**

7 I worry a lot about how **fast my daughter rides her bike.**

98.4
1 Ella **gently** stroked her new kitten.

2 Marvin played the piano **beautifully** last night.

3 Louis has worked **hard** to improve his English.

4 An eagle flew **high** above the ruined castle.

5 My stapler has **mysteriously** disappeared.

6 Kathy sang very **well** at the performance.

7 Tim shouted **angrily** at the TV when his team lost.

8 Sangita wasn't **badly** injured in the accident.

9 I went **straight** to my boss's office to talk to her.

10 Claudio passed the final test **easily**.

99

99.1
1 Ola played the most beautifully **of all the musicians.**

2 Carlo speaks English more **fluently than he does German.**

3 You've been working harder **since you got the promotion.**

4 Ahmed drove more carefully **when it started to snow.**

99.2
1 earlier / earliest
2 faster / fastest
3 more regularly / most regularly
4 harder / hardest
5 better / best
6 more stylishly / most stylishly

99.3
1 I usually get up earlier during the week.

2 A cheetah can run much faster than a human.

3 Juan comes here less frequently than he used to.

99.4
1 I should have looked **more closely** at my contract.

2 My employees **work less efficiently** when they're tired.

3 Who **performed better** in the test, you or your sister?

4 Joan gets up **the earliest** in our family.

5 My teacher said I should **try harder** in class.

6 Lena has to **travel the farthest** to get to our office.

7 Our cat can **jump much higher** than our dog.

100

100.1
1 Juan's cake was very popular. Everyone wanted more.

2 The two vases were only slightly different to each other.

3 Eric thought the test was fairly straightforward.

4 Phil's feeling remarkably fit considering how ill he was.

⑤ I don't think it's a particularly difficult mountain to climb.

⑥ The house at the end of the road looks really unusual.

100.2

STRONGER:
remarkably, **really**, **extremely**, **very**
WEAKER:
fairly, **slightly**, **barely**, **not particularly**

100.3

GRADING:
slightly, **fairly**, **very**, **not particularly**
NON-GRADING:
completely, **totally**, **absolutely**, **utterly**

100.4

ENTIRELY:
totally, **thoroughly**, **completely**, **utterly**
ALMOST ENTIRELY:
largely, **mainly**, **mostly**, **virtually**

100.5

① Marta's painting is virtually complete.
② I thought the lecture was fairly interesting.
③ Beatriz was absolutely thrilled to hear my news.
④ Craig looks completely different from his brother.

100.6

① Unfortunately, the hotel we stayed in was utterly awful.
② We found the music festival completely brilliant this year.
③ The students' handwriting was barely legible.
④ The food in the canteen is remarkably good.
⑤ It was nearly impossible, but we reached the summit in the end.

100.7

① The play had almost started **by the time we found the theater.**
② It's perfectly acceptable to **wear jeans to work on Fridays.**
③ This old phone is absolutely **useless without its charger.**
④ We were completely exhausted **when we reached the summit.**
⑤ Jon is extremely talented **and should study art at college.**
⑥ Timothy has essentially finished **writing his PhD thesis.**

101

101.1

① It looks like Sanchez is about to score!
② I've just knocked over that vase. I'm so sorry.
③ We've already packed everything for the move.
④ The chicken's not ready. It's still cooking in the oven.
⑤ Sarah looked like she was about to fall asleep.
⑥ The bus hasn't arrived yet. I'm going to be home late.

101.2

① Future
② Past
③ Past
④ Ongoing
⑤ Ongoing

101.3

① I have **just** received a letter from an old friend.
② Mizuho has **already** been to Paris three times before.
③ Have you been introduced to Tonia's parents **yet**?
④ The judges are **about to** reveal the winner of the competition.
⑤ I've **just** finished my final exam. It's such a relief.
⑥ I haven't finished the book you lent me **yet**.
⑦ Maria has **just** told me she is quitting her job.
⑧ The concert had **already** begun by the time we arrived.
⑨ Lisa has **just** returned from her trip around South America.
⑩ I was **about to** leave, when I remembered the oven was still on.
⑪ The new block on Park Street isn't finished **yet**.
⑫ Hurry up, everyone! The train is **about to** leave.
⑬ I've **already** told Anna that the meeting has started.

101.4

① Vanessa is still working **for the bank, isn't she?**
② We have already spent **all the money we saved.**
③ Has Zahra visited **the National Gallery yet?**
④ Giuseppe's restaurant **is still the best in town.**
⑤ Clive looks like he's **about to give a speech.**
⑥ We still haven't heard **back from the plumber.**

101.5

① Mesut still hasn't given back the $30 I lent him.
② Leroy is still the best player on the team.
③ Has Timo shown you around the new office yet?
④ The guests have already eaten all of the birthday cake.
⑤ I've just seen your brother walking out of the police station.
⑥ Jess is still living in Aberdeen, isn't she?

102

102.1

① Ola goes to the gym **very often**.
② It **hardly ever** rains in the desert.
③ I **regularly** visit my gran.
④ I **usually** go shopping on Saturday.
⑤ She **frequently** goes running.
⑥ We **always** go to France on vacation.

102.2

ALL OR MOST OF THE TIME:
nearly always, **very often**, **usually**
SOME OF THE TIME:
regularly, **sometimes**, **occasionally**
NOT OFTEN OR NOT AT ALL:
rarely, **hardly ever**, **almost never**, **never**

102.3

① Karen is hardly ever in the office on Fridays.
② I visit my parents about once a year.
③ The photocopier at work is nearly always broken.
④ Mira goes to the gym three times a week.

102.4

① Benny's very reliable and **is almost never late for work.**
② Carlita goes swimming at **least five times a week.**
③ Ella often stays at work **until after 10pm.**
④ I come from central Australia, **where it hardly ever rains.**
⑤ When do you usually **finish work in the evening?**
⑥ Ania plays badminton with her cousin **every Sunday morning.**

103

103.1

① It was so windy **that we couldn't fly a kite.**
② You children are so **much better behaved than mine.**
③ The bride wore such **a stylish dress for the wedding.**
④ It was so hot that we **all decided to go swimming.**
⑤ I've never seen such a **beautifully decorated cake before.**

103.2

① The cake Carlos made for the party was so tasty.
② Your exam results are so much better this year.
③ This store sells such lovely clothes.
④ Your brother owns such a beautiful villa.

103.3

① Colm's job looks **so** interesting, but it's very badly paid.
② My new phone's **so much** better than my old one.
③ Everyone had **such** a great time at the school reunion.
④ Hank is **so** generous. He gave me a watch for my birthday.
⑤ The new intern works **so much** harder than the old one.
⑥ It was **such a** shock when our boss said he was leaving.
⑦ Lorna's **such a** talented musician.
⑧ The weather was **so** bad that we decided to cancel the barbecue.

103.4

① My little sister is **such a** good dancer. She should take classes.
② The match was **so** disappointing. No one scored.
③ The weather is **so much** warmer in Florida. You should move here.
④ Kirsty's **so** funny. She always makes me laugh.
⑤ Sandra is **such a** good cook. Everything she makes is delicious.

104

104.1
1. If you're **too** cold, close the window.
2. Do you think we have **enough** money to buy this house?
3. Bob was **too** tired to concentrate on cooking the meal.

104.2
1. I'm not **rich enough** to afford those shoes.
2. Michael is **too young** to watch that movie.
3. The water is **warm enough** to go for a swim.
4. My neighbor always plays his music **too loudly**.
5. This bookcase is **too heavy** for me to move.
6. My French isn't **good enough** to understand Pierre.
7. The exercise was **too hard** for a total beginner.

104.3
1. We have **enough** time to catch the last bus.
2. If you're not warm **enough**, you should put on a sweater.
3. Do we have **enough** food for all the guests tonight?
4. The tickets for the rock concert were **too** expensive.
5. Norbert isn't tall **enough** to reach the bottle.
6. The café wasn't **too** far, so we walked there.
7. The professor spoke **too** quietly for us to hear.
8. I'm not rich, but I earn **enough** to pay the rent.
9. I tried my best in the race, but I wasn't fast **enough**.

105

105.1
1. There's a café **by** the church.
2. The meeting is **on** Monday morning.
3. Mia was nervous **before** going in to speak to her boss.
4. Dan put the flowers **on** the table.
5. Peter works **at** the local airport.
6. Julie gave her teacher her homework **after** the lesson.

105.2
1. **Before** leaving for work, I wash the dishes.
2. I have an English class **on** Tuesdays.
3. I don't know what to listen **to**.
4. Al passed **without** studying for the exam.
5. Kumi's listening **to** the radio.
6. Emma's house is **by** the park.
7. Their office is next **to** the library.
8. **After** finishing work, I go swimming.
9. Jon wants to study Spanish.
10. I live **with** Pete, Dan, and Ed.

105.3
1. My aunt is really good **at** making her own clothes.
2. My new house is **near** the National Museum.
3. In spite **of** the bad pay, Eleni loves her job.
4. You've been looking **at** that phone all morning.
5. Instead **of** going to college, I became a carpenter.

105.4
1. I'm not used to waking up so early each morning.
2. My son is planning to go to college in New York.
3. I'm sorry I haven't got around to replying to your email yet.
4. Jean-Pierre used to drive a red sports car.
5. Martin decided to quit his job at the library.
6. Virginie confessed to stealing the bottle of wine.

106

106.1
1. The dinner is **on** the table.
2. Julian lives **in** the United States.
3. Mesut wasn't **at** the party.
4. I went to meet Ula **at** the airport.
5. Carmen works **in** France.
6. I bought it **at** the supermarket.
7. Mary stayed **in** bed all morning.
8. There are 20 rooms **in** the building.
9. Put the toys back **in** their box.
10. We went to London **on** the train.
11. Marta left her keys **at** home.
12. Ben is sitting **on** the sofa.
13. The students are all **at** their desks.

106.2
1. Marina works at Z-Tech, the **software company on Park Street.**
2. You have some lovely **posters on your kitchen wall.**
3. My uncle Tony lives at **number 16, Nelson Avenue.**
4. We keep the lawnmower **in the shed behind the house.**
5. The college library can be found **on the ninth and tenth floors.**
6. I usually buy my bread at **the bakery across the road.**

106.3
1. The castle sits **in front of** some ugly modern buildings.
2. I placed the final box of books **on top of** the others.
3. Alan is working in the garage **under** a car.
4. Ian put his bag on the seat **opposite**.
5. There's a lovely park **near** the castle.
6. The library is **between** the bank and the café.
7. I found Craig and Robin hiding **behind** a tree.

107

107.1
1. Jan has a bath in the evening before she goes to bed.
2. **During** the week I wake up at 7am.
3. We'd better hurry. Our flight leaves **in** two hours.
4. It often gets far too hot **in** the summer in the city.
5. I'm free **on** Wednesday and Thursday this week.
6. I usually make coffee when I get up **in** the morning.

107.2
1. I'm meeting Eliana **at** 6pm.
2. Joe has his final exam **on** Friday.
3. She started work here **in** August.
4. I go to Angelo's café **at** lunchtime.
5. Pat works from home **on** Thursdays.
6. I always have a nap **in** the afternoon.
7. Their wedding is **on** August the 15th.
8. The performance starts **at** 4 o'clock.
9. Maria usually goes skiing **in** winter.
10. My daughter was born **in** 1996.

107.3
1. Americans celebrate **Independence Day on July 4.**
2. The best time to spot **a barn owl is at night.**
3. I often go walking in spring, **when the weather improves.**
4. I usually clean my apartment **on Sunday morning.**
5. Magda usually stays with **her family at Christmas.**

107.4
1. The store will be closed **until** the end of August.
2. Simon usually goes to bed **at** half past eleven.
3. The train leaves **at** quarter to seven.
4. What did you do **during** the summer break?

107.5
1. I usually go for lunch **between** 1 and 2pm.
2. I'm planning to work here **until** I retire.
3. Martin has worked here **since** October.
4. I lived in Spain for a couple of years **during** the 1970s.
5. Guests should leave their rooms **by** 11:30am.

107.6
1. The café is open **between** 8am and 6pm.
2. I'll be writing this essay **until** 10pm.
3. I've been working here **for** about five months.
4. We're traveling around Mexico from July **to** September.
5. Mabel's lived in Madrid **since** she was a child.
6. Camilla **has worked / has been working** here since July.

108

108.1
1. We went for a walk with our children this afternoon.
2. I get a lot of work done when I travel by train.
3. My aunt's written a book about the town where she grew up.

108.2
1. *Macbeth* was written **by** William Shakespeare in the early 1600s.
2. Takumi went to the theater **with** his wife last night.
3. We found our way to the castle **without** too much difficulty.
4. I ordered boiled potatoes **with** my steak.
5. Most tourists travel around Tokyo **by** metro.
6. We need to talk **about** employing some more staff.
7. Sarah managed to finish the project **without** any help.

108.3
1. We usually pay for **our groceries by card.**
2. Chris went to an interesting **lecture about Madagascar.**
3. We're looking for a house **with a view onto the sea.**
4. This wonderful piece of music **was composed by Chopin.**
5. We're going on vacation **to Kenya without our children.**
6. I took a photo of a fox in **my backyard with my phone.**

108.4
1. Julie always sings with such enthusiasm.
2. Pete's written a book about his childhood.
3. I decided to buy the laptop without thinking.
4. You can get fit by playing a sport.

109

109.1
1. There has been a big increase in people studying science.
2. You can always count on Dave to leave the place clean and tidy.
3. Andy sold his old car to one of his neighbors.

109.2
1. We haven't paid for the meal yet.
2. Emilia was angry about the dirty rooms in the hotel.
3. I'm waiting for a response to the email that I sent.

109.3
1. I was so proud **of** Katie when she passed the test.
2. There are lots of advantages **to** working from home.
3. This company is advertising **for** a new secretary.
4. Is everyone ready **for** the big exam tomorrow?
5. Stephanie has a very positive attitude **toward** her work.
6. The roadwork caused problems **for** many drivers.
7. I was so impressed **by** the room service.
8. My boss told us **to** be more punctual in future.
9. I don't agree **with** my husband about many things.
10. My son is afraid **of** spiders.
11. They've found another problem **with** my car.
12. Esther has talked **about** moving abroad for years.

109.4
1. I saw Leonard talking **to** a police officer yesterday.
2. There's been an increase **in** the number of thefts.
3. These animal toys should appeal **to** children.
4. Sangita is annoyed **with** her housemates.
5. My grandfather loves to talk **about** his childhood.

109.5
1. Ella is really upset **about** losing her mother's necklace.
2. Bill is anxious **about** giving a speech at the conference.
3. I have an excellent relationship **with** my manager.
4. My teacher asked me what I know **about** Roman history.
5. Erik has sold his bicycle **to** one of his cousins.
6. I've been having a lot of problems **with** my internet router.

110

110.1
1. There's a deli and a bookstore on Maple Road.
2. Would you like a first-class or standard-class ticket?
3. Pete's great with the customers, but he's very clumsy.

110.2
1. The movie was disappointing, **but the special effects were amazing.**
2. You can contact us by email **or by telephone.**
3. Bill's never traveled abroad, **nor does he plan to.**
4. My sister lives in Paris, **and my brother lives in Lyon.**

110.3
1. I've been to Ottawa, **but** I've never been to Vancouver.
2. It was raining, **so** we decided to go to the art gallery.
3. While walking, we saw an eagle, a puma, **and** a bear.
4. Ben has to choose between studying math, art, **or** psychology.
5. I did not like the food at the restaurant, **nor** did I like the decor.

110.4
1. Kim was feeling tired, so she went to bed.
2. My son doesn't live at home, nor does my daughter.
3. I was planning to go swimming, but I forgot my swimsuit.
4. Len's 76, yet he still plays soccer with his grandchildren.

111

111.1
1. The children ran out to play **as soon as it stopped raining.**
2. We bought Jim some binoculars **because he likes bird-watching.**
3. Adam failed his test, **even though he worked hard for it.**
4. Someone stole my purse **while I was at the restaurant.**
5. Sam usually eats **when he gets home from work.**

111.2
1. Eli decided to go jogging, **even though** it was raining.
2. Ella put on some sunscreen **so that** she didn't get sunburned.
3. **When** I finish this report, I'll give you a hand.
4. You need a passport **in order to** enter most countries.
5. **Even though** I prefer coffee, I decided to have a cup of tea.
6. Paolo decided to have a nap **because** he was feeling tired.
7. I made the dinner **while** my wife cleaned our apartment.

111.3
1. I read a newspaper **while** I was waiting for the train.
2. My dad bought some paint **so that** he can decorate the kitchen.
3. I'm not going out **until** I've finished my homework.
4. Sally's moving to Spain, **even though** she can't speak Spanish.
5. **When** you've written the report, can you send me a copy?

111.4
1. The concert **will begin** as soon as the singer **arrives.**
2. **Even though** I arrived early, there were no tickets left.
3. Miguela is learning to juggle **in order to** impress her friends.
4. Can you give me a call when **you arrive**?
5. I usually eat **when** my roommate gets home.
6. I went to the supermarket **to** buy some groceries.

112

112.1
1. Andy is tall, whereas his cousin is quite short.
2. I like visiting the mountains, especially in the winter.
3. Bill loves going fishing, just like his dad.

112.2
1. Selma has curly brown hair, **just as her grandmother did.**
2. Due to the bad snow, **all the trains this afternoon are delayed.**
3. As no one bought any tickets, **we've canceled tonight's show.**
4. Andy hated the movie, **though I thought it was okay.**
5. People in Japan drive on the left, **whereas we drive on the right here.**
6. We had to drive slowly **because of the icy conditions.**

112.3
1. Lianne loves football, **whereas** her brother hates it.
2. I was late for the interview **because of** the traffic.
3. The professor was sick. **As a result**, the lecture was postponed.
4. Frank is a zookeeper, **yet** he is terrified of mice.
5. I get on well with Saul, **so** we are going on vacation together.

112.4
1. Magda loves gardening, **especially** in the spring.
2. Omar visited Rome **because** he loves ancient history.
3. There are a lot of environmental problems **because of** the bad pollution.
4. **Thanks to** her music teacher, Selma became a great pianist.
5. I wanted to come this morning, **but** the tickets had sold out.

113

113.1
COORDINATING CONJUNCTIONS:
or, **nor**, **so**, **and**, **but**
SUBORDINATING CONJUNCTIONS:
after, **because**, **although**, **in order that**, **even though**

113.2
1. time
2. reason
3. cause
4. time
5. reason
6. condition
7. condition

113.3
1. I have to send an email before I go home.
2. You can borrow my laptop as long as you look after it.
3. You can't go to the party unless you clean your room.

113.4
1. Leo screamed **when** he saw the spider in the bathroom.
2. Toby doesn't know what he'll do after **he leaves** school.
3. Emma put on her coat **because** she was feeling cold.
4. I was planning to go for a walk, **but** it started raining.
5. I'll call you as soon as **I know** any news.

114

114.1
1. I had a lot of fun with my coworkers at the office party.
2. I much prefer nonfiction, such as biographies, to fiction.
3. My girlfriend disapproves of me eating fast food.

114.2
1. The police are looking for a man in his **mid-twenties**.
2. I've **misplaced** my glasses. Have you seen them?
3. The actor's performance was **substandard**.
4. It was **irresponsible** to drive so quickly.
5. Clara is trying to **disprove** the allegations against her.
6. The teacher said their behavior was **unacceptable**.
7. The student's handwriting was quite **illegible**.

114.3
1. We found Alexandra's cakes totally **irresistible**.
2. I **misread** your name. I thought it said Davies, not Davis.
3. Les failed the exam, but he can **resit** next semester.
4. Andy was **dishonest** about being fluent in Portuguese.
5. Emily was struggling to **untie** her shoelaces.
6. It's **illegal** to drive without wearing a seatbelt.
7. This cake is really **undercooked**. It's almost raw inside.
8. Don't be so **impatient**. The train will come soon.

114.4
1. I realized I had the wrong key when I couldn't **unlock** the door.
2. Ed's so **unreliable**. He's always late.
3. You can **reapply** for the course next year.
4. Ola was **uncertain** what to think about Jim's haircut.
5. I think she **undercharged** us. It should have cost more.

115

115.1
1. This wooden box should be **really useful for storing our documents.**
2. Karl's dog looks dangerous, **but it's actually quite harmless.**
3. Our accountant has been **accused of** incompetence.
4. The evening's entertainment **included some wonderful music.**
5. My brother's a pessimist **and thinks things will deteriorate.**

115.2
ADJECTIVES:
-able/-ible, -al/-ial, -ful, -ic/-tic/-ical, -less, -ous
VERBS:
-ate, -en, -ize, -ify
NOUNS:
-ance/-ence, -dom, -er/-or, -ism, -ist/-ian, -ity/-ty

115.3
1. Alan works for a **management** recruitment company.
2. The café serves a selection of **seasonal** vegetables.
3. The fish are **plentiful** in local rivers.
4. Kids love taking **inflatable** toys to the beach.
5. I found the music festival very **enjoyable**.
6. She always shows great **commitment** to her students.

115.4
1. We want to express our appreciation for all your work.
2. The new couch is really comfortable.
3. Unemployment is a real problem in my city.

116

116.1
1. It's difficult getting used to the city **after living in the countryside.**
2. I'm getting my hair cut this **afternoon at the salon across the road.**
3. Bill got used to the weather **in Australia surprisingly quickly.**
4. Sian's getting new **windows fitted in her apartment.**
5. Gill's still not used to driving **on the left in Britain.**
6. We have our house painted **about every 10 years.**

116.2
1 It took me a while to get used to the cold water in the lake.
2 Joel is used to the cold. He grew up in Finland.
3 You can get your car washed at the gas station.

116.3
1 I hated working nights at first, but then I got used to it.
2 Olga grew up in Moscow, so she's used to cold winters.
3 I used to work as a lab technician before I became a teacher.
4 Nico has his hair cut at the barbershop on Main Street.
5 I got my locks changed after our place was broken into.

116.4
1 Sheila always gets a pizza delivered on Fridays.
2 I'm not used to living in a rainy country.
3 I have my teeth cleaned by the hygienist once a month.

117

117.1
1 for instance 2 moreover 3 then
4 to begin with

117.2
1 Then I switch on the **oven and find my ingredients.**
2 Next, I put all the ingredients **in a bowl and mix them together.**
3 After that, I pour the mixture **into a baking pan.**
4 You can add extra ingredients, **such as nuts or dried fruit.**
5 Finally, I put the cake into **the oven for about 25 minutes.**

117.3
1 Furthermore, you should choose the type of house you want.
2 For example, do you want to live in an apartment or a house?
3 Does the property have, for instance, a balcony?
4 In conclusion, you should think carefully before buying a house.

117.4
1 **Additionally**, they provide employment to many people in the region.
2 **Furthermore**, many species are in danger of extinction.
3 **Meanwhile**, the logging companies continue to destroy vast areas.
4 **In conclusion**, forests are in need of urgent protection.

118

118.1
1 Really? I find him quite dull.
2 I didn't think it suited her, actually.
3 I'm afraid I disagree. I don't like them.
4 I don't agree. I think it looks great.
5 I thought it was predictable, to be honest.

118.2
1 To be honest, I much prefer the city.
2 I don't agree. It was incredibly boring.
3 I'm afraid I disagree. I think it's really overcrowded.

118.3
1 Anyway, she's still a really good writer.
2 I'm afraid I don't think she is.
3 As I was saying, I think she is very talented.
4 I don't think I agree with you, actually.
5 By the way, have you ever read her first novel?
6 You have a point about her books costing too much.
7 Actually, I thought the main character was awful.
8 I see your point about the main character.
9 I told you I wouldn't like Claudia's new novel!

119

119.1
1 It seems my car has broken down again.
2 It would appear that the cat has knocked over the vase.
3 I don't like modern art. However, I don't mind this picture.

119.2
1 Although the restaurant is **nearby, I rarely eat there.**
2 However, whenever I go there, **I always have a good time.**
3 Of course, all the dishes **are made using the finest ingredients.**
4 On the one hand, it's very expensive, **but on the other hand, it's good quality.**
5 I might go out tonight. **Alternatively, I could relax in front of the TV.**
6 Despite feeling tired, **I decided to go out with my friends.**

119.3
1 It seems you haven't completed all the paperwork.
2 She could potentially be a really good actor.
3 It appears that someone forgot to lock up the office.
4 To a certain extent, we believe Manuel is right.

119.4
1 The figures suggest that we are losing a lot of customers.
2 Despite the delays, I enjoyed myself thoroughly.
3 On the one hand, I'm rich. On the other hand, I'm not very happy.
4 To some extent, crime has increased in the past year.

120

120.1
1 You know, that's a great idea.
2 Sort of. I can hold a basic conversation.
3 Well, I do have plans later.
4 Let's see... I could probably make you 100.
5 Wow! That's amazing.

120.2
1 Let's see... I've been working **in IT for more than 10 years.**
2 Well, I enjoy working with **my team on large projects.**
3 So, I think we can all agree **that the project is a success.**

120.3
1 Really? What are you going to do there?
2 Well, I'd like to work as a waiter.
3 You know, that might be hard work.
4 I suppose so, but I will practice my French.
5 Of course. But do you speak any French?
6 Good question. Not yet, but I'd like to.
7 Oh right. What else do you want to do?
8 Let's see. I'd like to travel around France.
9 Wow! That sounds like a great idea.